FROM PIERS TO ETERNITY

A Story of Two Love Affairs

HAZEL PRELLER

With an introduction by Jay Preller

IndePenPress

First published in Great Britain by IndePenPress

All paper used in the printing of this book has been made from wood grown in managed, sustainable forests.

ISBN: 978-1-78003-650-2

Printed and bound in the UK

Indepenpress Publishing Limited
25 Eastern Place
Brighton
BN2 1GJ

A catalogue record of this book is available from the British Library

Cover design by Claire Spinks

This book is dedicated to my husband Jay, without whom this really wouldn't have been possible, and to anyone who has ever stepped onto a pier, felt the sea breeze on their face and seen the sparkling waves under their feet.

You will understand the magic.

CONTENTS

INTRODUCTION

The inspiration for this book was borne out from the devastation caused by the catastrophic fire on the Grand Pier at Weston-super-Mare in July 2008. The speed at which the pavilion was engulfed took everyone by surprise – one minute it was just smoke billowing from the roof and the next it was a pile of twisted metal, totally unrecognisable. In the weeks that followed, there was an almost palpable feeling at the loss of the pavilion, from tourists and residents alike. Both Hazel and I felt a great sadness too, as the Grand Pier had a special place in our hearts.

Although we were initially internet friends, we had our first meeting at the entrance to the Grand Pier in 2007. We went on to have our first kiss at the end of the pier and our love has blossomed since that moment. Only a few weeks after the Weston fire, we heard the news that Fleetwood Pier in Lancashire had burnt to the ground too. As we stood on the Grand Pier studying the twisted wreckage, we discussed the tragedy at Fleetwood and idly wondered how many piers there were left in the country. We jokingly said that we had better hurry up and visit them if we wanted a kiss on each one before they all burnt down!

After some research we discovered a list detailing 55 piers that were still standing, although some of these were closed to the public. We also realised that there didn't seem to be a recent book of these quintessentially English seaside structures. So with an equal mixture of excitement and trepidation, it was agreed that we would physically visit every remaining pier in Great Britain and make a written record of our journey, hoping to complete it before the pavilion at the Grand Pier was completed (scheduled for 2010). There was of course, one condition which *was* set in stone... that we would have a kiss at the end of each pier!

Jay Preller

CHAPTER 1

Off to a Good Start: Mumbles and Penarth

And so it was that on a gloriously warm autumnal Sunday in September we headed optimistically towards the two piers of South Wales, Mumbles and Penarth, to log our first two 'official' kisses. Looking back it seems all very innocent and little did we realise just what a can of worms we would open on our quest, or how the initial simple notion of having a kiss at the end of every pier would snowball!

To travel so far into Wales was a first for me. I had only ever been as far as Cardiff and up into the valleys where the grim ghosts of mining villages cling to the hills, and as such I had a very blinkered view as to what Wales was really like. Once out of Cardiff I realised the errors of my ways and I would like to apologise unreservedly to the Welsh, and congratulate them on keeping these delights so well hidden – don't worry, I shan't tell anyone! Once through bi-polar Port Talbot (on the one side idyllic rolling bracken-covered hills, on the other dark satanic industry) and having negotiated regenerated Swansea, we approached Mumbles and the Gower Peninsula by tracing the sweeping curve of Swansea Bay. The approaching traveller can spot Mumbles Pier on the horizon, reaching tentatively out from the dramatic cliffs and intriguing islands, but it was still a long way off, with the town to be investigated first.

As with all the piers, they cannot be taken out of context from their urban hinterland because that is the very reason for their existence – to understand one you have to know about the other, and Mumbles is no different in that respect. Hugging the pleasing bend of Swansea Bay it is a thriving, neat and well-appointed little town. Attractive, mainly Victorian buildings crowd the little streets right up to the wide promenade. The prom is the modern usage of the Victorian tramway that once linked the town with Swansea, bringing miners and industrial workers out on their rare days off for White Funnel steamer excursions. The Gower was, and still is a popular holiday destination because of its little hidden sandy beaches and an abundance of mussels, oysters and winkles. It was seen as the perfect place to visit for a day of clean air, tranquillity and calm after the hard labour and dirty steelworks of neighbouring Victorian Swansea and even now is a delightfully quiet retreat from life's hustle and bustle.

When we visited the promenade it was very busy, and we picked our way through the families enjoying their Sunday constitutional, and strolled from the town towards the pier past russet-coloured mud and the wooden skeletons of ancient boats. It was a deceptively long way and eventually we passed the old lifeboat house hiding against the cliff, and the modern one on the seaward side before we reached the pier.

The original 255m (835') long pier opened on May 10th 1898 was designed by W. Sutcliffe Marsh and cost £17,000 to build. It was originally meant to be little more than a landing jetty with a bandstand and amusement stalls to entertain the embarking and disembarking passengers from steamboat excursions. Piers vary immensely in their construction, something we hadn't even considered, but in our pier naivety we carefully investigated every aspect of this one!

Mumbles Pier has a boxed lattice skeleton of steelwork on fairly unremarkable cast-iron piles and is then topped off with a wooden planked deck. Apart from a Swiss-chalet style lifeboat house with its own slipway and a walkway that was added at right-angles in 1920, the basic structure has changed little over the last 110 years, although the deck-side, like most piers, certainly has. As we were painfully aware, fire is the first big enemy of piers but amazingly for this mostly wooden structure, Mumbles Pier has avoided any major alarms. Being hit by ships piloted by myopic captains appears to be the second most common accident likely to damage a pier, but again Mumbles has had an accident-free history. Like most piers, it was sectioned in 1940. This involved removing a midsection of the structure to prevent it being used as a landing stage by the enemy, and for many piers it was quite some time before they were rebuilt and returned to use. Mumbles

9

reopened on 9th June 1956 after substantial repairs were completed and a three-tier landing stage of concrete and steel piles had been added at the pier head (the end furthest from the land).

AMECO Ltd (an amusements company) have been running the pier since 1937 which has helped enormously with its upkeep, but despite ongoing maintenance the pier is in need of major rebuilding work and in 2008 AMECO estimated they would need £4 million pounds to accomplish this – running a pier is not a cheap matter! It is fortunate that piers seem to have retained their appeal over the decades and Mumbles Pier is visited by plenty of people for various purposes. We handed over a small charge at the entrance, (slightly more if we'd been going fishing from the landing stage pier head) and began our stroll along the planking between beautifully ornate wrought-ironwork rails, thankful that there didn't appear to be a surcharge for kissing at the far end!

Halfway along the pier on the town-facing side, the 1920s' lifeboat house is now closed off and although the building itself is quite quaint, it has to be said that the right-angled walkway is downright ugly compared to the rest of the pier. There was a more modern curiosity when we visited – a small test drilling rig nestled in between the slipway and the pier, with two industrious men resolutely ignoring nosy bystanders and comments from vocal teenagers!

The pier is curiously bare of anything – looking at photos from years gone by, there were once some strange oversized fibreglass creatures cunningly masquerading as swings and slides to entertain the children, but little else – and this seems rather at odds with the watercolour beauty of the sweeping bay to the left and the wonderful Enid Blyton-style islands (complete with lighthouse, caves and hidden beaches) to the right, although they are the perfect backdrop for an end-of-pier kiss!

At the landing stage pier head it was remarkably busy with fishermen of all ages periodically casting and reeling in. It was great to see the older ones sharing hints and tips with the boys, one of whom was ecstatic at catching a substantial fish all on his own while his dad was elsewhere on the pier. We had our first official end-of-the-pier kiss totally unnoticed, ruffled by the gentle Welsh sea breeze and then mused at how enormous the task ahead of us seemed now!

As we turned and headed back up the pier we investigated a large section of the pier that had been fenced off. Here the need for extensive and expensive repairs was painfully obvious and it could be seen where the planking had become rotten and in places removed completely. Much of the wrought iron on the pier here was unloved and badly rusted, in places misshapen with years of over-painting. And there, resting on a jumble of rotten timbers was one of the original animal amusements, a large monkey lying on its back, looking a bit incongruous amongst the decay.

However, the rest of our visit was quite pleasant and it was lovely to see the pier so busy and visited by so many people. At the landward end is a lively amusements arcade and thronging restaurant, and as we circumnavigated these on our return journey we agreed that it would not be difficult to restore the damaged section of Mumbles Pier, and indeed it should be done as quickly as possible to keep this wonderful structure open for as long as possible.

We strolled back along the promenade and nearly forgot that we were meant to be visiting two piers that day, so increased the pace and hurtled back along the motorway to visit Penarth, a seemingly inconsequential little town overshadowed by Cardiff. I had been to Penarth one grey morning some years previously as a passenger of the MV *Balmoral*, but seen very little of the rest of the pier from my position on deck and felt that it would be good to return and have a proper look. That would be *if* we could only find the place...

Signposts are not at a premium for this small Victorian town, and it took several frustrating U-turns before we located the town centre. Now tantalisingly close we had to track down the seafront... Where was it? Plunging suddenly down a steep side road, the promenade came into view, bordered at the sea's edge by multi-layered, multi-coloured angel cake cliffs of green, red and grey and an unprepossessing pebbly beach. Now to find a parking space...

Depositing the car at the top of Alexandra Park we walked downhill through the old gardens, hearing disembodied voices of itinerant teenagers in the bushes and hedges, quite bizarre against the neatly-trimmed Victoriana. At the bottom we walked around a corner and suddenly, there it was! We felt like we had been transported back in time, looking at this stately and beautiful Art Deco painted pavilion sitting at the landward end of the pier.

Penarth was originally a major coal port and it became even busier during the Victorian paddle steamer era, taking not only day trippers but also visitors from exotic places such as Birmingham and the West Midlands.

Steamer trips regularly went up and down the River Severn and across the water to Weston-super-Mare, where on a clear day the original Birnbeck pier at Weston could be seen. To make the most of this new trade and to cash in on its new found fame as 'the garden by the sea', construction of a pier began in 1894. Designed as a 198m (650') jetty with a promenade by H.F. Edwards it opened on February 4th 1895, a simple cast-iron construction with a timber deck. Owing to an increase in steamer passengers, in 1907 a wooden pavilion housing a dance hall was built at the pier head and shops installed along the neck. A concrete landing stage and the wonderful pavilion that graces the entrance today were added in 1929, but it was not long before disaster struck.

In 1931 a fire began at the seaward end and within minutes it had spread along almost the entire length of the pier. Eight hundred people on the pier were marooned at the pier head and had to be rescued by a local pilot cutter and yachtsmen. The buildings, deck and shops were rebuilt, and although the far wooden pavilion was not replaced, the pier carried on being a popular attraction. A 7,000 ton ship collided with the pier shortly after World War II, destroying a large section and repairs took two years to complete at a cost of £28,000 – piers were not a cheap commodity even in days gone by!

In 1981 White Funnel Steamers ceased operation and there was a great worry about the future of Penarth pier but the Paddle Steamer Preservation Society came to the rescue, and the MV *Balmoral* and PS *Waverley* still visit regularly. Like most piers it remains a popular spot with fishermen, and with strolling families taking the air as they are the perfect place for young and old alike because of the flat terrain.

Today entrance to the pier is free, and as we walked through the open gates to the pier we passed the original old turnstiles lurking in the shadows. Penarth pier is like an old maiden aunt – trim, neat, tidy and a pleasure to visit because of the aura of days gone by! The planks are well maintained and the pier is spacious, with small refreshment stalls at the landward end. At the pier head the landing stage is closed unless there is a visiting boat, but there is a good view across the Bristol Channel to the island of Steep Holm (the steep one) now home to a nature reserve, and Flat Holm (the flat one) with its lighthouse and unmarked, unconsecrated graves of Thomas Becket's murderers. If you squint, Weston-super-Mare is visible almost directly opposite and to the right the Napoleonic fort on Brean Down, which could easily be mistaken for another island.

Thwarted from getting right to the end of the pier we huddled into the railings and kissed in a stiff breeze under the Welsh flag, as a flotilla of blue-sailed tiny yachts bobbed around and went nowhere in particular in the sea. We strolled back hand-in-hand, again admiring the neatness of the planking and the magnificent pavilion. Sadly it is no longer used as a theatre, although there are plans afoot for it to be renovated and reopened as a multi-purpose entertainment centre in the near future. Much like any building of advancing years, it was already becoming apparent to us that piers have to adapt and change in order to survive in the modern climate, and Penarth was no exception to this. With two piers now visited, we wondered where we would end up on our next pier weekend!

Poignantly as I drove to work along Weston seafront the next morning, the demolition team were assembled and had already begun to remove the first of the sad, twisted girders from the Grand Pier...

CHAPTER 2

Houston, We Have a Problem...

Rising early a fortnight later on September 27th, I checked my car over and we set off for Kent to visit Jay's family and to sneak a kiss at Deal and Herne Bay piers, with perhaps Southend-on-Sea squeezed in if we had the time. It was a foggy morning but traffic wasn't too bad, and I optimistically said it would burn off later...

All went well until a pit stop at Reading Services. By now the weather was superb – a scorching September sun burnishing the autumn leaves and berries. As we pulled out of our parking space, full of anticipation for the weekend ahead, the car died and rolled to a stop. I called the nice man from the breakdown services who was a mere ten minutes away, and despite his initial optimism he left nearly four hours later close to tears and admitting defeat, while we waited for the relay truck to take us home!

Still, mustn't grumble – the fog *had* burnt off and we'd had five hours of sunning ourselves while admiring the autumnal treasures, circling buzzards and jays stuffing themselves with berries in the trees. 'Pierfect' it was not, but we were still talking, and determined not to let this put us off!

CHAPTER 3

Small but Perfectly Formed: Burnham-on-Sea

Every cloud has a silver lining, and so we made the most of being unexpectedly at home to visit the pier at Burnham-on-Sea, just down the coast from Weston-super-Mare the following day. It was another foggy start, but I was sure it would burn off later...

Burnham-on-Sea could be viewed by some as a poor-man's Weston-super-Mare but is a small seaside town in its own right with all its own charms. With mostly red-brick Victorian buildings creeping from the seafront back inland and a bustling shopping street, Burnham was once at the end of the Somerset and Dorset Railway, which led to it becoming a thriving town during the late 1800s. Unusually, the railway terminated right at the end of the main street and almost in view of the seafront, which was ideal for the genteel Victorian promenaders. Although now it's reliant on car-borne visitors since the demise of the railway, many stay at the numerous caravan and touring sites nearby, and Burnham-on-Sea still appeals.

The long, elegant promenade overlooks masses of sand on the beach and has sweeping views across Bridgwater Bay and the distant Devon hills (via the cubist blot of the Hinkley power stations). The views are available providing you can of course see *over* the enormous sea walls, built to defend the town from the fierce tides of the Severn estuary.

It is mooted that it was because of these fierce tides that the pier at Burnham was built in the manner that it was, although first you have to find it! We tend to think of pleasure piers as being gracious long-legged constructions that stretch out into the sea, hoisting their skirts high above the waves, and I'm sure we weren't the first people to walk along the promenade at Burnham having the following conversation.

"This really is pleasant – and the sun *is* burning the fog off after all. I was right!"

"Quite a nice little town too. Oh, here's the seafront. Lovely view!"

"Yes... but... where's the pier?"

"It's here, right in front of us!"

"Oh." (A pause to take it in, then incredulously,) "Is that *it*?"

For many pier enthusiasts (including many of those in the National Piers Society), the Burnham-on-Sea pier simply *isn't* a pier, merely a pavilion on legs. Nowadays you cannot promenade around the outside of the building, and it would be a very quick walk if you could, owing to its lack of length. If you *do* regard it as a pier (and in all fairness, that was its intended use and it *does* have a pavilion providing entertainments for all the family, and it *is* on legs out over the sea), then Burnham-on-Sea qualifies as being the shortest pier in the country. In fact if the internet is to be believed, it is the shortest pier in the world, although it was surprisingly difficult to establish just how short it actually is. When we later met its owner Louise Parkin, even she was unsure of its length, although we later established from records that it is a mere 36m (117') long.

This bijou creation is an Edwardian pier and it is not just its length (or lack of it) that makes it unique. Built between 1911 and 1914 it was the first concrete structure of its kind in Europe and was made largely of granite chippings that were brought from Penryn in Cornwall. It is believed that its length and construction were to combat the treacherous currents and tides of the sea at this point on the Somerset coast, although it would appear that there is little surviving documentation to explain why the pier was built in the first place or who was behind the original design. Some people believe that because most shipping went further up the coast to Weston-super-Mare's older Birnbeck Pier, Burnham Pier was purely a whimsical experiment and not built for any serious purpose. The pavilion design has been compared to those of Isambard Kingdom Brunel's railway stations at Bristol Temple Meads and Bath Spa but the original purpose of the pavilion is also a mystery. We did track down a photograph dating to c.1911 showing people walking around the outside of the pavilion, which in our mind just goes to back up its status as a real pier!

The pier was derelict by 1968, when it was bought and subsequently renovated to its beautifully kept and presented state. We found it smothered in floral displays, with plenty of places to eat and drink whilst sheltering from the brisk wind. Inside there is a luxurious amusement arcade with plush carpet and sparkly mirror displays and even at half past eleven on a Sunday morning, surprisingly busy with holidaymakers hoping to make a fortune from their small change!

We walked to the back of the arcade for the ceremonial end-of-the-pier kiss, which was rather novel as there is no longer access to the open walkway for the public, then we celebrated by getting £1 in 2 pence pieces to play on the machines. It was another first for me – I had never as much as even won my stake back before, but suddenly my luck changed. Armed with 50p worth of change the coins kept falling from the machine and before long I had 94p! Despite the temptation to put it all back in a machine in a desperate bid to win enough to mend my car, I resisted, and together with Jay's 6p winnings we had our £1 back and called it a day.

Outside, the sun had yet again burnt off the fog and spectral swirls of mist rose from the warming sands, already dotted with people enjoying a late summer day at the seaside. Looking back at this little pier hugging the sea-wall, I realised I had developed rather a soft spot for it, and wondered if this was the beginning of something more serious! Leaving it behind us we jangled our change as we walked back along the promenade. We'd had a successful weekend after all, even if it hadn't been *quite* what we had intended!

CHAPTER 4

When Is a Pier Not a Pier? (Or – Ap-pierances Can Be Deceptive!)

Visiting Burnham-on-Sea had raised more than a few questions – so just what *is* a pier? Where should we be going? What should we be looking for? The plot thickened... According to the National Piers Society (at the beginning of our quest) there are still 55 standing piers, although not all of these are open to the public because of their structural condition. Owing to the 2008 fires at Weston's Grand Pier and Fleetwood it initially left 47 open to walk on at the start of our challenge which sounded simple enough, but as I researched these remaining piers I came across an article about Gravesend Pier, and then a reference to Harwich Ha'penny Pier, neither of which featured in our list! After much frantic checking I got in touch with Tim Mickelburgh at the National Piers Society, who admitted that the definition of a pier was debated often at meetings and that Gravesend was discounted because it was on a river.

That seemed fair enough, but surely Clevedon, Weston-super-Mare and Southend-on-Sea were also (technically) on rivers as they are sited on estuaries... And does a pier have to have amusements on it? Should you be able to walk round the outside? What should it look like? Why hadn't we thought about any of this before?!

Looking back in time, most (but not all) piers in this country were originally built as landing jetties to facilitate those early tourists wanting to visit somewhere new via steamer before the heady days of railways had even started. Some piers had to be extremely long to cope with enormous tidal changes and shallow shelving beaches, but as the fashion for walking along the piers grew, so did the desire to be over the water. Once promenading along the piers became popular as a way of being seen in public, seating and then bandstands soon followed, giving us the traditional view of a pier that we think of when they are mentioned.

So technically speaking, and after a lot of talking, we decided that a pier needs to consist of legs (properly known as piles) out into the water and have a walkway or deck on the top. This could be made of wood, cast iron, concrete or a combination of materials but to our mind (and here we may upset the purists) it shouldn't be a solid wall because then it becomes a sea-wall, harbour-wall or jetty. It doesn't have to have amusements on it, but it should at least have benches for the weary promenader to rest on and admire the view... Or should it?!

In Scotland we discovered that there still are piers (by name), but these are all for functional purpose only and so we would classify these as landing jetties. But should we include all of these in our quest, or simply those on the list of the National Piers Society (which even they have admitted they don't all agree with!) or should we make up our mind as we visit each pier?

Being single-minded, stubborn and naively optimistic, we decided we *would* include Gravesend and Harwich (and any other neglected piers we discovered on the way), whilst investigating all of the still-standing piers on the National Piers Society list. We now had a list of 57 piers to visit in just under eighteen months and tentatively decided that it wouldn't hurt to ask for access to some of the piers that were shut-but-still-standing on the off-chance owners would say yes.

It would be wonderful if I could say that we had come up with a foolproof formula by which we could define a pier, but we haven't – sorry! I dare say you will argue fiercely with us over some of the decisions reached when we visited some of the piers, but if the experts have been unable to define a pier (now is that a jetty or a pleasure facility on piles?!) then we two lesser mortals stood no chance!

CHAPTER 5
Deal Or No Deal? (And Herne Bay...)

A fortnight into October and the weather was still unseasonably warm and sunny. The car decided to go further than Reading Services and the journey to Kent was thankfully uneventful. Our first port of call on a pier-filled weekend was Herne Bay, a delightful example of a traditional seaside town revelling in the last balmy days of summer. There is a long esplanade filled with seaside attractions for all the family – shops and amusements on the landward side, the attractive clock tower and elegant formal sunken gardens where ice cream and fish and chip-eating visitors sat out of the wind on the seaward side. Looking out to sea, the new Neptune's Arm breakwater points almost accusingly towards what was once Herne Bay's crowning glory, the pier. Today it is in two very distinctive parts – the decorative original pier head stands derelict and alone, forlornly out at sea. Poles apart in both condition and style, the 1970's grey building-block pavilion sits on what remains of the shoreward end of the pier.

The traditional approach of the promenade had lulled us into a false sense of security and we realised this would not be a traditional pier visit! Passing through the wide Edwardian entrance, somewhat out of character with the rest of the structure and looking not unlike the tiled surrounds of an old public convenience, we walked along the horizontally-planked deck towards the pavilion building, which was unusually built to house a leisure centre and were pleased to find that there is still access to the end of what remains of the pier.

Sidling past the imposing sides of the slab-sided (and decidedly unattractive) leisure centre, we emerged at the rear where it felt like being on the stern deck of a cruise liner rather than a pier. We looked out over the utilitarian railings to where the forlorn remains of the original pier sat some 1,036m (3,400') away with a modern backdrop of sci-fi wind turbines bustling on the horizon. It appeared to be yearning to join back up with where we were standing... or was that one of the first signs of pier madness? We mused on what Herne Bay Pier must have originally been like as we watched jet skiers skim between us and the end of the pier, before having a cruise-style kiss in the autumn sunlight.

The original pier at Herne Bay was one of the earliest and longest of its time, with the original plans for a wooden pier approved by Thomas Telford. The 1,107m (3,633') construction opened in 1832 and despite being made of wood it cost a staggering £50,000 to build! It catered for steamer passengers travelling between London and Dover and had to be lengthy because of the shallow shoreline, but by the following year a powered trolley-way was built to carry luggage backwards and forwards. However, only seven years later it was discovered that the wood-boring toredo worm had devastated the piles and cast-iron duplicates were inserted in their place. Fate dealt further blows for the pier, when in 1862 steamer services ceased to visit and then in 1870 the pier was found to be so decayed that it was sold for scrap and removed.

In 1873 a second pier was opened – designed by Wilkinson and Smith it was intended to be primarily for promenading and was just 97m (320') long with a theatre and shops at the shoreward end. The steamers visited on a trial basis nineteen years later, with some success, and so a third structure designed by Mattheson was built to incorporate the existing pier and opened in 1899. It was now considerably longer – at 1,154m (3,787') it was now the second longest pier in the country after Southend-on-Sea, and the railway built by the Stockton-on-Tees constructors, Head, Wrightson and Company, was kept and used to carry passengers and their luggage out to the steamers. Due to mismanagement, the local council became the new owners of the pier in 1909, building a new pavilion at the shoreward end in 1910 (and those 'convenient' entrance gates). The old theatre was destroyed in 1928 by a fire and further changes occurred in 1939 when the pier was sectioned and the electric trams ceased operation. Following the war a large storm damaged the pier and although it was repaired, the pier closed in 1968 when it was declared too dangerous.

At the shoreward end the pavilion remained open until its destruction by a fire in 1970 while work was being carried out at the pier's entrance. The replacement for the old pavilion was a new sports and leisure centre (a somewhat unusual choice), which quite coincidentally Jay had worked on helping to construct, back in 1976! It was officially opened by the Right Honourable Sir Edward Heath on 5th September that year and has remained well used ever since. Although the pier neck was still standing and local anglers campaigned for it to be restored, a severe storm in 1978 meant most of it collapsed into the sea, leaving the birdcage pier head isolated out at sea where it remains today. It was later discovered that the bridges put in to repair the World War II sectioning had left gaps, weakening the structure so that it only took a few winters before the storm did its worst.

Despite this disaster and the building of the incongruous leisure centre, there are earnest plans afoot to get the pier neck reinstated and Herne Bay Pier rebuilt as a modern enterprise for all the family to visit and not just fitness enthusiasts! For once, I was quite interested to read facts and figures surrounding the proposals (not being terribly mathematically inclined!) and cannot understand why more towns are not more energised into repairing their piers and getting them opened. Piers in large towns and cities such as Brighton and Blackpool annually attract two million visitors a year, and if entertainments and amusements are available, each visitor could easily spend £20 per head. You don't need a maths degree to see that this results in an impressive total income each year of £40 million! Smaller towns such as Southwold and Clevedon can expect 500,000 visitors per annum to their piers, and surprisingly piers without entertainments on them like Swanage and Saltburn get around 200,000 visitors a year, showing how magnetic the appeal of walking down a pier can be! Herne Bay wants to attract some 500,000 people a year to its redeveloped pier and current costs have been set at around £12 million. These plans have been supported by the Waverley Society who have pledged to visit should the pier reopen, bringing in more revenue, but unfortunately the local council are unable to provide funds for the rebuild, meaning money will have to come from independent or European sources. It looks like being a while before this project gets underway, which is a terrible shame for Herne Bay – a stunning proposal has already been put forward, featuring a T-shaped pier-head design which would definitely add to Herne Bay's charm and tourist potential.

We thoughtfully walked back along what little is left of the pier onto the old-fashioned seafront, past the traditional seaside sights – gardens, ice-cream eaters and gorgeous curved brick bandstand shelters, deckchairs and sunbathers, old ladies discussing the state of the toilets in towns they'd visited and a man teaching his son to throw stones at the beach signposts... On to Deal!

We were looking forward to visiting Deal, having heard lots about the fab food in the café on the pier head. We also knew it was in the process of being refurbished, but were confident it would have been completed by now, so we disembarked from the car and began our walk along the seafront. Deal is very much like an east coast seaside destination with steep curving shingle banks leading down to the sea, and a decidedly blustery seafront with Georgian buildings set well back with no traditional seaside ornamentation to speak of. That's not to say Deal is an unpleasant place to visit and promenade, it isn't, it's just... different. We couldn't find a fish and chip shop either, as we were a bit peckish by now with all this seaside air, so settled for an ice cream instead as we neared the pier. For the life of me I can't quite think what the pier designer Sir William Halcrow was thinking of when he drew up plans for Deal Pier in 1954, nor quite why it's managed to secure the coveted 'Pier of the Year' award for 2008, but I may be persuaded with a bit more of a look... This concrete pier was built to replace the original structure that collapsed in 1940 and was the first new pier to be built since WW2. Did Sir William have a secret desire to design a motorway bridge or inner city flyover? It's certainly a novel look for a pier!

The first pier here was built in 1838, designed by Sir John Rennie (the railway engineer) but due to a cash flow crisis only ever made half its proposed length. It stayed open for 20 years until a severe storm unceremoniously dumped the pier onto the beach in 1857. Pier saviour Eugenius Birch designed the second structure, cast iron and 335m (1,100') long with a wooden deck adorned with seating, two ornate tollhouses and a tramway to take luggage to the three-tiered steamer landing at the head. It opened in 1864 and was added to over the next 30 years with a reading room and salt baths in the 1870s and a smart seaward end pavilion in 1886. Deal Pier succumbed to boat collisions several times in this incarnation, requiring lots of repairs.

It wasn't until 1940 when the Dutch ship *Nora*, already crippled by a wartime mine, sealed the fate of this popular Victorian pier. The *Nora* ran aground to the south of the pier but the rising tide repeatedly smashed it into the piles resulting in the bulk of the pier collapsing into the sea. Churchill gave the army permission to demolish the remains, leaving just the shoreward tollbooths. These were removed in 1954 when Halcrow's pier was built entirely from reinforced concrete (incidentally, Sir William Halcrow was more used to designing Mulberry harbours, air raid shelters, tunnels and dams) and the Duke of Edinburgh came to open it in November 1957. Now 313m (1,026') long it has kept the landing stage at the seaward end, although weirdly the lower tier always stays submerged. For mermaids to get to the café perhaps? We couldn't quite work that one out!

The concrete flyover (sorry, neck) being made of concrete means you can't glimpse the sea below, which I don't mind too much as I can get queasy seeing waves break beneath my feet! It's lined with what appear to be bus shelters and fishermen, notices telling you NOT to do things, municipal rubbish bins and concrete lamp posts adorned with yet more signage. When we got as far as we could go, it was apparent that the new £1.2 million restaurant and café (intended to be a 'lasting and striking landmark' according to the local paper) was still incomplete and there was no access to the end – or food! We had a perfunctory (although still loving) kiss in the last bus shelter, surrounded by rubbish and the smell of fish bits in the air, before surveying the building work, submerged landing stage and rotting fish guts under the seats. Fishermen seem to be the only people who really enjoy Deal Pier, classed as an internationally recognised fishing venue – there were lots of them lining both sides of the neck.

I am trying hard to find something nice and positive to say about Deal Pier, honestly I am, but even the notice saying it's the same length as the ill-fated RMS *Titanic* is incorrect (she was only 269m or 882' long, the pier is 313m or 1,026')... Amazingly, Deal Pier has over 600,000 people walking along its flyover every year and goes to show how important *any* type of pier is to a seaside town, as it's estimated that these visitors also bring approximately £16 million to the local economy[1]*! As we walked back out under the entrance gate, I suppose the glass bowls on the top of the lamp posts were quite pretty in a post-war sort of way. And the fishy statue at the

---

1   * data from Herne Bay Pier website 2006

entrance was quite pleasing, and on the bright side at least there's no worry of it burning down!

CHAPTER 6

From End to End (Graves- to South-!)

We spent the night in Margate, and before turning in walked along the seafront, a very grand affair. Margate has a superb sandy beach lined with decorative sea wall dolphin lamps and backed by highly ornate Georgian architecture. It's seen better days in places, especially now that Dreamland fun fair is no more, and the skeletal remains of the wooden rollercoaster haunt the deserted park (and my nightmares – I can remember trying to get off this at the age of 6 because it was so terrifying!). However, it still gives a good impression of a decent seaside town, and quite honestly it's crying out for a pier. "Why is she waffling on about Margate?" I hear you protest... well, Margate once boasted a pier too, and is sadly one of the 36 resorts that is now pier-less. It wasn't called Margate Pier, as that title was already taken by the magnificent, still standing and lighthouse tipped harbour wall, so it was called Margate Jetty and provided amusements and a landing stage for the steamers.

Piers can be remarkably resilient, and this one was no different. It steadfastly refused to die, being hit by a storm-driven wreck then battered by storms until it was broken. When it was decided it should finally be destroyed, the pier was still standing after several attempts to blow it up, so it was finally down to the armed forces to remove it completely in 1978! So from pier-less Margate we departed the next morning in thick fog – so dense you wouldn't know where the seafront was! In a kind of déjà vu experience we blithely remarked that we just knew it would burn off later as we headed towards Gravesend.

No, it's not technically a seaside town, being firmly ensconced on the banks of the River Thames but it actually has not one but two piers! The Town Pier has, just 500m away, a sister, the Royal Terrace Pier that technically has always been a boating jetty. It was named 'Royal' following a visit from Princess Alexandria in 1863, and is still used today as a working jetty.

If pier-purists don't want to include Gravesend Town Pier in their list, then they should move along quickly, but I think this is a mistake, as Gravesend Pier is actually a little gem. It is also the oldest surviving cast-iron pier in the world, and the first to use iron cylinders in its construction (but if you're not going to count it, Southport takes that title, built in 1860!). The Town Pier was designed by William Tierney Clark in 1834 and built on the site of the Town Quay, designed to be a landing jetty for ferry-boats across the river, but following the rail boom of the 1850s was superseded and fell into disrepair as the boat trade declined. Fortunately in 2002 Gravesham Borough Council began an extensive restoration project where all the ironwork was dismantled and taken to Telford for cleaning. Once repainted or replaced it was returned and reconstructed, with the pier re-opening as a bar and restaurant. Now there is a beautiful 48m (157') wooden decked pier resting on a beautiful series of arches atop piles – it almost resembles half a miniature bridge from London.

We basked in the (yes, you've guessed it) brilliant autumn sunshine as we walked down a glassed-in walkway (with sliding doors for fair-weather promenading), in between elegant but not over-elaborate Corinthian columns which took us to an outdoor area, separate from the main bar and dining area. From here there are superb views for diners and walkers alike, out across the river towards the Isle of Grain and down to the Royal Terrace Pier. Whether or not the Town Pier should be classed as a pleasure pier or not, it's a beautiful and tasteful example of how, with a bit of thought (and money!) you can preserve a little piece of history in an up-to-date-way. We relaxed at the end, watching a flotilla of swans glide past, partook of our kiss and ambled back. Go and visit this little jewel, it's a delight!

As the temperature rose due to the baking sunshine, we left Gravesend for Southend, the capital of Essex-ness and the epitome of seaside summer holidays. It's an odd conglomerate of a place to drive through – a bit like the university quarter of Manchester – but soon stops at the coast and a bank of amusements. Seaside towns that cater for masses of holidaymakers are going to have a certain element of tackiness, and as such I think it's a bit unfair to criticise it. Come on, that's what going to the seaside is traditionally all about isn't it? Fish and chips, amusement arcades, loud music, candyfloss, bright lights, donkeys, fast rides, a beach and a pier. It's all there for a cheap and cheerful relaxing weekend, and if the sun is out it's incredibly easy to feel you've hit the jackpot and had the best time ever!

If Southend-on-Sea *does* have donkeys, I'm sorry I missed them, but on every other point it fulfilled all the criteria with its glorious sticky, noisy tackiness – and *what* a pier! I felt like writing to Deal, sending them a photo of Southend and underlining the words 'THIS is a pier!' in technicolour marker pen – you have to see it to appreciate just how long it really is. The 1.432 miles of pier (that's 2,158m or 7,080') proudly march out into what is technically the Thames estuary. Pick a bad day when the tide's out and what you'll get are miles of stinky, squishy lunar mud landscape as far as the eye can see. Pick a good day (and we were feeling smug here, because we were already celebrating the heady sunshine) and the tide is in, the sea glistens like an aquatic glitter ball and you really feel like you're walking over tropical oceans.

Southend Pier is the longest pier in the UK and the world, and inspired the great Sir John Betjeman to say 'The pier is Southend, Southend is the pier'. It's also one of the earlier piers to have been built, originating in 1829 as a wooden pier just 183m (600') long. To be so short unfortunately rendered it useless at low tide, so in just four years it had been extended to 2,133m (7,000')! The advent of the railways brought huge numbers of Londoners to the town, so in 1885 it was decided to replace the wooden pier with an iron one. Designed by James Brunlees (remember this name, he crops up later!), the new pier took three years to complete and was opened in 1890, complete with an electric railway. Seven years later the pier was further extended and altered to keep pace with visitor demands and became its current awesome length.

The pier became 'HMS Leigh' during the Second World War after being requisitioned by the Admiralty, but returned to its former use after the war in spectacular fashion. The electric train is recorded as carrying 4,713,082 passengers during the 1949/50 season with another million visitors entering through the turnstiles! The first of five fires occurred in 1959 and destroyed the pavilion and shoreward end. Fortunately boats were on hand to rescue the 500 people who were trapped on the rest of the pier and no one was hurt. Despite making repairs the decline of the pier began, fuelled by cheap foreign holidays where the good summer weather was guaranteed. By the mid 1970s, spiralling costs to maintain the pier meant the threat of demolition became very real.

The council decided on a 15-year restoration plan, but in 1976 a serious fire ravaged the pier head, requiring the services of not just the fire brigade to put it out but also tugs and crop-spraying planes. Boats and the pier railway evacuated stranded people to safety. Just a year later another fire badly damaged the shoreward end and meant the pier was closed for safety reasons soon afterwards. Piers being the evocative things they are meant a local action group drove forward a rebuilding programme that started in 1984 and saw Princess Anne opening the pier two years later. However, later that same year a ship collided with the pier, effectively sectioning it near the pier head and then in 1995 another fire destroyed the shoreward end bowling alley and railway terminal. Locals refused to let their pier die and resolutely began rebuilding yet again.

A spectacular new lifeboat station was built on the pier head and opened in 2000, complete with water and waste pumping facilities. Fire damage was also repaired and the toilets and shelters along the length of the pier were refurbished to compliment the new glass and metal entrance structure at the other end, complete with a museum. The last fire occurred in 2005 and destroyed the pub, toilets, shops, pier-head railway station and some 30m of pier deck. In 2008 however, work started on the repair of these blighted sections with the bill to re-deck and build a new station likely to cost £2.25 million.

The fantastic futuristic glass and steel entrance to the museum nestles in between various fun fair type amusements and baffles lesser mortals like myself by appearing to have no way in. However, once steered in the correct direction, it became obvious and we were impressed to find a museum and gift shop downstairs and ticket office upstairs. The choice is now left to the visitor – will you walk? Walk one way and train back or vice versa? Chicken out and take the train both ways? Or be a hero and walk there and back? If you choose the latter it may be advisable to wear stout walking shoes, pack an expedition-sized rucksack of provisions, water, spare socks, thermals, sunhat, sun block, compass etc... you may be gone for a while! It's only once you've bought your ticket to walk both ways, do you realise the error of your ways, as the doors open and there is the pier, stretching off into the hazy distance. Oh dear...

We set off, aided by a ramp down onto the main body of the pier and pacing ourselves as the sun beat down mercilessly. To our left, the little electric train trundled off towards the pier head with a full load of visitors, cheerfully pulled along by the aptly named *Sir John Betjeman* and resplendent in blue and white livery. We strolled along the planks admiring the functional railings and evenly spaced lamp posts stretching away into the distance – nothing fancy here! On the horizon the T-shaped pier head appeared huge and indistinct, the lifeboat station looking more like a fun fair and roller coaster in the heat haze. There were plenty of other fellow walkers but we wondered how many of them would be walking back too!

The length of the pier has strategically placed shelters where you can hide from the menace of the sun (or the wind, depending on your luck) and above the eerie silence, occasionally the hallucinating traveller can hear cries praising the purveyor of head-freezingly cold fizzy drinks that can be found in vending machines in these shelters. They're real, not mirages! We stopped to appreciate the quiet and calm half a mile out from shore. I can be precise because at intervals there are small wooden signs reminding you just how far you have to walk back to the shore. The 1 mile sign is particularly awesome!

At this literal milestone we paused and looked at the scenery – Southend seemed far away and silent, the end of the pier rapidly approaching and a light sea-breeze ruffling our hair. Over the side of the pier was another world, the water looking deceptively shallow as the tide slowly seeped out, amazingly clear and revealing some hidden delights. There were huge mussels and barnacles clinging tightly to the metal pier legs, tufts and fronds of seaweed sprouting like unwanted clumps of ear hair from in between the crustaceans. And there... oooh, and there, look! Lots of rather large fish, gliding like aquatic seabirds in and out of the seaweed trees, seemingly chased by their equally flighty shadows while we looked on from our lofty perch. I guessed that they might be bass, something backed up as we passed a knowledgeable fisherman pointing them out to his son. Once spotted, we saw more of these wonderful creatures who seemed particularly fond of nonchalantly circling the pier legs – maybe we were lucky because the water was so calm.

As we approached the end, damage from the recent fires became very apparent. After the pier's fiery history the right-hand side of the T-shaped head is just a skeleton of girders now, with all decking removed for the foreseeable future. Past the temporary station for the pier train you can clearly see the charred and blackened timbers clinging to the rusted skeletal framework of the pier. Fortunately there is also plenty of evidence of the pier's rebirth, thanks to the dedication of the people of Southend who have refused to let their pier succumb to the ravages of fire. Walking to the pier head, we noticed lovely new planking, smart silver railings, plenty of benches and LOTS of space to relax before the trek back to land. Here we found the new lifeboat house and RNLI gift shop, a wonderful modern piece of architecture made from wood, glass and steel covering different levels. We walked up to the top deck and leant against the rails to have an end-of-the-pier kiss under the old silver bell in what felt like a *Titanic* moment, then watched the fishermen picking weed from their lines, the old people picking crumbs from their teeth and the pigeons and starlings popping in and out of the decking under our feet – it took a while to work out where they were coming from!

We paused at the well-used temporary café and toilet facilities before we picked our way back along the warm wooden planks towards the land, leaving the gently lapping tide behind us in favour of a smooth mudscape, where brightly coloured boats perched lopsided looking at their artistic reflections in the left-over puddles. As we walked, the sounds of everyday life began to filter back in – the squeals of people on the clattering funfair rides, the trundling of the train and the hum of the traffic along the seafront road. As we emerged into the hurly burly of a hot Southend Sunday, we looked back at the pier stretching off into the late afternoon haze and marvelled that not only had a pier been constructed that was so amazingly long but also that we'd walked that distance. Twice! It had been a weekend of very different piers, contrasting in more ways than one, but all quintessentially English and well worth going to. We were now well into our stride visiting our list of piers and wondered where we would be journeying to next.

CHAPTER 7

The Modern and the Classic: Southport and Lytham St Anne's

We decided to carry on visiting piers over the winter thinking that to cover 57 structures in eighteen months or so seemed an awfully large target, especially when we had only been to six so far. We also had no fixed order to visit the remaining piers although we had grouped them into manageable packages that could be done in a weekend. Feeling brave, therefore, we plumped for heading north to the Lancashire coast on this ominously wet October weekend to see the delights of Southport and Lytham, then to see the remains of Fleetwood pier and the three Blackpool piers. As we hurtled up the motorway my trusty co-pilot suddenly exclaimed "Bloody hell, there's another one!" as we shot past the sign for Wigan Pier. I sighed and carried on... (Yes, it's called a pier but technically it's a landing jetty.)

We made it safely to Southport on the western side of Lancashire, a rather grand town of wide streets, attractive tall Georgian buildings and neat gardens that looked wonderful even on such a wet and windy autumn day. We found a car park and proceeded to be blown along the bleak and windswept promenade with the wide expanse of waterlogged beach to our left and the deserted fun park to our right. Saying that the promenade was windswept perhaps wrongly implies that it was dull, grey and boring, as it was anything but. There has obviously been much money spent on decorating the seafront leading to the pier, and I'd love to return on a warmer day to see it all shining in the sun. There are dark blue curling wave shaped railings, cosmic Aeolian sculptures that swung slowly in the gale representing various weather and space related geniuses (we found Galileo and Beaufort), patterned paving and contemporary colourful kite-topped lamp posts, eventually leading us to the pier.

Deceptively the pier doesn't look that long at all – it is the second longest in the country, so this was quite surprising. It is delicate and plain, the neck garlanded with simple hoops, each crowned with a lamp and there is an understated modern wedge of a pavilion to one side of the pier head. And then... an enormous tram, looking like a push-me-pull-you National Express coach trundled along the length. Amazing! And that's not all, for we realised that we weren't looking at the entire length of the pier, it stretched at least the same distance to our right, over land back to the town! We reckoned that there can't be many piers in the country where you can climb steps to access the walkway at various points along its length – we joined the pier at about the halfway point. It's probably also the only pier that goes over a busy road, garden and a golf course before it even reaches the beach. Originally the entire length of the pier stepped over the beach to the sea, but over the years the coast has silted up and the beach has become reclaimed land and built upon. We walked over wet shiny decking to where the pier crossed the road and looked back towards the distant town, taking in the complete 1,107m (3,633'). What is even more amazing is that just eight years after it was first built it was 1,335m (4,380') long and was the longest pleasure pier in the world!

Southport can be regarded as being one of the first true pleasure piers that was built, the preceding ones having started out life as boating jetties and then metamorphosing in their use. For nearly twenty years there had been talk of building a pier at the seaside town, but it wasn't until 1859 that an agreement was finally reached about how to proceed. Remember James Brunlees? He designed the original Southport Pier, but has a much more important part to play in the history of piers, having invented the Brunlees pile jetting system. Instead of just trying to hammer a pile or leg into the sand, Brunlees used a jet of water passed down the centre of the pile to force out sand on the seafloor. As the sand was displaced, the pile sank lower until the required depth was reached and the water switched off. Sand moving back into the space held the piles solidly, a very clever use of the powers of nature – try pulling your foot out of wet sand, the grip is amazing! Using this new method of sinking piles meant the whole pier was constructed in just a year and it opened in 1860 having cost £8,700 amid celebrations that included fireworks and illuminations. With its cast-iron legs so expertly sunk into the sand it also became the first iron pier in the country (unless you are a fan of Gravesend pier in which case it was the second!). Although it was a great success, passengers for the inevitable visiting steamers complained heartily about having to haul their luggage so far along a pier with no shelter from the wild weather. A track was laid down the centre of the pier in 1863 for a baggage cart but now people complained that it blocked their progress – you just can't please everyone – so it was moved to one side of the pier and fenced in. Later this track became a steam tramway to ferry people the new extended length of the pier and for a while, everyone was happy.

Already having weathered one disaster in 1865 when two people were thrown from the tramway and killed, the pier then suffered storm damage in 1889 that swept away the pier-head tea-rooms, followed by a fire in 1897 that destroyed the pavilion. The new century saw new additions – the pavilion and entrance were both redeveloped and the old steam tram was replaced by a smoother, quieter electric tram in 1905. By 1929 the severe silting up of the channel leading to the end of the pier meant that steamers could no longer call there and this was also the time when much of the beach was reclaimed for building land. Another fire caused damage in 1933 and then the outbreak of World War II amazingly saw the pier merely closed without being sectioned, used instead as a base for searchlights to spot German bombers. After the war the supply of DC electricity to the town was stopped and the tram ceased to operate and was replaced by a diesel alternative in 1950. In 1959 a serious blaze levelled all the buildings on the pier head and meant the pier had to be reduced to its current length of 1,113m (3,650'). Slowly the pier began to decline in popularity and condition, until in 1990 the local Sefton Council applied to have it demolished. Yet another example of the resilience of these structures and how much they are held dear to people, the council were defeated by just one vote and the pier was saved!

It cost a massive £7 million to refurbish, much of the money coming from grants and the first phase of the redevelopment (repairing the structure and building the new pavilion) was completed by 2002. The new pavilion was designed by Liverpool architects Shed KM and to my mind looks like an enormous bird-watching hide with one airport-style, floor to ceiling glass wall looking down the coast. The second phase involved the new half-hourly electric tram that was built specifically for the pier at a cost of £300,000 and completed the transformation along with new lighting and entrance to turn the pier from an old-fashioned and unloved embarrassment to a modern, interesting and enjoyable pier experience, the hard work rewarded with the title of Pier of the Year in 2003 by the National Piers Society.

We battled along the pier, clinging to each other like limpets for fear of being blown away in the wind, battered by the sideways sleety rain. The pier is still devoid of shelters from the merciless weather, the only very brief respite coming from the passing tram! Beneath our feet the neat planks were modestly adorned with over 2000 brass plaques of sponsors to one side of the unobtrusive tram tracks. Arriving at the pier head the rain and gale force wind amazingly paused for a moment and we looked out across the distant grey sea, wind turbines to the south on the horizon and Lytham away to the north. We kissed with numb lips, clutching onto the wet railings as the wind began to pick up again but had time to admire the modern wavy silver sculpture there before scurrying into the pavilion to thaw out!

It's by no means the biggest or grandest pavilion you will find at the end of a pier, but it has a wonderful airy feel to it and successfully combines the old and new of seaside experiences, as we found in the arcade full of old-fashioned slot machines! Here you can find out just what the butler saw, play one-armed bandits and have a go at some wonderfully simple looking but fiendishly difficult vintage games using old pennies bought from the kiosk. Moving on there is a very informative display about the history of the pier and also of the wildlife that can be spotted clinging onto the beach on a day like this! We can heartily recommend the café, and as we sampled Aunty Joan's delicious and filling leek and potato soup we gazed out over the wet sands and appreciated the hugeness of the angled glass wall. We were entertained by dapper black and white oystercatchers, picking their way in between the razor shells strewn across the beach. If they're not powered by random bursts of electricity they certainly look it, although Jay decided they scuttled around like miniature Hercule Poirots on their 'tiny leetle legs' whilst wearing immaculate waistcoats!

We stepped outside, relieved to find that the air was still and dry and so declined the offer of a waiting tram in preference to a speedy oystercatcher-type walk back along the pier. As we emerged from the security of the pavilion we were assaulted by gale force winds and an onslaught of slashing rain that had been there all along! We tacked sideways out of the path of the tram and its grinning driver, holding on tightly again to prevent an unscheduled flight to Blackpool. A family went past and we all exchanged those knowing 'whose crazy idea was this?' smiles through gritted teeth, as the man happily flew his Labrador six feet in the air and the two women struggled to stop the baby in his pushchair from being hurled out to sea. Because of this, it took twice as long to walk back to the car and when we got there cranked the heater up to maximum to ensure our clothes dried out and hypothermia was kept at bay!

We decided that there was enough daylight left to visit Lytham St Anne's before 'sunset', although the rain storm sweeping over the north-west that day meant we'd seen precious little sun since Birmingham. On arrival though, after driving along what must be one of the longest beach promenade roads in the world, we were glad we had made it. When you eventually arrive after miles of windswept grass lawns, bandstands, benches and quaint seaside properties St Anne's is a real delight. We splashed past Italianate gardens with fountains, painted and beautifully decorated bandstand-style wind shelters and an evocative memorial to lost lifeboat-men and were finally faced with the most ornate and beautiful pier we'd seen to date, tastefully painted in green and white (complemented by green and white beachside railings) with a fabulous mock Tudor entrance reminiscent of an Agatha Christie-era railway station.

St Anne's Pier had a humble start, and took six years to finish, finally opening in 1885. Designed by A. Mawson and costing £18,000 it was narrow and modest with a single shelter at the seaward end supported on iron columns with lattice girder-work and was primarily a steamer landing stage extending 278m (914') into the sea. Once the enthusiasm for pleasure piers had taken hold, the pier was extended and widened and by 1904 also sported a new 1,000-seater 'Moorish' style concert pavilion, bandstand and other attractions and the mock Tudor entrance with its red brick, imitation beams and gables. It also boasted beautiful wrought-iron railings along its length, which can still be seen today.

Six years later a magnificent glass Floral Hall opened at the pier head, drawing more visitors than the concert hall, which gradually declined. Fortunately for St. Anne's Pier, the hall was effectively saved by Yehudi Menuhin who gave a sell-out concert in April 1975 and secured the renovation of the building. Now restored to its original beauty, Princess Anne visited and the pavilion was regularly packed to capacity. However, as is often the way, this success story was soon to end in tears, and tragically only a few weeks later a serious fire resulted in the loss of the end of the pier, and everything on it. Permission to demolish the end of the pier was refused but another fire in 1982 completely destroyed the Floral Hall and now demolition of the unsafe part of the pier was inevitable. This reduced the pier to its current length of 182m (600') and the stumps of the piles that were once at the pier head can still be seen (and walked round) at low tide. Further refurbishment was carried out to the remaining section of the pier in the 1990s and it remains a popular attraction of St Anne's.

We marvelled at the outside of the pier until the rain started again sending us scuttling into the pier through the mock Tudor entrance. Once inside it's the perfect covered amusements centre for all the family (especially given the inclement weather of good old England), with seaside snacks, slot machines, two-penny coin drops, cars for the toddlers and even a ten-pin bowling alley! The whole interior is light and colourful with doors onto mini-balconies along the pavilion length. Then we faced a bit of a disappointment as the doors leading out onto the decking were locked tight shut and we couldn't find anyone to ask if they could be opened. Peering through the doors it looked tantalisingly close, with the original stumps of the end of the pier like a mother duck hovering not too far away, but we decided to make do with our end of the pier kiss by the doors – at least it was dry!

We strolled back, pausing to have a go on the small-change arcade games before heading back to the car. We listened nervously to the weather report for Sunday and were relieved to hear the outlook was dry – hurray!

CHAPTER 8

A Ghost and Three Ladies – Fleetwood and Blackpool

We would like to take this opportunity to tell you one very important lesson in life – NEVER trust a weatherman! Sunday dawned windy and cold with heavy blustery showers. We made our way to Fleetwood with the intention of walking to the pier and then catching a tram into Blackpool, so stopped at the Ferry Café for fortification in the shape of a bacon barm and a steaming mug of coffee before venturing out into the quiet of the morning. Fleetwood is sadly now very much a shadow of its former self when it was a bustling fishing and commercial port and ferry terminal and also a popular holiday resort for the Lancashire mill working hinterland.

All that remains of the golden heyday now are the shadows of the past, windswept architecture from a grander era, the trams squeaking and rattling like ancient ghost trains plying their trade. Having said that, there is still a lot going on here and it is well worth a visit – the ferries still come and go as does a depleted fishing fleet and some cargo vessels. The seafront promenade has some lovely new artwork to illustrate Fleetwood's history. You can walk along shoals of little silver fish set into the pavement and a touching 'Welcome Home' statue complements the prominent red stone lighthouses that are encircled by the tram tracks. I had been to Fleetwood a long time ago and could remember where the pier was on the sea front, having done some beachcombing on the pebbles around the land-bound piles. We were expecting a scene of devastation and ruin following the serious fire at the beginning of September 2008 but as we rounded the point we were shocked beyond words.

There were no traces whatsoever that a pier had ever existed in Fleetwood at all. No signposts, no burnt planks, no rusted pillars. The only clue to anything at all having been there was a small section of tiled flooring surrounded by some security fencing, and strangely the ghostly charcoal smell of old fire lingering in the air.

Fleetwood's Victoria Pier was one of the last built during what is considered to be the 'golden age' of piers, running from 1860-1910. To have a pier had been debated since 1892 but it was not until 1910 that the 149m (492') pier was completed, wooden decking on iron columns with amusements at the shoreward end. A pavilion was added in 1911 and Fleetwood Pier remained fairly unchanged right up to World War II when a small cinema was added in 1942 and the planking replaced in 1946. Then in 1952 the pier's fortunes took a turn for the worse as a huge fire ripped through the cinema. Much like the conflagration at Weston-super-Mare it could be seen up to 20 miles away and all that remained was tangled metalwork. Unperturbed, rebuilding started straight away and the pier reopened afresh in 1953.

However, growing popularity of Blackpool as a resort with its three piers meant Fleetwood as a resort slowly declined, but against all odds Victoria Pier kept going and in 1972 had a £70,000 facelift. There was little of note in the following 30 years of its history although the pier continued to decline until 2000 when it closed after the owners went into liquidation. New owners took over the pier in 2003 and redeveloped it complete with bars and a restaurant but eventually the pier closed again and was sold at auction for £500,000. There were new plans being debated hotly in the press when, at 4.30 am on 9th September 2008 smoke was spotted coming from the closed pier. In its final days the pier had been boarded up but had proven a magnet for vandals who had repeatedly broken in and caused damage to the inside and exterior. Over 60 fire-fighters attended the blaze, but the pier was gutted by the time they arrived. Within three weeks Wyre Borough Council ordered it to be demolished post-haste and the demolition company moved in to remove the sad remnants of the jewel of Fleetwood's crown. The week we visited, the council revealed that the pier would not be rebuilt. Looking at the dates, we had missed seeing Fleetwood's Victoria Pier (albeit the remains) by days, now just feeling the ghost of it in the air on the promenade, but we kissed for a pier that had been sadly lost.

We glumly returned to the tram stop and took a step back in time as we boarded one of the wonderful old trams to Blackpool. It banged and rattled its way along the coast slowly filling with damp locals and very wet, improperly attired tourists. As we approached the start of the Golden Mile illuminations, the rain was hammering on the outside of the windows, the condensation was becoming tropical and a fug of northerness was building up inside the tram. We descended deeper into depression as we passed under a string of illuminations advertising a well-known burger chain and watched families dragging their children past sex shops blatantly advertising their wares, listening to the people on the tram extolling the virtues of their holiday here while increasing our knowledge of expletives.

We stumbled off the tram into watery sunshine and a vicious biting wind and decided to visit the three Blackpool piers in reverse order, starting with the 'newest' first, the South Pier which was built in 1893. Walking quickly along the promenade to our destination to try and warm up a bit, we noted the new seafront developments that were being carried out, smartening up the seaward side of the promenade and distracting visitors from looking at the rather sad, tatty and down-at-heel shops and amusements on the opposite side. Not all of Blackpool's attractions are tacky – and it has been dubbed the Las Vegas of the North by many for good reason. You could get a tan at night from the number of flashing lights adorning the buildings here, and Blackpool Tower really is worth a visit if you've a head for heights. If thrills and spills are your thing then Blackpool is the destination to top all destinations, it's a funfair by the sea!

It had humbler beginnings, providing a breath of fresh air for the thousands of mill workers in Manchester and surrounding areas, allowing them to take a weekend break, or longer if they were lucky, using the newly constructed railways. North Pier was built first in 1863 closest to the railway station, Central Pier opened five years later, and such was the popularity of the resort that South Pier was built in 1893. Each pier developed its own identity and style of amusements for the throngs of tourists and this uniqueness has been retained today, even with all the flashing lights, noisy amusements and cheap thrills.

South Pier was originally called Victoria Pier when it opened in 1893 and had been designed by T.P. Worthington who, like Brunlees had invented a natty way of driving pier piles into the seabed to speed up the building of these seaside structures. Using a jetting technique like Brunlees,

Worthington's Screwpile System used a steam-powered pump to increase the water pressure and thus sank the piles faster than before. The pier cost £50,000 to build and was constructed of iron and steel to a length of 150m (492'). As well as a pavilion the pier had 36 shops, a bandstand, an ice-cream vendor and a photograph stall.

Little adaptations were made over the years but fires in 1958 and 1964 destroyed the original Grand Pavilion which was replaced with a more modern looking theatre that was well visited by paying customers and stars alike. As theatres became less popular, it was replaced with an amusement arcade and some hair-raising rides, which replaced the demolished buildings at the pier head in 1998. It's a good place to look back at the rides in Blackpool's famous Pleasure Beach, although I wonder how many people know this began in 1896 and was originally just a carousel ride in the sand dunes! Today South Pier doesn't really look like a pier from the promenade and it's only from the side that you can see the Victorian traces of this once grand lady.

The colour scheme for this old girl is a rather fetching shade of red and cream, demonstrated best on the buildings of the delightfully named Laughing Donkey concession at the entrance. Look behind the buckets and spades and hoardings and you can see some rather beautiful Art Deco statuary, in the shape of a stylised horse, looking down at the proceedings. The noise was deafening as amusements vied like technological sirens in an attempt to part us from our money as we entered the pavilion.

Walking through, we soon emerged into the fun fair experience that visitors to Blackpool are keen to participate in. Considering the Pleasure Beach is such a short distance away, the pier was remarkably busy for a cold and wet October weekend, with people queuing up to be stretched, fired up into the air on an enormous bungee rope or get rattled around on the rides at the end of the pier. A word to those who don't like to see through the floor beneath them (myself included), here at the end the planks have been replaced with some of that lovely metal walkway material, the type that you can see through and doesn't look very substantial... The tide was bashing hungrily at the piles some way below as, heart in mouth I tiptoed with Jay to the end of the pier for our kiss, then hot-footed it back round to solid decking on the other side, which affords a good view of the other two piers and Blackpool Tower in between them further up the wave lashed beach. Although it was cold in the strong wind at least the sun was doing its best to shine and the rain had stopped, restoring our faith in weathermen after all! I like to look at all the angles of a pier (although I draw the line at being dangled over the edge on a rope) so I can see all aspects of it, from the pattern on the piles and type of decking used to how many pigeons are in the eaves and finding loose 2ps in the amusement arcades. To begin with we both thought pier piles were all the same, but now began to notice that, just like the piers, they are all different.

Peering under the gaudy exterior of Victoria's skirts you can see her original pins, strong and sturdy iron legs with some rather pretty brackets at the top ornamented with flowers and curls – no expense was spared in making even the utilitarian parts of a pier attractive to look at should you happen to glance seawards. Nowadays I don't expect there are many people who would notice these details – today it was just us and a po-faced seagull perched on a cross member below the decking.

Walking up the revamped prom with its sparkling curved silver railings, like frozen waves stopped before they broke over the footpath, we made our way to the second of Blackpool's *grandes dames*. Sandwiched between South Pier and North Pier is the equally imaginatively named Central Pier who flaunts her wares as more traditional than South Pier, and is probably the more photogenic of the three, thanks to the enormous big wheel on its deck – you can't miss it, especially if you visit at night when the entire thing is illuminated. The pier was added to Blackpool's seafront in 1868 to provide additional facilities for the rapidly growing number of visitors, who were demanding more of the town than the original North Pier could provide. Designed by Lieutenant-Colonel John Isaac Mawson (I've tried to find out if he was related to A. Mawson who engineered St. Anne's Pier, but to no avail) and built by Laidlaw's of Glasgow (who had also erected the North Pier) it reached out nearly 463m (1,518') ending in a 122m (400') wide low-tide jetty at the pier head for those inevitable steamer visits. The piles were cast iron and were put into place using Eugenius Birch's screw pile method which involved screw-tipped piles being twisted into the sand until they hit the bedrock.

Originally looked on as being 'the people's pier' because of the provision made for dancing thereon, it was frowned upon for lowering the tone of the area by the more genteel Victorian visitors to Blackpool, but was a big hit with passengers from the steamers coming from Llandudno, Liverpool, Barrow, Morecambe and Lytham. Central Pier kept up this reputation for being a fun pier by adapting over the years. It featured roller skating in 1909, a joy wheel in 1911, speedboats and a car ride in 1920 and – wait for it – an automatic chip dispenser in 1932! We don't even have those now! Perhaps fuelled by these automatically dispensed fried fancies, the open-air dancing peaked in the 1930s, but gradually declined and ceased in the 1960s after moving indoors for a short while. Eventually the dancing pavilion was replaced by the fabulously named Dixieland Palace. Sadly this survived only five years, being totally destroyed by a serious fire in 1973, but emerging from the ashes in the guise of the current arcade and nightclub. The low level jetty was also removed in the 70s when the length of the pier was shortened to 341m (1,118') but popularity of this pier has never really waned as it has constantly been updated to cater for the changing tastes of the public.

The seaward end theatre was modernised in 1986 and the iconic Ferris wheel added in 1990. At 33m (108') high it meant the pier had to have substantial strengthening added to the superstructure, which cost around £750,000 to carry out.

All the money has been well spent, for on a day like this in a town with a huge funfair and enough amusements to keep even the pickiest visitor occupied for hours, Central Pier was busy. Granted, not as packed as I've seen it in the summer, but busy nonetheless, and if statistics are to be believed, this pier gets in the region of 2 million visitors a year! I am going to keep pretty quiet about my last visit to Central Pier – it was in a past life and I actually got escorted off the pier by no less than three security guards... and all for the heinous crime of having a dog with me! Hoping that I looked very different these days and that the guards on duty had moved on to pastures new we slipped on to the pier through the left-hand entrance and began our walk to the end, bypassing the warehouse-style corrugated entrance to the arcades, with flags and an enormous sign telling you where you are in case you weren't sure!

Central Pier has a pretty sky-blue and white (with a hint of primrose yellow) theme going on and the most exquisitely detailed wrought-iron bench backs we've ever seen. The continual seating runs along much of the length of the pier with this glorious ironwork making up the rails as it goes – pretty and functional! The amusements on the pier are not only crammed into every single available space, but are definitely of the more traditional visiting-fun-fair type, with shooting stalls next to the likes of dodgems, a helter-skelter and that enormous wheel dominating the whole affair. Weaving our way in and out of the kiosks we followed the more functional modern railings (and then some of the old ones again) as they curved round the theatre pavilion. This gentle sweep gave the air of an old paddle steamer out at sea and we attempted to be equally elegant as we made it to the end for a salty windswept kiss under the watchful gaze of the Tower on the seafront, and then retraced our steps in order to visit the last of the Blackpool dames.

Strolling past the imposing tower, North Pier drew closer and revealed itself to be the stateliest of all the piers in Blackpool, more of a duchess than a dame. As we approached, a rainbow arced across the slate-grey clouds behind the pier and the sun shone on the elegant green and white simplicity of the delicate architecture. This is the oldest of Blackpool's piers and gained its name from being so close to Blackpool North railway station where many of the original visitors to the town came from, although it is now also the most northerly of the piers too.

It was designed by good old Eugenius Birch, and was only the second of the fourteen piers he was responsible for engineering. It opened in 1863 with a landing jetty added a year later and then further extended in 1867 to a length of 503m (1,650'). It had its own steamers that went to the Lake District, the Isle of Man, Llandudno, Southport and Liverpool. Given that there were so many excursions and piers, the Irish Sea along the Lancashire coast must have been extremely busy back then! North Pier was so popular that it was enlarged with the addition of an Indian-style pavilion and amusements added in 1874, but it had to be extended again in 1875 and in 1877, with wings added to the sides and newfangled electric lighting installed.

The pier's history has not been without a certain amount of chequering, with ships colliding with the structure and the pavilion burning down not just in 1921 but again in 1938. The current 1,500 seat theatre also caught fire in 1985 but was saved by singer Vince Hill who spotted the blaze and helped extinguish it (although it may have been just a ploy to get himself mentioned in books for years to come!). A considerable sum was also spent on redeveloping the entrance buildings at this time and adding a tramway to get to the end of the pier. Although storms meant the jetty had to close for several years, it was successfully reopened as a helipad for a short while, before the MV *Balmoral* resumed visits in 1992. It was awarded the National

Piers Society 'Pier of the Year' accolade in 2004, the only one of Blackpool's piers to have been decorated in this way, and when the summer sun ventures out is still Blackpool's favourite spot to sunbathe on a stripy deckchair.

The entrance to the pier is an eclectic mix of classical colonial-style kiosks in green and white, and a huge glass-fronted arch and colourful signage that wouldn't be out of place on a Mississippi paddle-boat, but they strangely work! To get onto the main body of the pier we walked past the amusements, flashing lights and traditional fortune teller to purchase a ticket. In their heyday, most piers would charge a penny toll for promenaders, but these days there don't seem to be too many piers with admission fees, and where they are in place this is a nominal charge. The more we have researched piers, the huge cost of running and maintaining these structures has become apparent, and even with amusements and the 2 million plus visitors to North Pier every year, we could see that every penny from these charges would be well spent.

Stepping through the doors is like stepping back in time, from the gaudy, flashing lights and sounds of the amusement arcade into the sea-spray tinted fresh air with just a hint of seagull cry and landward noises. The long pier stretches away towards the sea, pleasantly wide and empty but with plenty to look at! There are cute cupola-topped, octagonal kiosks overhanging the side of the pier, selling traditional seaside nick-nacks (winkles anyone?!), and elegant wrought-iron benches along the sides of the smooth, solid planking. The windswept tramway station is still at the landward end of the pier, leading to the little rusty rails that run down the centre of the pier and overlooked by huge imposing metropolitan double-headed lamp standards.

Strolling down the substantial planking, arm in arm, it was easy to imagine North Pier full of elegant promenading couples taking the sea air, stopping to rest in a brightly coloured deckchair or sampling local seafood doused in vinegar – this really is a grand pier! At the end of the wide sweeping deck, the pier broadens to accommodate amusements, and we were surprised to find a beautiful two-storey traditional carousel inside the first shelter, complete with galloping horses, organ and fairground lights. There are bars and refreshments and a huge, elegant glass sun-lounge on one side and then the theatre, which was gearing up for another evening performance while we were there, as proof, if it were needed that this pier is thriving with amusements for all the family.

We snuck a kiss at the end of the pier and returned slowly back towards the prom, having a second look at the ornate ironwork of the benches and lamps and the gorgeous little kiosks. Looking north reveals the more sedate side of Blackpool, with the imposing red brick Metropole Hotel towering above a stern sweeping concrete sea-wall that protects the seaside residences along the coast from the wild winter waves back towards Fleetwood.

Once we'd negotiated the amusement arcades again, I had one more mission to accomplish, to find a little piece of heaven that is a Holland's meat pie! Fortunately I didn't have far to go, as there was a chip shop promising one of these bijou delicacies at the front of the pier, so we ventured inside, if only to warm up a bit! If you've not had a Holland's meat pie, they're hard to describe – a greyish nugget of moist meatiness (and no, I don't want to know what it is) lies encased in a small round case of squishy pastry, with the most delicious, searingly hot liquor gently caressing it. To the inexperienced, it's this juice that could put you off one of these pies for life, for if you're not prepared, it can squirt out and leave you with a face full of second-degree burns! However, I happily (and carefully) tucked in, the pie being as good as I remembered. Jay however, was not impressed, and declined any more, settling for chips instead but we were happy with our visit and agreed that we *had* found some pier delicacies along the Lancashire coast as we bounced back on the tram to Fleetwood!

CHAPTER 9

The Clevedon Cobweb

What do you do on a cold, blowy and dull November day when nothing seems appealing? Go to your nearest seaside and blow away the dust of course! Along the short stretch of the West Country coastline where we are it is possible to visit five very different piers in just one day, and we are lucky enough to live slap-bang in the centre of this pier universe at Weston-super-Mare, with Burnham-on-Sea to the south and possibly the prettiest of the country's piers just to the north at Clevedon. Raved about by Sir John Betjeman, Michael Heseltine, the National Piers Society (although if we're sticking to their rules this shouldn't be counted because it's well up the Severn estuary and technically not on the sea!) and anyone who has ever visited, this little jewel of a pier nestles quietly on an uncluttered and unobtrusive seafront, just waiting to be discovered.

Clevedon had been a relatively quiet town centred around fishing and farming until the Elton family turned it into a select seaside resort in the early 1800s. Grand Regency houses sprang up throughout the town as the well-to-do from Bristol came to take the sea air, and Brunel ran his Great Western Railway down from Bristol in 1841 which opened up the West Country to people from London. A branch line to bring visitors directly into Clevedon was opened in 1847 and a further light railway run by the Weston, Clevedon and Portishead Light Railway transformed it into a popular and thriving resort by 1897. It is a delightfully untouched town, even the newer housing estates rub shoulders comfortably with the older buildings without the awkward architectural blunders that can happen in other rural towns. Whilst the centre of Clevedon is worth a visit (and perhaps also the 1912 Curzon cinema, the oldest continuously operating picture-house in the country), our seaside amble to view the pier starts at Salthouse Fields, now a busy recreation area and play park some half a mile from the pier.

The promenade is raised above the field, which boasts a model railway, donkey rides in the summer and a huge play area out of the wind. Up on the promenade there are stunning views across the boating lake (once an open-air swimming pool for the hardy Victorians) to Cardiff and the Welsh mountains. Today the wind was blowing icily from the west, making the flags snap and crack as they strained to break free from the flagpoles along the sea wall. We walked briskly past the deserted skateboard park, tennis courts and pitch-and-putt, and on past the lure of a scalding hot coffee at the diminutive amusement arcade to our right and the multicoloured rocky beach to our left. Clevedon has a diverse coastline, classified as a SSSI (Site of Special Scientific Interest) with pebbly beaches, little cliffs and a spectacular area of raised striated rocks nearer the pier, as well as the ubiquitous stretches of Severn estuary mud when the tide goes out! Once past the Victorian bandstand we dropped down to the promenade leading to the pier with the Regency buildings to our right that stop abruptly, as if surprised to find the water's edge there. There are no seafront amusements here, just a quiet walk past elegant but sea-scarred railings on a paved surface that reflects the same curved design up to the pier.

And to the pier itself – the only 100% standing and functional Grade 1 listed pier in the country (Brighton West pier is the other, but is now a skeleton in the sea), and quite unlike any other pier either. Sir Arthur Elton, one of the later benefactors of the town described it as a cobweb above the waves, and it is not hard to see why, looking at the elegant arches tiptoeing out 257m (842') into the Severn. The Clevedon Pier Company was founded in the 1860s to obtain an Act of Parliament to build a pier here, making the most of the hundreds of visitors brought by train to the town and to capitalise on the huge steamer trade of the time too. The building started in 1867 and must have been quite a feat of engineering with John Grover and Richard Ward's elegant design being erected by 60 men during tidal changes of up to 12m (40') and in a vicious tidal current that can reach speeds of up to 10 knots (11.5 mph or 18.5 km/ph) as it goes in and out twice a day, made worse by the fact this part of the coastline has no protection from the elements.

The contractors were fortunate to come into possession of a large quantity of 'Barlow' rail, from an abandoned project of Brunel's to build a broad-gauge railway in South Wales. These patented hollow, light, slender but strong and versatile iron rails were perfect for bolting together and curving into the slender arches needed for the pier, and it took two years to use up the piles of metal that were stored on the beach then manhandled and craned into position 15m (48') above the shore. Once the pier was completed, work turned to constructing a shoreward approach, toll house and accommodation for the Piermaster. This was designed by Hans Price, a much celebrated architect from Weston-super-Mare, who came up with a fashionable ornate, castellated, elongated, octagonal Scottish castle creation. The pier opened amid a huge gala celebration on Easter Monday, March 1869 overseen by nearly a thousand locals and more than two thousand people from Bristol and Exeter, including five hundred passengers brought in on one train from Bristol!

The pier proved to be well-used for nearly twenty years by steamers that provided the quickest route to Wales, until in 1886 the Severn Railway tunnel was opened, and on passing into the hands of the council the pier underwent a facelift which included a new pier head and a six-level, cast-iron and wooden landing stage built at an angle to the main pier to make it easier and safer for steamers to berth and for passengers to embark safely despite the wildly fluctuating tide level. The pagoda-style pavilion was also added and the pier re-opened to a new flourish of steamer traffic, including the White Funnel fleet. The life of the pier continued uneventfully – no fires and not even a collision occurred, despite the hazardous nature of the estuarine waters, although the landing stage was replaced in 1913 with the present pre-cast concrete construction (funny how concrete is thought of as being a modern building material!).

Since the 1950s, piers had been subject to structural tests by the Ministry of Transport for insurance purposes, and Clevedon Pier was no different. Six plastic 'bags' (each 50ft long, 5ft wide and 2ft deep were filled with 10ins water to give a pressure of 50lbs/square foot) were used for each span to simulate a load, then emptied and dragged to the next span. It was on 17th October 1970 during one of these tests that the seventh span buckled and collapsed, dragging the eighth span down into the sea with it.

Making national news, the pier was instantly closed, its future uncertain. Some suggested it should be demolished which sparked much protest, and the Clevedon Pier Preservation Trust was established and began a huge fundraising campaign to restore the pier. In 1980 a Public Enquiry was held to determine the future of the pier, backed by the then-Poet Laureate Sir John Betjeman who said Clevedon Pier was 'the most beautiful pier in England. Its demolition would be a tragedy'. Politician Michael Heseltine also intervened to prevent demolition, and eventually judgment was passed in the favour of the Trust. From 1984 after considerable sums of money were raised from fundraising and grants, the rebuild of Clevedon Pier started. Despite the original contractors going into receivership, such was the determination of the Trust to see their pier back in action that a new firm were found with help from English Heritage and the National Heritage Memorial Fund – it took some £4 million in total to save it.

During the summer of 1988 the new parts were towed into place and reassembled, then re-decked with planks that were sponsored by members of the public. Amid much celebration the pier re-opened in May 1989, with cruises on the *Waverley* and many people dressed in Victorian costume – a real step back in time! Work was still needed to fully restore the pier head and pagoda, and this was finished in May 1998 with another Victorian extravaganza and grand opening by Sir Charles Elton, the great-grandson of the original pier owner!

Today the pier has lost none of its charm despite the days of the mass audiences arriving by steamer or railway being long gone. The castle-like nature of the Tollhouse perched on craggy rocks is slightly lost due to being overshadowed by the equally dark and Gothic pigeon-strewn ruins of the Rock House Hotel (later the Royal Pier Hotel, destroyed by fire in May 2003). The hotel was built in 1823 as a guest house but upgraded in 1869 to provide accommodation for people disembarking at the pier. It deserves a mention because the upgrade to the hotel was also designed by Hans Price. The pier's eight delicately arched spans stretch out across the choppy water and end in a latticed box pier head, topped with an elegant green and white pagoda and two matching smaller shelters.

Unlike any other pier we have seen, the accent here is on the arches and delicate nature of the whole structure – the decking and walkway, despite having solid wooden sides and lamp standards is hardly noticeable and the eye is drawn all the while to the curves supporting it. Look back at any other pier and the norm is a flat, solid, substantial construction on a mass of straight upright piles and cross-hatched supports. We ventured into the Tollhouse to pay our £1.50 entrance fee, which may seem expensive but goes towards the continual upkeep and insurance of the pier, which alone can cost in excess of £100,000 a year.

Stepping out onto the landward end of the pier you feel a little like a bowling ball, about to roll down the ramp onto straight, flat decking that looks rather like an old-fashioned bowling alley! (We found out later that it has actually been used as such for a fund-raising venture – what a brilliant idea!) The decking itself consists of simple, widely-spaced planks laid in the direction of travel that afford a scary view of the milkshake coloured torrent below. Each one is covered in tiny brass plaques, evidence of the support afforded to the pier to get it rebuilt. At either side of the deck along the entire length of the pier are wooden high-backed benches interrupted at intervals with short elegant, sturdy, black wrought-iron Victorian lamp-standards topped with white globe shades. Brass plaques are everywhere, from the planking on the deck to the backs of every bench – spend a while spotting the famous names and see if you can find ours, kindly donated by the pier's current Pier Mistress, Linda Strong, when she heard of our travels around the country!

As we strolled along (me clinging on for dear life because of the seemingly huge gaps in the decking) we took in the views up, down and across the Severn estuary. To the right there are wooded cliffs, rocky cakes iced with houses on the top, and in the distance the two Severn bridges can be spotted glinting in the sun. We (carefully!) leaned over the side to see the beautiful green arches dipping into the rushing, grabbing tide that greedily pulls at the girder work, complete with the maker's name still embossed on them. Watching the water here gives an idea of how fast and merciless the current can be too and we felt real admiration for the team of workmen who assembled this stunning pier against the elements.

Looking to the left we could see back along the promenade to the boating lake and then in the distance, the islands of Steep and Flat Holm on the horizon. Directly in front is Wales – on some days it appears crystal clear and you can see every detail. There is something very special about the light quality here and it is worth visiting the pier for a walk as the sun is going down, as it boasts some spectacular sunsets across this wide expanse of water.

The pier was quite busy when we visited, despite the howling icy winds, and as we approached the pier head had to navigate our way around several well-wrapped fishermen and their enormous rods (stop tittering at the back, I'm on about their tackle! Oh for goodness sake, you're incorrigible!). Clevedon Pier is a popular haunt for sea anglers and a wide variety of species can be caught here and the recent catches including an impressive cod were displayed on a poster at the pier head. The central feature here is the beautiful pagoda which has a tiny tearoom on the first floor which provides a simple array of snacks for visitors. Everything is adorned with really beautiful and intricate green and white wrought iron, which we took time to examine as we sipped our fizzy beverages outside the café! Outside the pagoda at roof level are stunning ivy-leaved swags in green, complicated but still delicate white floral railings all around the top 'deck' and even the spindles up the steps are wrought-iron works of art with more flowers incorporated into the design. Green and red columns support the pagoda and these are topped with substantial ostrich plumes – the columns on the building have Corinthian tops and sport a five-pointed, almost Eastern-style star. Rich red and yellow squares of stained glass complete the period feel.

But the stunning attention to detail doesn't end here – there are two identical four-sided shelters too that are not just utilitarian windbreaks with benches inside but another excuse to cover everything with more wrought iron! There are anchors holding up the roof, each one adorned with a little six-pointed star that to my mind looks like a starfish, and arch-topped windows, all in the same green and white colour scheme with a hint of red. Access to the landing stage is underneath the pagoda, and today the pier is often visited by the *Waverley* and *Balmoral*, retaining its original use and bringing new fans to this architectural gem on the North Somerset coastline.

At the end of the pier we stopped to read more of the 10,000 plaques that seem to cover every surface (they're several deep here!) and looked at the view, which today was rather fuzzy. Even here there is attention to detail with the same colour scheme picking out the railings and chains and full-height lamps, so everything has a decorative edge. With the wind threatening to blow us back to the land with a dose of hypothermia we had a warming kiss before strolling back up the other side of the pier to read some of the other plaques!

Back inside the Tollhouse there is a selection of tasteful gifts and mementoes to browse through, and an interesting bijou art gallery upstairs, many pictures include the beautiful lacework of the pier, often by sunset. It is worth looking at the pier at night-time too, something we have since done for a Valentine's Day fundraising event. Walking along the pier by the lamplight of the golden orbs, which pick out the brass plaques on the decking making them sparkle like a seaside yellow brick road, is hugely magical. At the end the Pagoda beams warmly from ruby and gold windows like a welcoming lighthouse and the lights of Cardiff sparkle like a new constellation – the perfect place to celebrate another pier kiss and we urge you to try it too!

CHAPTER 10

Romance on the Riviera – Paignton, Torquay and Teignmouth

The first weekend in December dawned cold and crisp but clear, the sun dawning golden in a duck egg sky as we headed off down the M5 towards the English Riviera, past chestnut cattle rimed with frost and steaming gently in the fields like something from a picture postcard. Pier visiting might not seem like the most obvious thing to do on a December weekend, but most piers are open all year round and we decided to make the most of the gorgeous weather.

Devon has been a popular holiday destination for the English tourist for many decades and acquired its reputation of Riviera-ness by way of the balmy climate and beautiful secluded beaches, comparable (apparently) to those in the South of France, and is still a favourite with sun-seekers and holidaymakers of all ages today, but is not perhaps, as well-known for its piers.

We travelled first to the pier that can claim to be the furthest south in the country, pulling up in Paignton with the sun still beaming and the sky a stunning crystal blue. Away from the heaving crowds that pack the streets in the summer, the visitor can now appreciate this seaside resort, full of interesting shopping streets, russet brick buildings and a wide, spacious seafront – so wide it's hard to believe it IS a seafront! Having said that there are lots of things to do here and there are often events being held on the beach lawns, but today it was free from impediment and we were soon on the wide promenade overlooking the sea. The seafront is spectacularly broad with a pleasing curve that hugs the edge of the wide, sweeping bay and the pinky-brown beach slopes gently down to tempting wavelets sighing onto the sands. It is partly the colours here that make this part of the coastline so appealing – the sky is a wonderful forget-me-not blue, the sea mirroring this with added diamond sparkles and the beach glistens in shades of pink and terracotta, with a sprinkling of pearly seashells and vivid green sea lettuce – stunning!

To add to the enjoyable ambience of the mile-long stretch of beach, Paignton Pier sits demurely in the middle, tiptoeing some 229m (750') out into Tor Bay. It is long, straight and uncomplicated – neither fancy nor gaudy, with simple pairs of unadorned piles running along its length. The main white and grey pavilion and buildings sit quite low in the centre of the pier, tempting the visitor to explore further, which we duly did!

Paignton Pier was really a second-best option for the town following a remarkable attempt by businessman Arthur Hyde Dendy in 1871 to buy and move nearby Teignmouth Pier to the resort to provide a much needed tourist attraction for the Victorian promenaders. Huge technical problems forced Mr Dendy to abandon this venture, so plans for a new pier made from iron instead of wood (Victorian one-upmanship?!) were drawn up by George Soudon Bridgman and construction began in 1878. Considering how long it takes construction projects to be completed in this day and age with modern machinery, it never ceases to amaze me how quickly piers were constructed in the Victorian era, and true to form, Paignton Pier opened for business in June 1879, a grand 238m (780') long.

No expense was spared, and the new pier provided popular entertainments in a superb pavilion at the pier head that boasted state-of-the-art lighting, a moveable stage, organ and grand piano for concerts, balls and performances and in 1881 a billiard room was added, along with a roller-skating rink for the more adventurous visitors. Unusually the pier wasn't built with the steamer trade in mind as the coast was well served by the new Great Western Railway, and it wasn't until Dendy's death in 1886 when the pier became owned by the Devon Dock, Pier and Steamship Company that paddle steamers began to call in, bringing more visitors from the resorts of Brixham and Torquay.

A huge fire in 1919 destroyed the glorious pavilion and pier head, and these were never replaced, which led to a protracted period of decline that saw the pier sectioned in World War II. With the 9m (30') gap replaced after the war, the pier remained open, but it wasn't until 1980 that the pier was rejuvenated and given a new lease of life. Building work widened the shoreward end and gave Paignton the pier that visitors see today, and probably like us, they will think that there are lots of buildings on the decking, but this is not the case!

We bypassed the Portacabin-style entrance and made our way along the spacious deck towards the peculiar pseudo-pyramid (but not unpleasant or out of place) entrance to the main pavilion which, instead of being the several buildings linked together that it appeared to be from outside, turned out to be just one long building, housing the traditional all-weather amusements demanded by today's seaside visitors. Owing to the gorgeous weather, we decided to forego a peek inside the pavilion and followed the walkway outside instead. Tor Bay is a beautiful location for a pier, and there are stunning views in all directions of the pretty rose-red coastline and the marine traffic towards the horizon, especially in the sparkling December sunshine! The walk along the pier was also a delight – despite its modern revamp there are lots of interesting things to look at. The way is lined with elegant Victorian-style lamp standards and what initially look like municipal metal railings, but these have been cleverly transformed into something much more stylish with a beautiful swirly floral panel at the bottom.

Once past the end of the pavilion the outdoor amusements resumed, with go-karts, slides and a carousel, although there weren't any takers today, before we got to the end railings and looked out across the bay. We marvelled again at the stunning views, and how lucky we were to visit when the sea was so calm and the sun so warm, although after a few minutes of romance leaning on the seaward railings the nip in the air became apparent and we decided to head back to land and carry on with our trip along the coast before we got frostbite!

Leaving Paignton behind, we travelled a very short distance along the coast to Torquay, the hot-spot and focal point of the English Riviera for tourists and visitors of every age – and it really does have a lot on offer. Nestling tightly into its red, sandstone-lined bay, Torquay is a little sun-trap and was surprisingly hot (for December, at any rate) out of the light sea breeze. The town has a certain Victorian quaintness and some stunning architecture nestling alongside some more modern additions, a thriving harbour-side and some rather attractive landscaped gardens with a beautiful decorative fountain, which are a lure to old and young alike on such a sunny day!

Being careful to do a little research before we set off to visit each pier, we knew that Torquay's Princess Pier was one of those is-it-isn't-it piers, and as we rounded the fantastic ornate Victorian pavilion building (now a shopping centre and not to be confused with a pier pavilion) we initially thought we were in the wrong place, because we could only see a teeming, thriving harbour – where's the pier?!

We followed the strategically placed signposts and arrived on the western side of the harbour and were presented with a wide walkway which *looked* like a pier but was sat on top of the harbour wall. Or was it...? By all accounts Princess Pier is unusual and is regarded as a pier, not a sea wall, by the National Piers Society as it is apparently a latticework structure of girders with a timber promenade that was built in 1890. A concrete groyne and extra timbers and girders were added four years later and the substantial wooden landing stage was built in 1906, taking the length of the pier to 238m (780′).

With wrought-iron lamps and benches along a wide, spacious wooden decking, Princess Pier was a popular promenading spot, perhaps due to its simplicity. There was an entertainment centre built at the pier head, but a fire in 1974 damaged it to the extent it had to be demolished, and it has never been replaced. Major reconstruction work was carried out in the 1950s with the rest being done in 1978 – a task that was so complex it was entered for an environmental award the following year.

We stopped on the landward end of Princess Pier and pondered its inclusion as a pier, and first impressions were not very favourable I'm afraid – to all intents and purposes it looks like a walkway on top of a sea wall, and not like a traditional pier with sea flowing unimpeded beneath it at all. It may have piles driven into the seabed and a wooden decking adorning the top but we still weren't convinced!

However, we did walk as far as we could along (as there isn't really an 'end' to the pier, more the point where it runs out and turns back into the harbour wall!) and had a good look at it, and then walked back again and had a good disagreement about what we found! To our left as we walked out towards the sea we could see the very busy and bustling harbour, with yachts and motor boats jostling for space in front of the older buildings of the town, edged with some arty red sandstone cliffs, stacks and arches for geological interest. To our other side we watched a water-skier hurtling across the glassy waters of the bay, swinging around and coming to grief as he crashed back into the waves of his own creation! Up above, looking down on the sea front are tiers of white-fronted buildings in a variety of styles, but leaning heavily on the St. Tropez theme, helped by studdings of Torbay palms and pine trees here and there under a Mediterranean azure sky.

The pier itself was an extremely pleasant experience – a beautiful wide expanse of decking divided simply by a string of multi-coloured fairy-lights along its length. On either side, wrought-iron and wooden benches make up the sides of the pier, interspersed with wrought-iron column lamp standards fixed to the back of the benches and topped with a globe light. All the wrought-iron along the entire length of the pier has been painted white, and it picks out the stunningly simple star and circle design of the ironwork on the benches beautifully. Everything about Princess Pier is understated and simple, but adds to the regal experience of promenading in the sublime seaside air above the sea.

We walked as far as the curve and steps down to the sea wall, and Jay begrudgingly had an end-of-the-pier kiss (not because he'd suddenly gone off me, but rather he did not really feel it was a proper pier!) before we strolled back to the seafront, debating the inclusion of Princess Pier in our quest.

From the top it certainly looks and feels like a traditional Victorian pier, and has a lovely dignified feel about it – I would love to go back on a summer's evening when the fairy-lights and globe lanterns were alight – but lift the skirts of this topping and it really doesn't seem to fit the criteria of a pier at all. We both feel that there should be an unobstructed flow of water between a pier's piles for it to be a 'proper' pier and sadly this Princess is sat on a wall with just her toes in the water! We walked past the substantial timbers of the landing stage and made dry land, still debating the validity of this as a pier all the way back to the car and on to our last pier of the day at Teignmouth.

Teignmouth, to the east of Torquay, was a thriving seaside resort in the early Victorian era and as you approach along the windy roads and down the steep hills it's not hard to see what the appeal would have been as it is still there today. Once over the River Teign we travelled through the old town towards the seafront and parked up by the wide beach lawns known as the Den, overlooked by an impressive crescent of Georgian buildings and found the front of the pier.

Much like Paignton, Teignmouth Pier is a simple, straightforward affair – no glamorous shapely legs or elaborate buildings on the decking, but a functional seaside pier offering up some traditional seaside amusements on a delightful beach and coastline, so we ventured further to see what there was on offer – and at least it *had* legs!

Teignmouth Pier was designed by J.W. Wilson in the 1860s to provide the town with a fashionable promenading venue stretching 213m (700') out across the water and was built on cast-iron screw piles over two years, opening to the public in 1867. With men's bathing machines to one side of the pier and the ladies' to the other, Teignmouth Pier afforded a popular addition to the resort and survived the plot to transport it to the more popular resort of Paignton in 1871. It was extensively refurbished in 1876 and was then added to with an enormous shoreward pavilion in the late 1880s and a seaward end, more demure pavilion in 1890 and was a popular destination for steamer excursions from Weymouth and Plymouth at the turn of the century.

Teignmouth Pier had an uneventful life until 1904 when the entrance kiosks crashed unceremoniously onto the beach, but then all was quiet until 1954 when a fire destroyed the castle pavilion at the seaward end and the bridging section leading to the landing stage. This had to be removed and so shortened the pier's length by 23m (75'), but further work was needed when it was found that the rest of the pier was in danger of collapsing into the sea! Remedial work included new steel pilings being driven an amazing 24m (80') down into the bedrock, and the poor pier needed further work later when new sea defences resulted in the shoreward wooden piles being exposed right down to their bottoms. Emergency lorry loads of cement and sand were brought in and used to stabilise the landward end of the pier and make it safe once more.

Since then there have been no major dramas here, and the pier has remained a popular tourist attraction, and even as the sun began to dip towards the horizon and the December chill began to make itself apparent once more, there were plenty of people on the pier as we walked up to the 1950s-style red and cream entrance and into a wealth of amusements!

It has to be said that the somewhat spindly legs and jumble of buildings do make Teignmouth Pier look a little like a Dali creation, but once on board, you may not be back on land for a while, there's an awful lot to see and do on this pier!

Drawn magnetically to the red and white entrance that helpfully said 'Pier' in big letters we experienced a shift in relative space, not dissimilar to that experienced by time-traveller Dr. Who as he steps inside his Tardis, for Teignmouth Pier seems to be an awful lot bigger on the inside than it appears from the promenade! Packed with slot machines and amusements we were kept busy for quite a while spending 2p pieces and spare change as we meandered through the pavilion, and I was surprised to come across a 10-pin bowling alley in amongst the other machines!

We nearly came unstuck at this point, when we rounded a corner and found our way blocked with a temporary wall – no entry, pier closed. What? Thwarted! We looked at the other side, but it was horribly true – the rest of the pavilion and access to the outside section of the pier was barred to us due to repairs and winter refurbishment. I tried not to be too disappointed.

"Never mind, we can have our end of the pier kiss here can't we?" I suggested in a mock-cheerful fashion.

But Jay wasn't going to be put off and walked back to an unobtrusive employee sat quietly in a booth at the side of the amusements and explained our plight and asked if there was any way at all we could be allowed a few minutes access just to walk to the end of the pier and back. The employee (who asked not to be identified, which is why I have gone all careful with my narration!) looked thoughtful for a few moments, then got up and unlocked the door.

"I haven't seen you. If anybody asks, I don't know how you got through here. Just a few minutes, to the end and back, right?" We needed no further persuasion, and feeling rather like escaping prisoners, furtively looked over our shoulders as we slipped through the door and tiptoed over pots of paint and workmen's tools to the outside!

It was a strange experience to walk along a pier that was wrapped up and closed for the winter – a bit like tiptoeing past a regal sleeping old duchess and not wanting to disturb her, we found ourselves whispering and being careful where we trod! After a while we realised that this was not a sensible option. We were pushed for time and the wooden planking was littered with mussel shells, debris from foraging seagulls that were using the hard wood as a shell cracker to get at a tasty treat.

Despite the functional appearance there are some delights on Teignmouth Pier – although the railings look like general council issue and the lamp posts a bit boring, the addition of some lovely graceful seahorse silhouettes manages to instil an almost Art Nouveau air to this part of the pier. There are some benches made of interesting bits of wood that look like they may be old piles, and mysterious bits of rides under coloured sheeting. This air of mystery certainly made us want to come back and see the pier alive and buzzing as in our haste there are undoubtedly things we missed or didn't see in their best light.

In amongst the rides and kiosks, we found a boating lake and ghost train set-up (it's tiny!) and in amongst these sleeping delights we found an intriguing wooden and metal structure. On closer inspection we discovered it was a metal head section from one of the original cast-iron screw piles, dating back to 1865. Removed In 1973 it is now used as a donation receptacle to help with the upkeep of the pier – apparently Teignmouth was one of the first piers to allow free admission to promenaders which must be a bit of a two-edged sword. To allow free admission would have encouraged more visitors, but must have lost the pier a useful slice of income, something that is still an issue today, as we had already found.

We carried on crunching to the end of the pier and had a kiss with chilly lips in the last of the golden winter sunshine, before pausing to look at the sparkling ripples on a gorgeous turquoise sea for just a moment. Then it was time to trot quickly back, hands in pockets to keep out the cold, before we were missed. We were glad to be back in the noisy warmth of the pavilion, and after locking the door behind us went and said our thanks to the generous benefactor before heading back to the entrance. Only on leaving did we realise that this pier too is called The Grand Pier, and wondered if this was anything to do with the owners, the Brenner family, who were also the owners of Weston's Grand Pier until the current owners took possession. Beginning to feel the winter chill sidling into our clothes we beat a hasty retreat to the car, but also delighted that we'd had such fabulous weather for these three piers in December!

CHAPTER 11

A Seaside Solstice Set – Boscombe, Bournemouth, Swanage and Weymouth

The shortest day of the year, December 21st, saw us heading south again to cover piers in Dorset and uncover some more mysteries! It wasn't a bad day – no blinding sunshine or fog (that might burn off later!) but a standard winter light-grey sky, which was exactly the sort of thing you'd get on a winter solstice with the sun so far away!

We had an eventful journey – eventful if you like spotting birds and animals, as we must have seen virtually every type of farm animal in the country. Even goats and llamas...! First stop was Boscombe, once an esteemed seaside resort in its own right, before it was swallowed up in Bournemouth's spread. I have to confess that I didn't even know Boscombe had a pier, so I was looking forward to seeing it. We pulled into a car park halfway down the steep hill that descends to the sea, and walked over to look at the view.

If you were being rude, you might refer to Boscombe's pier as a bus-stop by the sea. It has a bus-station shelter running down the middle of it, neat planking and some natty municipal grey plastic bins for recycling and not much else. From our vantage point we could see that it opened out to a t-shaped seaward end with a flag pole, but that there didn't seem to be much else of note. Unperturbed, we walked down to look at the rather striking entrance, because although at first glance Boscombe Pier isn't the most exciting or architecturally beautiful pier in the country, it has struggled to survive and is lucky to be in existence at all.

Back when holidaying by the bracing coast was fashionable, Boscombe was thriving, and jumped on the let's-build-a-pier bandwagon in 1886 with the formation of the Boscombe Pier Company. A designer was chosen (Archibald Smith) and building began in 1888 with the first pile being driven in by Lady Shelley, daughter-in-law of the famous poet and obviously a very strong young lady! The pier cost a mere £12,000 to construct from wood and iron, and was 183m (600') long. It was opened by the Duke of Argyll in the summer of 1889 and was a simple affair, consisting of a promenading deck and a landing stage.

The exciting installation of a 'canal boat sized' whale carcass was put onto the pier in 1897. Previously found washed up on the beach, it provided a novel source of amusement to all and sundry. A local newspaper reported that 'boys took running jumps up its slippery sides and tobogganed down them'. This passed into childhood lore too, with a playground rhyme saying:

> 'Have you been to Boscombe?
> Have you seen the whale?
> Have you stood upon its back
> And smelt its stinking tail?'

I would imagine that an enormous rotting whale was only a positive tourist draw for a while, and ultimately the leviathan was auctioned to a local man for £27 and ground up for fertiliser!

Despite this wildly exciting period in its history, the pier was never really a success, something that seems to have been a curse of the pier since its inception, and it passed into the hands of the local Corporation in 1904. The council knew they would have to improve facilities to maintain public interest, and so buildings were constructed at both shoreward and seaward ends. In 1926 the pier head was rebuilt in the material of the day, high alumina concrete, and the pier was now 226m (740') in length.

In 1940 it was unsurprisingly sectioned to prevent the enemy sneaking ashore, with the intention of rebuilding it once raw materials became available again. However, it took fifteen years before this became an option, and the council had to apply to the Government for permission to rebuild what was by now a rusting skeleton hanging limply above the waves. The pier neck was rebuilt using reinforced concrete, in what has been called a 'motorway bridge' style. However, knowing how awful concrete piers in a motorway bridge style can look, I have to say that this is a very unfair comment, as you will see later!

Following this rebuild, no evidence of the original pier remained. The pier entrance, as it stands today, was built in 1958 while the pier neck was undergoing its bionic transformation, and was very much in keeping with the designs of the time. It consisted of a reinforced concrete platform and cantilevered roof which curved gracefully to echo the curve of the coastline, while the paintwork was cream, yellow and pale blue – very post-war! The pier reopened in 1960, and the Mermaid Theatre and restaurant were added in 1962 at the pier head. It was originally used as a roller-skating rink, but surprisingly even back in the swinging 60s the 'youth' decided roller-skating on the pier wasn't cool. The council had resisted installing amusements of a more traditional nature on the pier but realised that now they would have to reconsider. Despite opposition by some members (concerned about lowering the tone of the area), it was decided to go ahead. And so, on June 4th 1965 after a one hundred year ban on such devilment, a £50,000 amusements centre was opened. Now the pier had bingo (shock!), a rifle range (gasp!), a mini ten-pin bowling alley (tut tut!) and slot machines (no!). However, the council drew the line at 'What the Butler Saw' type machines, as apparently this was considered too risqué, even in 1965!

The pier struggled on with diminishing visitor numbers, until the pier head was closed in 1990 on safety grounds. Despite looking for help from a cash injection or partnership for redevelopment, money was not forthcoming for repairs and eventually the entire pier was closed in 2005 because it was too dangerous. However, people were not going to give up on Boscombe's pier, and in January 2007, work began on a £2.4 million rescue project – proof, if proof were needed that rescuing a pier CAN be done without needing a Bill Gates type fortune in the bank – take note, owners of derelict piers! New decking was laid down, lamp posts along the length and a durable windbreak with benches.

The entrance had survived well, and following some restoration was granted Grade II listed status. Just over a year later the pier re-opened – Wayne Hemingway, one of the country's leading urban designers, said it was 'one of the coolest piers in the country', and evidently, he should know! I'm not sure I'd class it as 'cool', but it IS a pier and it has been brought back from certain death and preserved for many more years to come, which surely must be a good thing.

And so to our visit! Overlooking the entrance, we admired the rather lovely curve of the roof and building beneath, rather like an oversize jelly bean. I am not generally a fan of 1950's-60's architecture, but it has an almost Art Deco style to it. There are glass brick type window panels at each end of the curve, and kiosks lead walkers to the entrance at the centre of the curve, the general paintwork colour a rather fetching royal blue.

We walked down the last of the steps and were inexorably drawn through the entrance and out onto the neck of the pier. Without a pavilion it does look as though there is something missing, but we carried on to the end of the pier, past lots of other solstice strollers and sturdy plastic waste bins! The pier is edged with functional, side-of-the-street type dull-grey railings, on the seaward side of this some anti-jump wires to stop foolish oiks attempting to tombstone off the pier. There are no fancy decorative lamps either, although the almost kite-shaped modern lamp posts are not out of place or unattractive. The windbreak in the centre is, again, very functional and follows the colour scheme of grey on the roof and royal blue panels above the floor, and is light and airy with clear panels and a gently sloping roof. It's worth taking some time to read all about the history of Boscombe and its pier, on the informatively and chronologically ordered displays on illustrated panels under the shelter. There are benches every so often along the length of the pier too, high-backed wooden seats in a very pleasing modern design that wouldn't look out of place in a museum's art installation – I liked them very much, and upon trying them out can recommend them for their comfort!

The end of the pier opens out into a wide decked space with a flag-pole and telescope at the end, and we walked to the railing and had a gaze out to sea (grey, no hint of royal blue today) before having our first pier kiss of the day. Walking back to the shore, we could see Bournemouth pier just up the coast to our left, temptingly close and within an easy walk. We exited the pier through that fetching entrance again, and spent a few moments admiring the modern roundabout opposite, cream bricks and two shiny black granite monoliths that appear to have come from an Arthur C. Clarke film. Ever since my first pier visit to Wales I have learnt not to have pre-conceived ideas of places and even architecture and art, and so as well as liking Boscombe Pier's benches and modern entrance, I have to say that I rather like the roundabout too!

We turned left and looked back to admire the structure of Boscombe Pier. It may be made of concrete but it actually has some rather nicely shaped arches along its length, gently curving above the waterline. From a distance the windbreak looks as though there is a modern suburban train running along it...

We turned our back on Boscombe Pier and began to walk along the broad promenade at the foot of the steep sandstone cliffs towards Bournemouth. These megaliths help to make the beach a wonderful sun-trap in the summer, and the sand is a pretty pale butterscotch colour and velvety soft. I can remember marching along this promenade on a stiflingly hot summer's day in my marching band uniform – it must have been for the Bournemouth carnival – but there are lot of things I don't remember seeing then, maybe my euphonium got in the way of sightseeing!

There are some rather lovely beach huts tucked in at the foot of the cliffs. Some traditional Bohemian ones with names and interesting paint schemes, and some rather quirky modern ones that look *exactly* as though they were made of life-size Lego bricks, complete with uniform terracotta tiled roofs and neatly hinged red or blue doors. Beach huts are another iconic seaside fixture – people spend thousands of pounds and wait years to buy one of these bijou *pieds à la mer*, then lavish time and money on personalising them. I would too if I had the spare money, I think they are a great place to spend time and help stick those childhood holidays firmly in your back-catalogue of memoires!

Speaking of icons, a little further along the promenade is Bournemouth's cliff railway. If you've never seen one of these curiosities before they are rather intriguing, although they can look a bit Heath-Robinson and scary to the uninitiated. Two little carriages fire up and down an improbably steep miniature railway line that clings to the side of the cliff, passing half-way up the incline with just a hair's breadth between them. These quirky engineering marvels were a fantastic invention that enabled the elderly, infirm, young and bulkily-skirted Victorian and Edwardian ladies a sedate way of going up and down to the beach, rather than negotiating the umpteen flights of precarious zigzagging steps that were the only other way of accessing the coastal delights.

Also known as a funicular railway or inclined plane there are approximately sixteen of these coastal, two-car delights left in the country, mostly powered by electric motors, but a couple still water-powered. I feel another book coming on...! Bournemouth is lucky enough to have three cliff railways, and this is East Cliff. It is 52m (170') long and has an incline of 68.9 degrees and unfortunately for us, only operational in the summer – go on, give them a go!

It wasn't long before we were approaching Bournemouth Pier. If there's ever a tsunami along the south coast, I'd wager that Bournemouth Pier will be the only surviving structure, as it is SO solidly built you can hardly see the gaps between the piles! Approaching this substantial edifice, it appears to be reached by a concrete bridge not dissimilar to Boscombe Pier. Closer still and we were marvelling at the sheer amount of stuff on the pier – no wonder it has such sturdy undergarments! There's a huge green-roofed barn, an air-traffic control tower and a crashed flying saucer... Really? This needed more investigation!

We strolled up the ramp to the paved apron of amusements in front of the pier, where restaurants, cafés and fish and chip emporia cluster to ensnare the hungry holidaymaker after a day making sandcastles on the beach. In between the modern seafront furniture lurk traces of the 'good old days' – here a tiled frontage to a building, there a grand Edwardian stone column now proudly advertising bingo, all beckoning the visitor towards the pier entrance towards headier seaside delights.

We sidestepped the odd shaped multi-sided amusements buildings and walked out onto the pier neck, experiencing a certain sense of déjà vu. No, the day hadn't suddenly become one of blinding sunshine and unseasonal temperatures; surely we had gone back onto Boscombe Pier? Here were the same concrete arches on groups of pillars, grey kite-like lamp posts and plastic railway carriage windbreak. We stopped and looked. No, there was Boscombe Pier waving back at us in the distance... one of them must be a clone pier!

But wait! The railings here are white, and the windbreak has gaps in it, and... it's NOT an emerald aero building Dorothy, it's a theatre, and what an imposing building it is too, certainly very characterful. We walked around the side of the theatre and looked over the rails at the steps going down the side of this solid pier, then continued past the air-traffic control tower to the crashed flying saucer... which weren't quite that of course, the taller structure at the back of the theatre on closer examination looks like the bridge of a ship, and tacked on the seaward end of this is a glorious rotunda, now called Key West, a busy bar and restaurant. The dove-grey domed roof is topped with a circular skylight window that looks like a white crown and adds an extra element of elegance to this rather lovely building.

Bournemouth Pier has had a chequered history, and repairs and necessary works are why it looks as it does today. The very first pier here was a simple wooden jetty that was built in 1856, but replaced in 1861 by a larger wooden pier, designed by George Rennie (brother of Sir John Rennie) that was opened to a twenty-one gun salute! It cost just £3,418 to build and had an admission fee based on the rateable value of residents – a very novel idea, but not one which would be terribly welcome nowadays!

Due to that nemesis of wooden piers, the teredo worm, attacking the wooden piles, a cast-iron replacement was erected in 1866 but just one year later a storm washed away the landing stage. The remaining neck was repaired and the pier was used for another ten years until a severe storm in the November of 1876 caused so much damage that it became too short to be used by visiting steamers. The pier was demolished, but a temporary structure was erected until salvation materialised in the shape of pier-god Eugenius Birch.

His new design took three years to be built, cost £21,600 and was opened by the Lord Mayor of London in August 1880. It consisted of a wide open promenade stretching 255m (838') down to a 34m (110') wide pier-head. A bandstand and covered shelters were added a few years later, an extension to the length in 1894 and a further extension in 1909, which took the final length to 304.8m (1,000'). Visiting boats and ships could moor along the sides of the pier at jetties that extended like wings, and visitors could enjoy amusements such as the jazz club or roller-skating rink!

Wartime sectioning put paid to any promenading until 1946 and then it needed a two-year refurbishment before it was reopened to the public. Further refurbishment and the building of the green-roofed Pier Theatre in 1960 meant that the super-structure of the pier had to be substantially strengthened. Extra concrete piles were installed, such was the weight of the theatre, but it proved to be a big success, with lots of famous acts performing over the years. The pier was also reduced in length to its current 229m (750') as the old structure was tidied up.

Strolling on a little further, the decking opens out and the planking points invitingly towards the sea. We walked over what feels like the deck of a ship to the 'bow', marked by a red flagpole, and rather unceremoniously, a grey rubbish bin and a couple of lamp posts where we had a kiss before turning round to admire the decking and pleasing curve of the building. In the summer this space has a small funfair on it, with a helter-skelter dominating the rides. There are still boat rides coming and going from the pier, a tradition started by the steamer *Fawn* back in 1868 and continued today with local providers and the *Waverley* and *Balmoral*.

The future of Bournemouth Pier would seem to be quite positive, as it is a popular venue in a thriving city and the current owners are keen to carry out surveys and maintenance as required. Back in 1996 they had planned a £13 million hi-tech total rebuild of the pier, leaving just the original girders, but neither the money nor other investment was forthcoming. Although it's nice to have a clean sweep now and again, we rather liked the mix of styles here which are in keeping with seaside traditions.

Setting off up the opposite side we realised quite how big the amusements building was that we had come round the side of, and spotting the time, realised we needed sustenance before having a bracing walk back along the promenade and journeying on to our next pier – Swanage here we come!

Swanage is a beautiful town, snuggling on the Purbeck limestone coastline, just around the corner from picturesque Corfe and its enigmatic castle and not far from Weymouth. With gorgeous stone buildings, stunning scenery and crystal clear waters this is one of the most idyllic parts of Dorset, and worth a visit whatever the time of year. We parked in the town and walked along the route to the pier, passing a rather wonderful mural on a building in *trompe l'oeil* style, complete with painted seagulls on the roof and little rats hiding in the shadows! There are benches along the seafront with fish-themed triskele designs on the ends (an ancient Celtic circular design consisting of three repeated shapes, as seen in the flag of the Isle of Man), and the same design can be seen picked out in coloured pebbles outside the Heritage Centre, a building that used to be the local fish market.

Swanage started life as a flourishing fishing village which became fashionable during Victorian times when the well-heeled came to promenade beside the sloping white sandy beach and partake of the fresh sea breezes. This coincided with a boom in the popularity of building with the creamy Purbeck stone, and Swanage became one of the centres for exporting the stone to other parts of the country, which is where the pier comes in.

Such was the requirement for the limestone that Swanage harbour was now used by shallow-draught ships to transport stone out to bigger vessels in the deeper water. The economy thrived and a more cost effective way of transporting the stone to London and other growing cities was sought, so in 1859 the Swanage Pier Act was passed to allow the Mowlem stone company to build a wooden pier out into deeper water. The finished pier, designed by James Walton of London was 229m (750') long and meant that wagons of stone came from the quarries by horse-drawn tramway, and were taken along the pier to be loaded straight onto the larger ships. Although it meant that men and horses didn't have to work waist-deep in water to load ships, the Swanage Pier and Tramway Company insisted that a toll be paid to use the pier, and this was considered expensive and resented by the local stonemasons.

In 1874 a steamer service from Bournemouth and Poole meant more and more people were visiting Swanage, and the pier was not big enough to cope with both businesses running at full pelt. It was decided that a new 'pleasure pier' should be built for the tourists, and in 1895 a new wooden pier was constructed, to a length of 196m (642'). Shorter than the stone-loading pier, it did not need the length as the visiting steamers did not need such deep water to berth. Swanage wanted to emulate Bournemouth and become a successful resort, and from May 1896 up to ten steamers a day brought people to visit via the pier, also contributing hugely to the income of the town. The new Swanage Pier Act said that the company could:

> 'construct upon it such saloons, pavilions, waiting,
> refreshment, concert, reading and other rooms,
> lavatories, shops, bazaars, baths, upper promenade
> and other conveniences as they, from time to
> time, think fit' (in other words, anything!)

In the event, the new pier remained fairly free of any of the above, but was still popular with visitors, and old pictures and postcards of the time show crowds of people promenading along it.

By 1885 the newfangled railway had arrived in Swanage and much of the stone-loading trade had been transferred away from the old pier, which managed to keep alive as a re-coaling station for the visiting passenger steamers. However, this alternative use was short-lived, and as steamer trade diminished the old pier fell into disrepair. There was talk of building a dance hall and beach huts on the structure in 1934, but despite this novel idea, the plans never reached fruition. By 1948 it was being used by the Swanage Swimming Club as a diving platform but soon became totally derelict and was completely closed. The final remnants of the old pier can be seen today, the curving relic of posts and cross-members jutting from the water to the right of the new pier, used now by perching gulls above the water and scuba divers below.

But what of the new, all singing and dancing new pier? With steamer traffic bringing tourists from Bournemouth and Poole, it kept reasonably busy right up until the Second World War, with only a minor hiccup in the twenties. In 1929 it was discovered that the wooden piles, although made of greenheart wood (solid and resistant to the attentions of hungry marine worms) were considerably decayed and needed urgent remedial action. They were subsequently lined on the outside with concrete, which would protect them from the ravages of tide and worm for some time to come.

In 1939 a 61m (200′) section at the landward end was blown out by the army, effectively preventing the pier from being used during the war, and the pier stayed that way until 1948. The missing section was rebuilt using concrete, and it wasn't long before the steamers began bringing trade to the town once more. Peacetime tourism continued without incident until the inevitable death knell of the cheap Mediterranean package holiday struck in the 1960s. The last boatload of tourists came in 1966, and with 'staycations' being seen as a bit naff, and a succession of owners who could not decide what to do with it, the pier fell into decline and disrepair.

There then followed an unhappy time of uncertainty for Swanage Pier. Purchased in 1986, the company then went into receivership and it wasn't until 1994 that an ardent team of volunteers bought the structure, and the Swanage Pier Trust began their dedicated rebuild and rebirth programme. Over £1 million was raised, cast iron was replaced and the old wooden decking replaced by ekki wood planks. I have to confess I had never heard of this, and having dug around a bit, discovered it's a dense African hard wood. Being so tough it needs a chainsaw to work it, it's impervious to the attentions of the tenacious teredo and gluttonous gribble worms and is therefore ideal for piers and other marine uses. Fifty of the original piles were replaced as well – there are one hundred and seventy wooden piles in total holding up the pier, and without this restoration the ever hungry gribble would soon reduce the pier to a spongy ruin. Intending to keep Swanage Pier as original as possible, the Trust know this replacement of piles will be ongoing, but is worth it in the long run.

I've mentioned gribbles and teredos quite a bit and wonder if you might like to find out exactly what they are? They will pop up a bit more as we go on and I felt I needed to know what the little blighters were! Mr Gribble worm is small and innocuous looking. In fact I think it looks quite cute. Do you remember those little rubber monsters with waving arms that children liked to stick on their fingers in the seventies? Well, they look just like that, even if they are only a couple of millimetres long! They are crustaceans that like to burrow into marine softwoods that are in free-flowing water, munching into the cellulose and turning it into food. Subsequently the wood turns spongy because of all the holes, and then collapses – not good if you're walking along the pier at the time!

Teredo worms are a well-known terror of the deep. They're also known as shipworms, or more tellingly 'termites of the sea' and cause no end of trouble to any wood that is immersed in seawater, leaving no ship, pile or plank untouched. It is in fact not a worm at all, but a small clam. It bores its way into the wood to eat the cellulose, but shores up its tunnel with a calcareous lining to stop it collapsing immediately. So impressed by this marine engineering technique was the nineteenth-century engineer Marc Brunel that he devised a tunnel shield to mimic the work of the teredo worm, and the same method has been used ever since in civil engineering projects, including the original Thames Tunnel! The only way to prevent your pier from being nibbled and gribbled is to use expensive, tough hardwoods, cast iron or everlasting concrete, and it explains why there are so few original wooden piers around today and where much of the money for their upkeep goes.

Enough of diversions! Let us go back to our stroll, and tell you of our delightful visit to Swanage Pier in the present day, without a gribble or teredo in sight! The pier is reached by passing the lovely blue-and-white pagoda roofed ticket office and you can see the last of the original horse-drawn tram lines in the roadway. We bought a promenading ticket from the

Pier Trust Office – it is possible to park on the quayside here too if it's not too busy, but we hadn't realised this, although it was good to walk through the town and get to know a little of the local area to help put the pier in context again.

Once through the gateway, we were greeted by a wide concrete apron leading onto the pier, and the unique sweep of this delightful structure. As we were discovering, every pier is completely different and has its own beguiling features that set it apart from any other. Swanage Pier goes out into the water and then does not one, but two kinks, before promenaders go up some steps to get to the end!

To walk along Swanage Pier is rather like strolling along a stately avenue in an old part of London – there is space, a sense of serenity and some beautiful 'pier furniture'. The gorgeous silver and blue wrought-iron railings echo the fish triskele pattern (albeit without the fish) and the lamp standards along the centre of the pier are tall, solid and stately, crowned with a white glass globe. The benches are thoughtfully positioned along the central line of the pier but face in either direction, to make the most of the sumptuous views to east and west, each one adorned with curls of wrought iron and solidly ornate feet.

As we walked, we couldn't help but notice all the little brass plaques on the planking, and our pace slowed considerably as we read little snippets of people's lives – loves, deaths and seaside reminisces that made us smile, sympathise and hold hands that little bit tighter as we moved along the pier. We asked at the gatehouse on our way out about the plaques, and were told that there were over 7500 of them and have been a valuable source of income to the Trust since their inception in 1995. The plaques continue all the way to the raised section at the end of the pier, designed to provide a higher level landing stage for the steamers, and it's reached by some elegant steps.

The widest point of the pier is 24m (79') across, with lower level landing platforms at the sides. Older photographs of Swanage show boats moored along the sides, which upon reflection give a more stable place to tie up so that your passengers can get on and off without being pitched into the sea! Surrounded by the beautiful ironwork, glinting plaques and sparkling green waves we had a lovely kiss at the end of the pier and stayed a while to appreciate the calming atmosphere and pretty views, before we slowly made our way back the way we had come.

Even on a dull December day there were quite a few people out on the pier, many just out for a stroll, others fishing from the side staging. Swanage is a cracking example of how to restore a pier and make it appeal to people all year long. The Pier Trust hold lots of events and fairs on the pier itself, sells tickets to anglers and scuba divers and have a thriving little shop that provides mementoes of the visit to passengers of the *Waverley* and *Balmoral* and other boatloads of tourists that still arrive in the summer. This all goes to putting Swanage Pier in the top ten of British piers in 2008. Ironically it was also in the top ten list of piers most seriously at risk or partial or total collapse for the same year – it just goes to show that not all statistics or lists should be believed one hundred per cent, as this pier looks like it is in safe hands for a while yet, and will not be falling into the jaws of the gribble or teredo worm just yet. Hopefully the 150,000 plus visitors a year will keep providing the much needed income, which runs to around £180,000 a year for maintenance and running costs. Hand over a pound if you visit and tell them to keep the change – it's not much to pay to keep this gorgeous seaside gem going, surely?

Saying goodbye to Swanage, we drove west to one of our favourite seaside towns of all, Weymouth. It is hard to resist the charms of this archetypal holiday destination – it was a favourite of King George III and his discreet partaking of the briny waters led to everyone else jumping on the bandwagon and spending the summer here too. The town has been in existence since the thirteenth century and was the probably the first landing place of the Black Death in 1348, not really something you want to brag about in your tourist brochures!

King George's influence was responsible for the sweeping Georgian and Regency buildings that give Weymouth such a splendid air and echoing the curve of the wide sheltered bay. George is still part of Weymouth – look back to Osmington in the east and you can see him on his horse, carved into the hillside. Although Weymouth has predominantly been a tourist town since the eighteenth century it is also a thriving fishing port, has a huge marina, cross-channel ferry to France, a significant military and naval history *and* a little rowing boat ferry across the busy mouth of the River Wey as it meets the sea. There is so much to do and see here, the gorgeous silvery sand is world famous for sand sculptures, and there is a festival here on the beach every year, with some spectacular creations. But we just could not think where the piers were. I don't remember seeing anything jutting out into the bay, not even a ruin – a frantic scrabble in the car for some paperwork shows that there are not one but two piers here – the mystery deepens!

We were lucky to find a little parking spot on a side street not far from the central part of the beach, and emerged into the watery winter light to go pier hunting. Our first destination was the Bandstand Pier, the result of an architectural competition held in 1938 and won by Mr V.J. Wenning. It was originally called the Weymouth Pier Bandstand, and opened in May of the following year. I searched my notes for some more clues as to where it was.

"It says here that it sits in the middle of the curve of the bay and breaks up the natural shape and that people have complained about it for years," I remarked. "But there simply isn't a pier here!"

As we looked around us, the horrible truth dawned. We were stood outside the front of an older looking amusements arcade on the seaward side of the promenade. Looking up, we could see the name quite clearly now, 'The Pier Bandstand'. Ah. This was it then – but following a little look around on all sides it would seem that something is missing. There's no pier. And there's no bandstand either!

Originally it was meant to be a venue for summer musical performances and dancing, something that was very popular in the short time before the Second World War and in the post-war years when people needed simple entertainments to take them away from the austerity and hardship they had just gone through. Postcards and photographs of the time show a rather curiously wide and stubby pier with a theatre-cum-stage construction at the seaward end and broad cantilevered shelters to either side of a wide area that was used as a dance floor. The pier itself 'intruded' into the bay on quirky stubby legs that looked like wigwams by a mere 61m (200') – hardly a dramatic eyesore surely? But then, as we've seen so often in current times, people don't like change!

People entered the pier through the Art Deco entrance that is still there today, marked by its period square windows and rectangular frontage, ending in sweeping curved walls and windows, typical of the era. There was, and still is, a large and elegantly simple 1930's clock too, which even today really complements the cream and sky-blue colour scheme. A two-storey building, the upstairs was a tea-room and café, with a wide staircase sweeping up to this top deck that led out to the open-air auditorium.

It must have been a really novel venue for dancing and enjoying the musical performances of the day, with bracing sea air and sunshine instead of the smoky dance floors people were used to. Originally there were glazed shelters to each side and a semi-circular bandstand at the stage-like construction on the seaward end. There was originally provision for some 2,400 seats that should have been protected from rain by the cantilevered roofs on each side – however, a design flaw meant that only one third of the seats had protection, leading to overcrowding in a downpour! On the plus side, this modern roof design meant that there were no pillars to obstruct the view wherever people sat, even if you were going to get wet!

Being built more recently, there are some fascinating statistics available concerning the construction of this pier. It used 3,050 tonnes of concrete, 80 tonnes of steel, 9km (that's 6 miles) of electrical wiring, 762m (2,500') of neon tubing and 1,200 light bulbs to get it up and running – and yet, it's so tiny!

So what happened to this little dancehall by the sea? It was so short it didn't need sectioning in the war, and carried on quietly without incident through the years, proving a popular place for concerts, bathing beauty contests and the like – at least it wasn't going to catch fire or get sliced apart by drifting oil tankers! By the 1970s the pier facilities included amusements, a gift shop and a restaurant, but by 1985 the council made the sad decision that the bandstand end was proving too costly to maintain and embarked on a novel way of solving the problem. How do you get rid of a pier in a fun way? Blow it up of course! There ensued a national competition, which was won by two schoolgirls (what do you have to do to win a competition like this, one wonders?), who subsequently pressed the button in May 1986 and wiped the little pier from existence.

We walked round the remaining bit of the pier, today used as a Chinese restaurant upstairs and amusement arcade on the ground floor, and stepped out onto the soft sand to have a look at what's left. We were sceptical that it should still be classed as a pier – was it still on legs? Did the sea come lapping round any remaining sturdy concrete legs any more? Could you walk around the outside of it? (Er, yes for this one, as long as you don't mind getting sand between your toes!) Were there amusements to delight and entertain? (That was a definite yes, it says amusements above the front door!) Sadly, we felt there was probably not quite enough left of this pier to really call it a pier any more. Or did it?

The back of the cream-painted building did still have one set of sturdy pins holding the upstairs deck above the sand, and if you look closely, on a very high tide the sea might possibly make it up the beach this far. (I can't believe we were that desperate to determine whether this was a pier or not that we were searching for seaweed under the suspended remains!)

However, our investigations proved inconclusive and we just couldn't decide but following a bit more post-visit reading, there may be a glimmer of hope on the horizon. In 2007, The Weymouth and Portland Borough Council put forward extensive plans to regenerate and redevelop much of Weymouth's esplanade in time for the 2012 Olympics, which although being mainly centred on London would see the sailing events held in Weymouth. These plans included tidying up the Victorian seafront shelters, providing a proper building to protect the sand sculptures and restoring and rebuilding the pier out into the sea. What? Yes! Rebuilding it!

The proposed plans for the entire esplanade make for very interesting reading, and are worth a look. Will they see fruition in the current economic climate? Only time will tell, but we have everything crossed. If it does go ahead, it would see features on the front of the existing building restored, the ground floor converted from its current use as an amusements arcade to a café, restaurant and toilet, and upstairs the floor would be extended out to sea with a curved wooden deck. Sadly there are no details saying how far out to sea it would go, but at least it's a start!

We mused over the remnants of the pier as we made our way into the building for our end-of-the-pier kiss at the back of the room. I'm not even sure if we were out over the beach at this point, but a kiss is a kiss and neither of us was going to turn down the chance to have another one, so we embraced and made the most of the opportunity at the back of the amusement arcade! The call of the penny falls machines lured us away from our mission for a few minutes, and we managed to secure a 2p profit, and decided to quit while we were ahead!

We had discovered one pier and now needed to find the other to complete our journey for the day, so left the Bandstand Pier behind and walked westwards along the promenade towards the harbour. We admired the distinctive Jubilee clock, erected to commemorate fifty years of Queen Victoria's reign, the facades of the beautifully elegant buildings and the gangs of seagulls threatening families and demanding chips with menace. We used our cunning and guessed the pier was somewhere in the area of the Pavilion theatre and harbour, a busy area that had possibly seen better days.

Once upon a time this part of the seafront-river mouth area was water, but as demand grew for mooring space, land was reclaimed and industries expanded. With the arrival of the railway, a boat train used to run right into Weymouth town centre and proceed cautiously along the harbour side to terminate on the quayside, depositing travellers right next to their departing boat. This continued until fairly recently when, as usual, it was considered not cost effective to run as there were less people needing the service. The huge cross channel catamarans now leave from the quay here – it's worth walking to the front of one and peering right under its huge hull. When we were there we could see a couple of ducks paddling around under the huge superstructure! Anyhow, I am digressing – we should be looking for a pier!

There is a record of there being a pier-type structure at this end of the harbour since 1812, although there is very little documentation to elaborate on the details, but what we do know is that in 1840 a pier was built on the northern edge of the harbour and in-filled with Portland stone and shingle concrete to make it a substantial structure and it was used mostly as a boating jetty. By now, we had walked up to the Pavilion Theatre, marooned in a sea of car parking and with remnants of railway line still in the tarmac to the right of it. Also visible here are the old railway platforms, a booking office for the ferry and lots of bits and pieces of fishing and boating tackle on the quayside.

It was possible that we were on the pier, but if we were, we could find no clues, so we decided to walk along the left-hand side of this peninsula of land to the end, and then back up the opposite side and see what we could find. What were we looking for? The history of the pier points towards a substantial and multi-purpose construction, rebuilt in 1860 from the in-filled stone one previously there. This time it was made of wood and projected some 274m (900') from the land, and a cargo landing stage was added in 1877 to cope with imports of potatoes coming from the Channel Islands (not what I was expecting!).

By now the railway was bringing hordes of visitors right onto the seafront, some wishing to board a steamer to foreign lands, so the Great Western Railway built a new landing stage and baggage handling hall to cope with the demands of travellers. So far, the pier had been a purely commercial enterprise, but in 1908 a theatre was built at the landward end – almost in the same position as the modern Pavilion Theatre, so we had been right to follow our instincts, although there really were no other clues to say we were on a pier!

During the 1930s the boat traffic really increased and meant that the pier needed to be rebuilt to cope with commercial demand and also to supply recreational facilities for the changing tastes of tourists. A new pier was constructed from reinforced concrete, now going 396m (1,300') into the water. It was 30m (100') at its widest point and 12m (40') across at the seaward end, and was opened by the Prince of Wales (soon to be King Edward III) on 13th July 1933. The platform was divided into two halves, one for all the business things – two railway lines, state-of-the-art electric cranes to handle cargo and the capacity at the dockside to cope with one passenger, two steamers and three cargo boats simultaneously! The other half of the platform was the complete opposite and a dividing fence kept the working riff-raff away from the strolling gentry on the other. For the east side of the pier consisted of a wide promenade with shelters to keep the wind at bay, changing rooms for hardy swimmers and an elaborate diving platform for the totally bonkers set! At night the entire pier was illuminated, and must have looked very impressive.

Sadly the original pavilion, The Ritz Theatre was consumed by a fire in 1954, but the current Pavilion Theatre was built as a replacement in 1960 and has hosted year-round shows and traditional end-of-the-pier entertainment ever since, which is a great accolade as there are only a handful of pier theatres left these days. The pier continued in its split personality existence quite successfully with additions here and there over the years. The car ferry started shuttling cars across the channel in the 1970s and the terminal was updated again ten years later, but there is little really here to remark upon...

We picked our way through the car park and avoided the customs shed, before finding a clue – a sign! Small and understated it simply said 'Pleasure Pier'.

We followed the enticing sign, along a channelled walkway, around a corner, then around another one and still we could not see anything that looked remotely like a pleasure pier! But wait, what's this? Dwarfed by an enormous ferry and jutting out from the main solid body of the pier we spotted the end-of-the-pier entertainment. There, on decking, on piles into the sea are the Cactus Tea Rooms, a double-decker Portacabin affair advertising cream teas, hot chocolate with cream and other artery-hardening traditional seaside treats. But unfortunately for us it was closed, so there was to be no thirst-quenching cuppa here and we sadly walked around the equally sad building. It had seen better days, with the paint faded and peeling. At the seaward end there were some surprising 1930's additions, curved railings, brick columns and the same Art Deco blue and cream colour scheme that we'd seen on the Bandstand building, here stained and worn from years facing the sea breezes.

We looked around and peered over the edge of the blue and grey railings down into the glorious jade sea to look at the piles of the pier. These too had seen better days, and were now eaten away in places and sprinkled with barnacles. We were surprised to see that they were wooden rather than concrete, considering the pier was a later build and the landward end is concrete, but trusting it to hold us up for a few more minutes, we had a kiss at what we guessed was the end of the pier. We left the faded delights of the Cactus Tea Rooms behind us, pondering on the choice of name (not entirely sea-side related!) and went to investigate the huge twin-hulled ferry tied up next door and laughed at the ducks playing games under its hull. We could go no further and followed the fence back towards the concrete footpath we had found initially. It was here, tucked away at the back of the customs building that I found my favourite bit of architecture on the pier.

Looking a little like an old telephone exchange morphed with some public toilets of the same era, with a roof-top terrace added, was this strange little building. There were no clues as to its use (although I'm sure someone reading this will know exactly what it was), the windows are small but now boarded up, access to the roof denied and no signs or faded letters left to decipher, although I am pretty sure it is 1930s in origin. Baffled, we headed back to the red brick and green topped Pavilion Theatre, feeling a little deflated – it was a pier in the end, but not really anything to rave about, which is a real shame for Weymouth, it could do with a proper pier here to round off a truly traditional day at the seaside, whatever time of year it is!

However, there is a post-script to add, because the council also had plans for the whole of this peninsula as part of their 2012 Olympic regeneration. It would appear that the entire area would be flattened and redeveloped to include a refurbished theatre, World Heritage Site visitor centre, a new ferry terminal, 140-bed posh hotel, 340 luxury apartments, 110 homes, a shopping arcade, offices, public squares, a substantial underground car park AND a public pier to the end. I have some questions regarding this proposal though – surely with all that on it the pier would sink anyway? And how can you have an underground car park under a pier? Won't the cars be in the water/below the water/subject to tidal extremes? I don't fancy coming back to my car after a day at the beach to find a foot of water on the inside and crabs playing in the glove box! The bad news is that these plans were proposed in 2006, and you would expect that by late 2008 there would be some sign of this project getting underway, but there was no evidence of this. Never mind, as with all sea-front developments, things take time, although it would be lovely to see all these plans reach fruition.

We celebrated our five-pier day with some excellent fish and chips just over the opening bridge, and watched it open to let the taller yachts go back into the marina at the end of a day at sea. As we strolled back through the town to the car we decided it might be nice to pop back pre-2012 just to see if anything had happened – I'll put that in my diary and let you know!

CHAPTER 12

Something Fishy on the Beach
(Or – Weston's Third Pier)

It's a new year, 2009, and we hadn't visited any piers for a month. We needed to get back on track and notch up a few more visits, but the weather was still grim and dull and grey, which is to be expected really, considering it was January. In retrospect I am glad that we visited piers all year round – not only did we see them when there were less people around but also it would have taken years to do all of them if we had just waited for the summer months!

I had been back at school for a couple of weeks, and had been sat musing out of the window in a moment of boredom. There was a building in my eye-line and it got me thinking. At home that night I did a bit of checking and excitedly told Jay we had another pier to visit. That Sunday we had a coffee in town, walked past the ruins of the sad old Grand Pier and carried on along the promenade. By the Beach Lawns is Weston's SeaQuarium, a sea-life centre to you and me, complete with rays, miniature sharks and an array of fish, crustacean and a decent helping of marine life. As well as this, it happens to be up on legs over the beach, is reached by a walkway, is open to anyone to walk around the outside and has a café inside. In other words, it's a pier!

I can hear the spluttering of the pier enthusiast, but wait! Don't judge me yet, hear the evidence! Better still, go and have a look...

The SeaQuarium was built in 1995 – staff at my school, which is just along the road, can remember being able to hear the piles being driven into the several million miles of sand on the beach. It's regarded as being the first seaside pier to have been built for some 85 years (not sure how Deal would feel about that claim to fame, although it IS the most recently built complete pier), but is not recognised as being a pier by the National Piers Society (although you will find it is mentioned in their 'Jetties' section. We thought a jetty was somewhere a boat tied alongside, and I'd love to see a boat try and moor next to *this* one!).

The construction was purpose-built to house the considerable weight of an aquarium and all its water and so there are quite a number of sturdy black piles under the concrete decking. There are some narrow diagonal bracing struts that mimic the ones on the Grand Pier and Birnbeck, which is a nice homage to 'proper' pier construction, and it is rather fun to be able to walk under the pier when the tide is out – this means you usually can, because here the tide goes out to Wales, stays there and nips in again when you're not looking. If you do happen to visit when it's a super high tide, the sea does come up to the little stone sea-wall, leaving behind it shallow pools of water that make for a lovely photo opportunity if the sun's out, as they act like mirrors.

Piers don't come cheap – this one cost £1.6 million or thereabouts, and it's not even particularly long (and I don't have a tape-measure long enough to tell you the exact measurement) but as we've seen with small piers, they can be just as interesting and full of character as the longer ones. With the SeaQuarium Pier, there is everything you could ask for. The pavilion has an interesting and very distinctive roof – lots of pointy bits surrounding a larger pointy bit and in traditional blue and silvery-grey paintwork. The roof has been described as a pyramid or as being diamond-shaped, but as we walked up to it and had a good look, decided it was a bit more complicated than that, as you can tell by my technical description!

We reached the pavilion by strolling up the gentle concrete ramp that leads from the promenade. It is edged with lamps that although modern are in the traditional Victorian globe-topped style. The railings up the ramp and all around the pavilion are simple, and if they had been left in corporation grey would have been very dismal, but like the roof, these have been picked out in blue and white which is much prettier and very seaside-y. Once at the top of the ramp we had to choose – go left, go right or go into the aquarium for a cup of tea (which when we visited was possible without paying an admission fee). We opted for the right-handed path, mostly because it got us out of a nippy wind, and began to circumnavigate the walkway. It is perfectly pleasant, although you are not as far out to sea as on more traditional piers, and before reaching the most seaward part of the walkway we had to navigate some noisy and smelly extractor fans, a dead pigeon and quite a lot of pigeon poo, but the view from the edge, just out of the wind, was... erm, muddy! There, a long way out was the tide, to our right the remains of the Grand Pier, and further behind it the end of Birnbeck, black against the horizon.

We had a swift peck and carried on walking around the other side of the pavilion, looking now towards Brean Down and the long-gone Tropicana building. Once the pride of Weston-super-Mare, the Tropicana was an outdoor swimming pool with the best high diving platforms in Europe, and shown on many posters of the resort in the 1930s and 40s. Sadly, it has gone the way of many pools these days and is empty, derelict and forlorn, and subject to the council, good folk of the town and various prospective buyers wrangling over what to do with it to no avail.

Our short and sweet visit and kiss were over. I'm glad we don't time these visits and grade them accordingly; this would have been done in minutes. But this little pier deserves a mention and a kiss, because it has been overlooked by many – go and see it and recommend it to a friend!

CHAPTER 13

Did You Bring the Lipsalve? (Or - How to Kiss on Ten Piers in Two Days!)

It was the first week in March, and we needed to do some serious pier visiting. So far we had been to 23 piers and were almost half-way, but were panicking somewhat, with the thought that we had the same number again to see before the Grand Pier in Weston was completed. By this point the old twisted ruins had been removed and workers were busy making repairs under the deck, getting ready to bring in new piles to strengthen the existing superstructure – we had no idea how long we had left!

I had also taken the brave (but necessary) steps to bid farewell to my sleek but unreliable old car and buy a brand new shiny one. Unlike the other one it has a tiny engine – but at least it goes, and doesn't cost a weeks' wages to fill with petrol! Charged with enthusiasm, we sat and looked at the map. I'd marked all the piers on a general map of the UK and we were then able to group them into 'weekends' so that we didn't have to try and fit too many in to the time available. We decided to do a distance trip and head east to Norfolk to visit Cromer, then to Great Yarmouth and Lowestoft, and finally Southwold in Suffolk, which seemed a reasonable weekend's work.

The weather was fine, the car all new and squeaky clean as we set off horribly early for the long haul up to Norfolk, and more pastures new for me. Fortified by packets of sweeties and a stack of music cds, the journey passed uneventfully (hooray!) and we sailed into Cromer five hours later on a bright and breezy day with no chance of rain. We parked high on the cliff top near the putting and bowling greens, activities that were so popular in the heyday of the British seaside holiday, and now populated by the older generation who prefer a more sedate activity in the bracing briny air. Keeping these green spaces has meant seafronts up and down the country have remained undeveloped though, which is nice. It gives the casual observer an uncluttered view of the coast and preserves the feel of the town because, like Cromer, on the other side of the road are the fantastic old buildings of yesteryear.

I had remarked when we drove into the town what stunning architecture there seemed to be on many of Cromer's buildings, and the road leading down to the Esplanade was no exception – grand Victorian designs with hints of Gothic melodrama all along the road! Cromer is very lucky as it's situated right on the top of some stunning cliffs. Down below are seemingly miles of sandy beaches stretching as far as the eye can see in either direction, making it a very tempting destination for the holidaymaker.

Unlike many of the Southern resorts, Cromer became popular in Victorian times, although it had always been a busy fishing town. Now famous for its crabs, Cromer used to have an industry that sought herring in the autumn, cod in the winter and lobster and crab during the summer. The Victorians, who did not like to get too close to nasty rough working types nor expose an inch of flesh unnecessarily were not really interested in the stunning beaches or catch of the day until it was on the plate. They came instead for the healthy breezes, and Cromer's position up on the cliffs made this an ideal place to take the air.

We did too as we walked down the gentle incline towards the pier at the bottom of the hill, past some witty lamp posts bearing sea-themed illuminations crafted from coloured light bulbs – we found seagulls and dolphins, but were particularly impressed with the shrimps (are they illuminated with pink bulbs?). At the bottom we could have zigzagged down to the Esplanade, but all that travelling coupled with sea air had made us hungry and we fell in through the doors of a restaurant that promised fish and chips, warmth and a lovely view out over the pier. The service was slow, the fish and chips not bad and the other clientele noisy, but we didn't mind, it's all part of the visit and flavour of the area, and so suitably refreshed and fortified, we left and headed downhill to the seafront and the pier.

Even though it was a breezy March day there were plenty of people having a stroll along the front, and Cromer should be really proud of its superb promenade. 'Cromer Prospect' was included in a public art scheme, and between 2005-2006 had £200,000 spent on it to transform it into this wonderful area. We headed towards the area at the front of the pier, and stopped in our tracks to watch an unlikely offender helping itself to dropped chips and morsels of food on the pavement. We were used to seeing crows, gulls, sparrows and starlings, and maybe the odd wagtail scavenging for leftovers, but here was a little turnstone in his patchwork plumage rooting around under the benches and around the litter bins. He must have been watching the gulls and decided to evolve!

Cromer is a town very proud of its lifeboat-men, and on Cromer Prospect at the front of the pier, this is really evident. There has been a lifeboat here for more than two hundred years, initially the push-it-into-the-sea-and-row-for-your-life type which the painters of yesteryear captured so well in their dramatic paintings. In the 1920s a lifeboat station was built on the end of the pier, and daring rescues over the next twenty years made Cromer famous across the country. Nowadays the lifeboat carries out around a dozen or so rescues, and an inshore lifeboat on the beach does the same. The tireless efforts of these volunteers have been immortalised on the Prospect and in the local church which dominates the skyline (and is the highest tower in Norfolk).

In front of the entrance to the pier is a beautifully constructed area, steps mimicking the pattern of the waves and in front of them a granite compass set into the pavement. Twenty-four points radiate from this compass, and each one ends at the sea wall with a memorial to a rescue by each one of Cromer's lifeboats. Lifeboat crew are not always remembered for their work in such a public way, and they deserve mention for their selfless acts of heroism. Progressing on to the pier itself we passed through a grand entrance between sturdy white columns guarded at either side by little squat rotunda of a pleasing Victorian style.

Amazingly there are records that there has been some form of pier or jetty at Cromer since 1391, albeit for fishing and boating purposes, with Queen Elizabeth I granting the right to the people of Cromer to export wheat, barley and malt for the upkeep of the town and rebuilding of the pier. There was a plain wooden jetty here from 1846 that was around 64m long (210') and it had very strict rules governing those who dared to promenade along its length – gentlemen were only permitted to smoke after 9 pm (once the ladies had retired for the night!). Fierce gales badly damaged the pier and resulted in it being dismantled.

A period of emptiness on the Cromer coast prompted the locals to badger for a new pier, and the 1899 Cromer Protection Act, although sounding like some kind of gangster outfit, meant that Cromer would get a new pier. Douglass and Arnott designed a fashionable new pier and Alfred Thorne started work on the grand design in 1900. In June of the following year the 137m (450') pier was opened, and had cost a mere £17,000. Two rival railway companies served Cromer and in those days many railways also ran steamers to coastal towns, so the grand opening of the pier was the perfect place for the Great Eastern and Midland and Great Northern to show what they could do. Dignitaries and VIPs from London, Birmingham and Bradford were hauled to the town by sea and deposited at the end of the pier, where the Blue Viennese Band played 'charming music' to all and sundry from the seaward bandstand!

The bandstand was removed in 1905 so that a pavilion for roller-skating could be built (although it was used for concert parties too), and this use continued until the outbreak of the Second World War. Access to the 1920's lifeboat station at the end of the pier continued with a 'temporary' walkway made of planks – I'm not sure what the Germans would have done if they had decided to try and come ashore via this gangway, take one look and decide it breached Health and Safety Regulations and abandon the plan? Probably...!

This part of the East coast is extremely exposed to the merciless rigours of the North Sea, and over the centuries much of the coastline and its original villages have been eroded away and lie beneath the grey swell of the waves. Cromer was not exempt from this punishment and severe storms repeatedly damaged the pier in 1949 and 1953, the latter gale demolishing the pavilion. If this had happened in modern times, I'm sure the government would have said 'tough, sort it yourself', but back then they granted Cromer enough compensation to rebuild the theatre and pavilion in time for the 1955 season! Further storms in 1976 and 1978 caused more damage and in 1990 another one rendered the amusement arcade little more than matchsticks, and it was not rebuilt.

Poor old Cromer Pier probably thought it had suffered enough, but a wayward 100 ton rig hit the pier and severed the neck in 1993. The lifeboat station and theatre were left marooned until repairs were effected and the temporary replacement buildings removed a few years later. The theatre now has a seating capacity of 510, a restaurant, a shop and a theatre bar. Cromer has established a tradition for 'Seaside Special' shows over three seasons, and also hosts musical performances of all styles during the year, with the local community using it in between times.

Today the pier retains its pleasant wide, spacious promenade, with neat white railings and little rectangular kiosks along the way to the theatre. Neat black Victorian lamp-standards adorn the deck, and some well-placed traditional benches provide resting places for the weary traveller who can't quite make it to the pavilion!

At the end of the wide promenade there were some benches incorporated into the curved white railings, and there in front of us was the impressive theatre, a dominating ribbed grey roof and enticing entrance. Sadly for us everything was closed, and we were unable to walk any further along the pier thanks to some barriers blocking our way – winter maintenance!

Behind the theatre we could see the equally impressive lifeboat building. Although of modern construction and decorated in mock-Tudor grey and white, it really assimilates into the rest of the pier quite well and it is fitting that the two important focuses (no, not the crabs!) of Cromer have been brought together in one grand place. A bit miffed, we had a decidedly unromantic kiss pressed against the metal safety railings, and decided this was one pier we would definitely come back to for a better attempt!

We turned back, and experienced the other view from a pier. I think this is one of the nice things about getting to the end of the pier. Walking out to sea gives a frisson of excitement as you leave the land behind you. Standing at the end with the wind in your hair and the salt spray on your face gives a taste of what it is like to be on a grand boat out at sea. Then turning back, you get a unique view of the host town, one which can give a different feel to a place.

Here we had a view of the cliffs that only fishermen or pier walkers would see. To the right of us the grand hotels and expensive buildings for the rich and privileged are perched uncomfortably and slightly disapprovingly not too close to the edge. To the left, the older part of the settlement has a wider assortment of buildings, smaller, more varied in appearance and certainly closer to the edge of the cliffs, as if the residents understand that there has to be some sort of symbiosis with the sea in order to survive. Slap bang in between these two sides of the town, and keeping an eye on the pier is the Hotel de Paris. A red brick Victorian excess of towers and gable ends it was originally built in 1820 as the seaside pad for one Lord Suffield. It was converted to a hotel ten years later and the impressive fancy remodelling carried out in 1895 by local architect George Skipper. There's not just an excess of architectural fancy bits here, I really wouldn't want to be the local window cleaner – there are simply *hundreds* on this place!

Leaving the pier we had another look again at the lifeboat memorials and surrounding area, and noticed that some cleverly hidden lights would illuminate the whole scene at night – Cromer Pier was given the 'Pier of the Year' award in 2000, and all without the added benefits of this fantastic artwork along the seafront. Both deserve high commendation – the Prospect for its sympathetic but effective decorations, the pier for refusing to give in to the wild tiger in the sea and remaining a fantastic example of promenading excellence!

We strolled along the Esplanade and found a heart-attack inducing set of concrete steps up to the cliff top and where we had parked the car. We stopped to catch our breath while pretending we had actually stopped to admire a particularly orange Harley Davidson, then got out the map, started the new shiny engine and set off back down the coast to Great Yarmouth.

Great Yarmouth. Which has more of an air of expectancy about it? Somewhere with 'Great' in the title or 'Super'? Am I now a victim of seaside town one-upmanship? Having 'Great' in the title certainly gives a town a sense that it will be grand, and we were looking forward to finding out whether Great Yarmouth would deliver. It was certainly in the running – it has not one but two piers, which is a start, although it very nearly only had one, following a fire on Wellington Pier in the early hours of August 30th 2008. Fortunately it was brought under control swiftly and the damage wasn't terminal, but it could so easily have been three piers that had been lost in the space of three months that year and not just the two.

Our first impressions on driving into the town and parking up by a crazy golf-course and a tennis court inhabited by skate-boarding teens in overly baggy clothing was that someone had stolen the sea. There appeared to be all the signs of a seaside town and a nice wide horizon, but no sea, just a HUGE expanse of creamy-coloured sand. Squinting into the afternoon sun we could just make out the merest smudge of grey water on the horizon – hooray! We were in the right place! We started to walk along the broad front in the watery spring sunshine, taking in the sights of another seaside town – no we weren't bored of them yet, there was so much to see!

However, Great Yarmouth was going to be a bit different to some of the other places we had already been to. The road in doesn't take you past any notable features, and once on the seafront, which is as wide as the stretch of sand leading to the sea, the only bit of the town that is visible is the front line of assorted buildings on the opposite side of the road! We did spot a particularly lovely building, an Art Deco palace called The Empire which still managed to stand tall and proud despite being a bit on the neglected side.

It's a shame that we were on a tight schedule for the weekend and couldn't go and explore the town in a bit more detail because this is one place that has oodles of history if you just look. It's the gateway to the sea for the Norfolk Broads and has been a seaside town since the eighteenth century. It used to be a major port and centre for the herring industry, but now that people prefer beefburgers to rollmops, the fishing boats have given way to servicing centres for offshore natural gas rigs, pleasure boats and the new kid on the block– wind turbines. We'd already remarked on these new sights just off the coast of so many seaside towns, and here was another one. We could see the huge white windmills of the delightfully named Scroby Sands on the horizon, turning lazily in the March breezes.

There's not just industrial things to go ooh and aah over in Great Yarmouth – if we had been there longer, we really would have found out more about the Romans, the royals, a clown in a geese-powered barrel, bloaters, zeppelins, Charles Dickens and some pretty horrific floods. As it was, the two piers were calling and we needed to go and answer their siren songs, so carried on along the 'Golden Mile'. Although some may confuse one seafront with another, I'm not sure how this could be the case here. Perhaps we should have looked closer at the signs on the way in as we may have seen that it said 'Great Yarmouth – Twinned with Blackpool'! There is indeed a mile of beach here, a pleasure beach with rides (albeit not quite on the same grand scale as its Lancashire twin) and over twelve amusement arcades within a two-square-mile radius. And of course, two piers! We were nearly at the first one, the Wellington, originally built in 1852.

We were not sure what to expect, and were a bit lost for words. There's not an awful lot of pier going out into the sea – there were some pier ribs sticking up out of the sand, giving the impression that the sand was slowly and seditiously going to consume the entire construction and spit the bits out when it had finished. The large pavilion sat on the entire leftover portion, and gave the impression that its immense bulk had forced the deck down towards the sand until there was hardly any daylight to be seen underneath it. This was not like any other pier we had seen before! Did the sea even come in this far? Did the pier legs ever get wet? Yet another pier mystery! And then there's the small matter of the pavilion itself.

It's... big. And cream, with a curved and vivid verdi-gris roof. There are odd curved inverted buttresses along the side and two Italianate bell towers topped with terracotta red sunhats. It's decidedly an exercise in Art Deco stylised design and demands that you look at it! Before we step closer to investigate, the smart golden lamp posts on the prom should get a mention and... what is that enormous Victorian greenhouse doing here?! Our investigation of some cute little beach huts painted up like the small wooden building bricks I had as a child was interrupted by the large glass house smack bang behind them. All closed up and with a children's entertainment complex inside it looked a bit strange, as though toddlers in a ball pit were an exotic exhibit from a travelling menagerie, but we soon found out that in fact this was Yarmouth's Winter Gardens, now a Grade II listed building and with a history that tied in with the Wellington Pier.

It's time for a history lesson to find out why Great Yarmouth has a giant greenhouse and an Art Deco temple on the seafront, so pay attention! In 1852 the Great Yarmouth Wellington Pier Committee were formed to build a pier on the seafront not only to provide entertainment for the hordes of tourists but to commemorate the recently deceased Duke of Wellington. Its 213m (700') wooden deck and discreet pavilion were designed by one P. Ashcroft and was opened in October of the following year. For a cost of £6,776 in 1853 you could get a pier that had fantastic ornamental railings and a 30m (100') promenading area at the pier head where all the best of Yarmouth's elite wanted to be seen. It even made a respectable profit of £581 7s 6d in the first year which was a tidy sum back then, but despite being hugely popular the Wellington Pier's days were numbered. Some bright spark decided that the town could do with a second pier at the north end of the beach, and when it opened in 1858 the tourists went there instead and the Wellington was given the proverbial boot.

In 1899 the local corporation had a cunning plan, stepping in and buying the pier for £1,250 then ploughing more money into updating the facilities thereon to provide entertainment for the growing numbers of visitors to the town. This also included building a new pavilion and in 1903 the new and improved pavilion with theatre opened. It was hugely popular and provided all types of entertainment, affectionately being nicknamed 'the cowshed' because of the tarred, rustic roof and glass-topped partition walls (and not because they played lots of moo-sic!). There seemed to have been lots of people in this part of the country with flashes of genius, for at the same time, it was decided to buy a huge redundant glass pavilion from Torquay for the grand sum of £2,400 and then bring it up to Great Yarmouth to be incorporated into the pier development as a Winter Garden. It was moved successfully without a single pane of glass being broken – try that today and it would take months of logistics intervention!

Wellington Pier and the Winter Gardens proved a popular venue for the next seventy years – no fire, plague or pestilence, but unfortunately by the 1970s major renovation work was needed, and three thousand pounds worth of replacement decking, steelwork and timber piles were installed. Thanks to the great British tourist now choosing to holiday abroad, the pier was losing its appeal and money, and in 1986 after several years of continued losses the council asked to close and demolish it. There was a huge public protest and the comedian and entertainer Jim Davidson took it on, but found that the cost of repairs and maintenance were huge.

Despite spending £750,000 of his own money on repairs to the inside of the pavilion, the outside was left neglected as money could not be found from anywhere to renovate it and eventually the building was left empty until it was sadly demolished in 2005. The front part of the pier was then redeveloped as an amusement arcade and the old theatre end of the pier was rebuilt as a large bowling alley. Amazingly, and in fantastic homage to the original design, there is very little difference in design between the old and the new pavilions. We didn't even realise that we were looking at such a new building!

Inside, the original one-hundred-year-old girders were restored and are now on show and the ten-lane bowling alley pretty much fills the space that used to be taken up with the auditorium and stage. As we approached the front of the building and looked up, our eyes were drawn to the impressive stained glass window at the top of the curve. This beautiful piece of artwork depicting ships sailing into Great Yarmouth's port was discovered when the original building was being removed. Subsequently restored, it now sits as a fitting memorial to the original pier pavilion and the thriftiness of the local people!

We got onto the pier via the promenade, marvelling at the height of the sand again, half expecting a sand worm from Frank Herbert's *Dune* to come rearing up out of the golden banks and eat a tourist. Sadly it didn't and we walked around this amazing new-old pavilion. It really has been built beautifully, the new facades, signs and lamps blending in really well with the classic design of the building. The new decking is lusciously smooth, there are plenty of tables and seating, and even though the railings are the kind of bog-standard grey ones we'd seen in so many other places, they really don't stand out. Perhaps it's that huge Clarice Cliff pavilion behind us that keeps distracting the eye!

As we neared the end of the pier – and it's not a terribly long one, but this really doesn't matter – the tide was gently sliding in and a large tanker sailed past heading north. We both loved the novel lamps along the pier, already alight and glowing with a soft sodium orange, almost like gas lamps. Each lamp post has a bunch of three lamps at the top, arranged in Art Deco simplicity, painted black and then topped with a burnished copper hat – totally delightful! There are still some old bits of the piers legs sticking up out of the sand and leaning on each other for support to remind us that this grand old lady was once a bit longer than she is today.

We finished our walk along the Wellington Pier with a soft kiss at the end and as we turned back and prepared ourselves for the Britannia Pier we noticed another substantial wooden jetty-pier construction sticking out into the sand in between the piers. With no way of getting onto it we were unable to find out what it was or had been – surely not another pier?! Before heading back along the promenade to the Britannia Pier we had a closer look at the Winter Gardens, marvelling again at how this enormous greenhouse could have been taken apart and shipped so far north unharmed. There is so much metalwork it almost looks over-engineered, and is scary to think that it moves in the strong winter winds, but a testament to its original engineers that it has lasted over one hundred years intact!

We set off back towards the Britannia Pier, now owned by the same company that own the Wellington Pier, Family Amusements Limited. It's worth having a look at the website for this pier, I had great fun navigating around the 3D image of the buildings – click on each one and the roof comes off to tell you what's inside! Compared to Wellington, this has a cheaper and cheerful approach, bright and breezy and only just skimming the sand like its counterpart along the promenade!

The front of the pier looks like a giant seafront kiosk – it's bright and flashing, covered in posters, neon lights, and adverts for burgers, hotdogs and amusements, you can't help but be drawn inside! It's also totally loaded with buildings – the pavilion and theatre is huge and looks like a giant silo from the American mid-west. Once you've negotiated the buildings and amusements at the front, squeezed past the giant pavilion and made it to the seaward end there's a children's funfair – and a view of the sea!

There are a couple of themes running throughout the Britannia Pier – if you like a drink, this is definitely the place to visit as there are an abundance of places to have your favourite tipple while you're here. The other theme (unfortunately for the pier) is one of going up in flames – don't stay too long, the Britannia Pier is on its fourth pavilion!

The idea for a second pier at Yarmouth was first put forward in 1856 and work began the following year, with George Allen's wooden pier opening in July of 1858. Approached by some impressive and ornate wrought-iron gates the pier stretched out 213m (700') onto the sands. Costing a whopping (and precise) £3158 11s 6d to build, it didn't last in this incarnation for very long as a schooner, the *James and Jessie* collided with it the following year and 15m (50') had to be removed – it must have been an extremely solidly built schooner and a rubbish bit of pier building to have resulted in so much damage! More bad luck followed with a severe North Sea storm shattering more of the structure. The pier hosted evening band performances and open-air concerts, but not much more for visitors and it soon transpired that the previous damage was causing an ongoing structural problem so the pier was completely demolished in 1899.

A replacement pier was drawn up the following year because Yarmouth as a resort was continuing to prosper and it was felt the town really did need a second pier (although I'm sure the owners of Wellington Pier would have disagreed!). Mayoh and Haley re-built the pier from steel and wood, a design that was whipped up in a jiffy and opened in 1901. It had a 247m (810') deck and a temporary pavilion, which was replaced with a grander building at the pier head that would seat 2000 the following year. It was to become a case of enjoy it while it's there, because in December 1909 the pavilion burnt down. It was rebuilt the following year, but burnt down again on 17th April 1914; although this time the local gossips pointed the finger of blame at the Suffragettes, who had been refused permission to meet there.

A third pavilion was put up in super-quick time, and three months later was open for business again! In May 1928 the Floral Ballroom was built (decorated in blossoms or for dancing gladioli?), but, unsurprisingly it burnt down in August 1932. Diligently, the locals rebuilt it again and it was re-opened in 1933, just in time for the pier to be closed because of the outbreak of World War II. The pier was sectioned in 1940 and then left alone for seven years before it was repaired and re-opened to the public. However, it wasn't long before – you've guessed it, another fire destroyed both the pavilion and the ballroom (now called the Ocean Ballroom) in April 1954!

Perhaps wisely, the ballroom was never replaced, but the fourth (and current) pavilion was rebuilt (hopefully from something fire-retardant) and reopened on 27th June 1958. Remarkably the life of the pier since then has been spectacularly quiet, and there have been no really news-worthy articles to report from then up to the present day. I bet the owners are extremely grateful for this, especially considering its flammable past! The current incarnation of the Britannia Pier is such that you could enter in a complete fug of despondency and despair, and be cheered up immensely within minutes (and that would be without supping from the massive number of bars that can be found hereon!).

As we ventured on board this cheery vessel, we found that despite its cheap and cheerful exterior, it was a bustling, happy and jolly place, for every member of the family to enjoy. We passed a bar and restaurant, then some kiosks, bowling and various amusements flashing and twinkling away.

Here in the huge theatre building, decorated in a fetching red and white colour-scheme, you can see such classic comedy delights as Cannon and Ball or that old stalwart of Great Yarmouth, Jim Davidson. If you listen carefully on a quiet day, you can hear, above the melancholy mew of the distant gull, the perennial call of the Chuckle Brothers too, echoing across the sands... *from me... to you...*! But we are just jesting, as it is fantastic that in this day when so many other seaside theatres close down due to falling numbers, that like Cromer, Great Yarmouth has such a thriving entertainment centre where there's something for everyone – long may it continue!

Because of the size of the Theatre pavilion, the pier head is extremely wide to accommodate the building and its attendant kiosks and amusements. It almost gives the impression of being back on dry land (although, like the Wellington Pier, dry land isn't really that far below you!), and as we squeezed around the side of the theatre, under more jolly red, white and blue flags, we found more amusements for the younger visitors. There's a cute little carousel, a water ride, a huge wibbly-wobbly slide and more places to eat (and drink!). At the end of the pier, fenced around with some freshly painted white railings, we surveyed the vast deserts of sandy beach to the left, the right and straight out to sea. There had at one time (last week?) been some safety railings down there, but now just a hint of the top remained, waving desperately as the gulping sands engulfed them completely. We're not sure that we'd want to fall asleep sunbathing here, and wondered how many tourists lay mummified beneath the beach, blissfully unaware of the encroaching sands as they slept!

Regardless of the menace below, we were on a crest of a wave, our emotions buoyed by this cheerful pier, and enjoyed a blissful kiss – a bit gritty with the blowing fine sand, but lovely nonetheless! With three piers visited, we were looking forward to tomorrow, going to Lowestoft and investigating two more very different piers before heading home. Little did we know how Sunday would pan out in reality!

Following a restful night in a lovely local hostelry that seemed to have a riot of songbirds in its car park, we set off to Lowestoft, Suffolk, the most easterly point of the UK. Much like its great rival Great Yarmouth, Lowestoft was initially a fishing port catching herring. Delving back into its history, it got its name from the Vikings – 'toft' in a place name means homestead, but also has lots of other noteworthy events that have happened since! I particularly like the idea that Roger Bigot was a tenant in chief here in the Domesday survey (although he does sound like a character from *Viz* magazine!).

Following the same historical path as Yarmouth, Lowestoft prospered in the late 1800s when the arrival of the railway meant fish could be taken further afield. It was comprehensively bombed in both World Wars, and was also a centre for soft-paste porcelain from the 1750s until the 1800s (not a good mixture, bombs and crockery). As a low-lying town, flooding by the sea has been a continual problem, and this is a particular hazard in the autumn and winter. Having said that, Lowestoft is also one of the driest areas in the country, but as you flock to the wide, sandy beaches in your bikinis and budgie-smugglers, be aware that it also suffers from cool onshore breezes and sea fog!

As we drove into the town fairly early on a quiet and sunny Sunday morning, we found a lovely car park down on the edge of the beach, not far from one of Lowestoft's main employers, Birds Eye. There's also a growing renewable energy industry here – not to everyone's delight, as there is a growing movement against the turbines installed out at sea, claiming they cause much destruction to the marine life during construction and are a hazard to migrating birds and insects. The opposing argument has produced some compelling evidence, however, that once established, these turbines become artificial reefs for a wide variety of sea weeds, sponges and anemones, which in turn become home for other marine life. Nature has a funny way of dealing with man-made structures and never fails to make use of whatever edifices we throw in its way!

We had a little walk to get to the seafront and the piers, and this gave us the chance to walk past the harbour, full of yachts and pleasure vessels, and the odd business-like vessel too. The last sidewinder trawler of the Lowestoft fleet can be found here – the *Mincarlo* is now a living history exhibit and open to visitors, here in the harbour. Once past the boats, we checked our directions and looked for the first place to kiss – Lowestoft South pier. Looking around we found a few signs and headed across a rather lovely square to the gateway. There has been quite a lot of money spent here, revamping the area for the new millennium and a new breed of visitor, and we walked across an area that I would imagine is great fun on a hot sunny day – there are squirty fountains imbedded in the paved flooring, to impart cooling wetness to squealing children (and the unfortunate parents dragged in too!). There's also an epic statue of a bearded man strangling a serpent and a rather lovely Edwardian-style pavilion, home to Tourist Information, a heritage exhibition and children's play area. Despite all this mix of eras, the square is very pleasant and welcoming, and there, tucked on the sea side of it is a low-key white building that houses amusements, fish and chips and a source of liquid refreshment!

It also announces that it is the entrance to the South Pier, so slightly trepidatious (for we hadn't seen anything that actually looked like a pier), we walked through the gate and along the side of the amusements building to a wide, tarmac area and walkway along a curving structure that bordered the harbour entrance and appeared to end with a little lighthouse. Topped with a solid and durable wall it looked rather like a sea wall or harbour wall... we needed to know more!

According to the flapping pieces of paper we unravelled in the morning breeze, Lowestoft South is considered by some as the south side of the harbour entrance. It looked like our fears were true; this was Torquay all over again, surely? However, read on and make your own decision, as there is quite a past to this construction!

Initially it does look like this pier was just an extension of the harbour wall. In 1831 two short piers were built either side of the harbour entrance. They were just 152m (500') long and engineered by William Cubitt for the Norwich and Lowestoft Navigation Company. In 1846 the South Pier was lengthened to 402m (1,320') and a reading room added in 1853-4 – this was destroyed by fire the following year but was replaced by a pavilion between 1889-91. So far, so good – the pier *did* have decking and benches for weary strollers, and the reading room and pavilion definitely class as amusements.

In 1884 following plans to upgrade the harbour a bandstand was added to provide entertainment for the walkers, and to the people arriving at the jetty by steamer. Old postcards show a thriving pier with a handsome black and white Swiss-cottage style of pavilion, little groups of Edwardian people promenading on the decking and strings of light bulbs to illuminate its length. It had elegant five-bar gate wooden railings and the supporting wooden piles are clearly visible.

In 1928 the pier was strengthened with concrete, but with World War II there came some dramatic changes. The grand pavilion was sadly destroyed, and the pier was commandeered by the army and became a gun battery. Two twelve-pound guns with fixed beam lights were installed in June of 1940. These guns were to protect the harbour entrance and were primed to attack any small craft, report enemy aircraft and shipping and to defend the town from German parachutists. The only events worth relaying during this time were that of a bomb grazing the watch shelter in 1942 (that fortunately didn't explode!) and earlier that same year a ship collided with the pier and caused enough damage to render the Number 2 gun out of action until August of the same year.

Following the war, life returned to normal and a new pavilion, designed by local architects Skipper and Carless was opened by the Duke of Edinburgh on 2nd May 1956. At around the same time a miniature railway was opened that ran the entire length of the pier – this must have been a wonderful addition to the facilities for those post-war summer holidaymakers! Alterations to the pier were made between 1974-5 and a 67m (220') leisure centre was added to the shoreward end at a cost of £220,000 and repairs made to the pavilion.

In 1987 following tests the seaward end of the pier was closed due to structural problems, and the following year it was announced that the pier would be incorporated into plans for a new marina, but when funds for this weren't forthcoming and only the pavilion had been demolished the pier stayed unloved for a couple of years. Following extensive repairs and refurbishment in 1993 at a cost of £30,000 the council re-opened the pier to the public. There was another major refurbishment in 2008 and it is in this current guise that it can be seen today. As we walked along the curving length, it was very hard to believe that this was the same pier of days gone by, as there seemed to be no clues left from the glorious past of this pier to show what it had been like, which was rather sad.

No longer do visitors promenade along wooden decking, instead there's a solid road underfoot and those seaworthy walls in fetching concrete. Lots of people fish from the South Pier, and there seem to be plenty of birds around too, from gulls to cormorants and a couple of ducks over on the harbour side. We made our way to the end of the pier, but sadly couldn't quite make it due to a severe case of anti-vandal fencing preventing access to the little lighthouse here.

We tiptoed over fishing rods and pressed our noses to the grey metal that barred our way. The end-of-the-pier lighthouse was hexagonal and had a rather fetching pagoda canopy supported by columns at its base. Over to the right was an eight-sided concrete base with some little steps going up, and it's likely that this was the base for the World War II Number 1 gun. We had a little kiss here, musing over whether we were stood on a pier at all, but looking at the historical evidence have decided it probably-is-might-be-oh-I-don't-know-alright-then a pier after all, but discussed this at length as we made our way back to the promenade.

On drier land, we left the pier square behind and headed along the stylish re-vamped promenade alongside South Beach to get to Lowestoft's Claremont Pier, 'a real pier' as many pier purists are crying right now! Well, yes, they have a point, although for how much longer this edifice will be here in Lowestoft is anyone's guess, as it has seen better days.

But the walk to the pier was very pleasant – the statuesque double-headed lamp posts lead the way past crashing waves and a sand-and-pebble-beach to a much older part of town, with grand old Regency buildings overlooking the flower beds. As we approached the pier we passed another impressively sturdy statue of reptilian throttling activity and some modern but pleasing-on-the-eye wooden and brushed steel benches, before finding we were walking on some coloured tarmac where herrings and waves heralded our arrival at Claremont Pier. In case we'd missed it, there is a really grand advert for this pier from the road; big silver arches like giant croquet hoops lead you to the front door!

The front of Claremont Pier is big and promises grand things – 'fun!' it says, emblazoned in big letters on the white façade. Behind the glass are the luring flashing lights of the amusements contained therein. Sadly, on the outside, it's not quite such a monument. Towards the landward end are a series of somewhat inelegant buildings – the first one is white with portholes, but it's got two grey corrugated ones tailing it, which we thought would look much better with a lick of white paint too! And there seems to end the 'best' bits of the pier. Beyond the buildings, Claremont Pier has been left to the ravages of the maritime elements, bare, unloved and unadorned apart from a curious bundle of lights on the end. What had happened to this once grand old lady?

Lowestoft's Claremont Pier is one of the country's later piers, originally built as a mooring for Belle Steamers between 1902-3. The steamship company was formed in 1898 and built Southwold, Felixstowe and the Claremont to serve their famous fleet of steamers that operated from London Bridge via other notable piers at Southend, Clacton, Walton-on-the-Naze, Southwold, Felixstowe and on to Great Yarmouth. It was designed by D. Fox and was originally 183m (600') long and 11m (36') wide, with its head in deep water at high or low tide for ease of access by the boats.

In 1912, the T-shaped head was extended and redeveloped with a new pavilion. The original piles were replaced with solid greenheart timber and it now stretched out to 232m (760'). It had a rather chequered life, with the number of steamers visiting dropping away as the railways took over in popularity and cheapness as a form of transport for holidaymakers.

The army moved in for the duration of World War II, sectioning the pier and using it as a training base until 1948 (they temporarily bridged the gap with a Bailey bridge to get to the end!). Once the war was over, the steamers never returned and the pier was not reopened to the public as no one wanted the responsibility of running it. However, this wasn't to be a long period of abandonment, as actor George Studd bought it the following year, and in 1950 a new concrete platform and pavilion were revealed to visitors.

A violent storm in 1962 washed away the T-shaped end and a part of the neck, reducing the length to 219m (720'), and then little happened to the pier until the 1980s, with the pier spending the intermediate years run down and closed to the public. There was a major restoration project that saw the neck of the pier and the landward end revamped and reopened, but the sad thing is that this pier has been left unloved in its entirety for a great many years, and it's surprising that it has stayed in as good nick as it is!

The wooden piles still look solid and sturdy and there is little evidence of rot on the decking or distortion of the railings that indicate there's something nasty going on structurally! Although the rest of the resort has had lots of work done on it and is very pleasing to the eye, the poor Claremont Pier sits on the promenade looking good from the front, but very tired from the side. In 2000 the council decided to have the two piers linked visually with an art installation created by David Ward. His work, opening in the Spring of 2001 is entitled *St Elmo's Fire*, on Claremont Pier is the odd group of sticks and lights that we had seen – if we'd come along at night, it would all have been made so much clearer! Apparently these lights fade in and out at random intervals and reflect on the water – there are also some on the South Pier and in the dark, depending on the weather and tidal conditions, these light reflections link up and create shifting and changing ethereal patterns on the water.

It was a quick kiss here – piers had started to become a personal thing with us, they were starting to develop personalities and characters – were we going mad? Whichever, it was quite disheartening to see a seaside town that had spent so much time, effort and money on making significant improvements to its seafront and attributes, but had left what could be a real asset neglected and barely useable. Come on Lowestoft! It's not too late to save your pier!

We found more interesting treasures of Lowestoft on the way back to the car – building-block beach huts by the side of the Claremont Pier painted in black and primary colours, neat and pretty gardens along the seafront, a wind turbine twirling lazily near the harbour and despite the drifts of sand everywhere the town was impressively clean and tidy. We're not being hypercritical here, saying Lowestoft should repair its pier – Weston's Birnbeck Pier is in far worse condition and nothing is being done to it at all, but it just seems a shame…

Once back in the car we got out the road map to plot a route back home (please note younger readers, a road atlas is made of paper and shows all the roads in the country – no electronic connection required!), and glancing at the clock realised it was still very early in the day – not even time for elevenses yet! I made a suggestion. 'Look, it's early yet. Why don't we go back via Southwold Pier, it's not that far, and it seems silly to not go, then have to come back again for another weekend. What do you think?'

Looking at the map Jay agreed it was feasible and we were soon on the way to one of the loveliest little towns in the country – and that's official! There is something about Southwold that is instantly captivating – it's a popular holiday destination tucked away on the Suffolk coastline and some one million people visit here over the summer season every year – thank goodness they don't all visit at once, the place would sink into the surrounding marshes!

I'm going to refrain from calling this town 'quintessentially English'. Everyone does and it isn't fair! There are so many reasons why Southwold is such a special place – it's never really expanded due to being surrounded by marshland or water, it's really proud of its ancestry and has lots of little 'village greens' as a result. When a huge fire devastated the town in 1659 many of the buildings were not rebuilt, and these spaces are where they were all those years ago. A large water tower dominates the Common (dating from 1890), everyone who's been there knows where the lighthouse is, you can't miss it! It was built in 1887 and is unusual in that it doesn't have a rotating beam but flashes on and off four times every twenty seconds.

And there's so much MORE to this little town! There's a boating lake, a harbour, a brewery that's been there since 1660, an amber museum, a fantastically painted old church made of flints, beach huts that originally cost £75 to build but now sell for over £75,000, Punch and Judy, some cannons from 1672 on Gun Hill, no High Street shopping chains, rather good fish and chips, a sandy and shingly beach... oh, and a pier!

We've met the Belle Steamer Company before at Lowestoft Pier, and the Southwold Pier Order of 1899 meant they could build a jetty for their boats here. The T-shaped design by W. Jeffrey was opened in 1900 and was 247m (810') long with the landing stage at the head. It served the boat passengers well enough as a basic landing stage for a couple of years until a wooden pavilion with refreshment rooms was built at the landward end. Steamers continued visiting until the 1934 when the scourge of the East coast, a large storm, swept away entire landing stage. This T-shaped section was never replaced, but the wooden pavilion was replaced in 1936 with a state-of-the-art two-storey building that is still there in all its Art Deco glory to this day.

In 1940 the pier was sectioned, but a drifting sea mine hit it and spectacularly took out another section! This was 'repaired' in 1948 at a cost of £30,000, which left the pier in one piece but not as strong or secure as it should have been. An October storm in 1955 decided to flex its muscles and washed away the far end of the pier. In February 1979 another storm reduced the length of the pier even further to 45m (150') and it remained in that state, a stump sticking out into the North Sea, until it was bought by the Iredale family in 1987.

They have really been the driving force behind getting the pier restored and in the state you see it today, along with the enthusiasm of a league of fundraisers that came forward from across the country to get their favourite seaside pier rebuilt. First, both floors of the 30's pavilion were fully restored, with a little amusement arcade (where I remember playing the original *Star Wars* arcade game many years ago!), and a diner. Determined fundraising then began in 1999, as did the rebuild! New piles were installed using the latest techniques and just two years later the pier was back to its original length, complete with a T-shaped head. New owners, the Bourne family took over in 2005 and have continued the good work started by the Iredales.

The pier was officially re-opened on 3rd July 2001, and the following year the *Balmoral* was the first ship to revisit for fifty years and the pier was named Pier of the Year. It consistently gets named as visitor's favourite pier, comes in various Top Ten lists of best or favourite piers or appears as photos in articles or on television programmes! We have to hold our hand up here to owning a rather lovely black and white print of Southwold Pier which adorns a wall at home!

As we turned off the main road onto the bouncy, windy road through the marshes to the town I waxed lyrically to Jay about how lovely it was here. I'd visited once but have family links to this part of the country – my grandma lived here as a child and various family members regularly visited, sending back sepia postcards of the town, which she kept and passed onto me when I was little. And it doesn't seem to have changed much, which I think is a good thing!

We rolled to a stop just next to the pier, opposite the boating lake in bright and breezy conditions, walked across the road and turned to look at the pavilion. It still oozes 1930's symmetry and simplicity, and there's nothing fussy about the frontage – in fact it's quite plain and just says what it is! The ground floor still houses an amusement arcade with more recent machines, but there are still the favourites like horse racing and 2p pushers, but sadly no more *Star Wars*. I wonder what the youth of today would make of it? (Now I sound really old!)

We walked around to the right-hand side of the pavilion and found the entrance – we anticipated from our first view that we were going to be saying 'wow!' a lot here, and this was going to be a visit quite unlike any other! Over the gateway is an automata sign – rotating metal fish and boats bob up and down around the words 'Southwold Pier', and it's all been powered by solar panels – that's neat! Stepping under, the pier revealed itself in front of us – seemingly traditional huts, simple white paintwork and dark roofing, a few people fishing, some basic strings of lights. All seems in order!

But there should be a sign that says 'Please leave your preconceived ideas at the gate' – this pier is nothing like you expect. Once through the gate, all the details become apparent. There are brass plaques just about everywhere, showing how much this pier has meant to people over the years – the support for getting it back up and running was phenomenal! It's worth taking time to read as many of them as you can too, some are touching, some show little glimpses into family life and fond holidays spent in Southwold and then there are the downright funny, and we smiled and laughed out loud several times!

We walked past the Boardwalk restaurant and bar, which provides wholesome home-cooked fare and has a bar, the Treasure Chest gift shop and then the Under the Pier Show. If you think you've seen every kind of pier amusement arcade, you'd be wrong – step inside! It'll be quite crowded, this is a popular spot on the pier and with very good reason. There are no gambling machines in here – but it is packed with hilarious and quirky creations by Tim Hunkin, who hand built delights such as 'Mobility Masterclass' (can you get across the motorway on your Zimmer frame?) and rent a dog for a walk around Southwold, seeing it from his point of view!

A while later, and with aching face muscles from smiling so much, we carried on along the natty diagonally planked decking to the Clockhouse café – as well as inside seating there is an outside area with a wooden and glass wind-break, a very clever idea. Then we came across the water clock, somewhere else we had to stand and watch for a while! This is a huge creation of bits and pieces, charting the progress of water from filling the bath tub to flushing the toilet and down to the bottom tank with a whoosh!

There are other quirky little details all over the pier, from the metal rubbish bin sleeves with little shoals of cut-out fish on them, to the mini band-stand and standard wooden benches surrounded with grey metal windbreaks that are surmounted by gorgeous bronze metal eels and wavy tops. Even the restaurant tables have different sea creatures on them! Everywhere there is attention to detail, but you'll only find it if you look, so the odd-ball sense of humour isn't in your face all the time. We walked past the last kiosk, Seaweed and Salt which sells kitchenware, toys, stationery, jewellery and local produce and made it to the end of the pier at last, having purchased a tea towel to assist with those boring domestic duties!

Here at the T-shaped head there's a real feeling of space, even with a few fishermen and families here this early in the morning. There's more to do too, you don't just have to get here and look at the view or back at the pier, although you should do this of course, they're both stunning! There are some little curios here too – a pier tide recorder, a quantum tunnelling telescope (have you ever seen a mermaid? You might here!), a weather station and a normal telescope. There's also another form of entertainment, whether by accident or design – try and get your small change onto the top of the rust-ringed concrete pile just off the end of the sea! With a slightly domed top, it looks quite a challenge, but there were coins on each of the buffers that stop the *Waverley* from bashing into the end of the pier, so it can't be that hard! It wasn't a challenge to have another kiss at the end of this delightful pier, in the spring sunshine, chilled by the wind off the North Sea we enjoyed an equally delightful kiss and turned to look at the view back to land.

There's a nod here to the origins of the pier – not only is it here that the *Waverley* and *Balmoral* tie up on visits, but up on the Seaweed and Salt cabin is a weather vane depicting the silhouette of an old steamer, sleek and seaworthy. It looks rather like the *Balmoral*, with squinty eyes and a bit of imagination (I'll apologise if it actually is!). Hand in hand we strolled back along the pier reading even more of the brass plaques before watching the water clock again as it struck the hour. We decided then that eleven o'clock meant it *was* time for elevenses and adjourned to the Clockhouse for a coffee and a tea-cake and sat outside to enjoy it. The wind break did a fantastic job of keeping the strong sea breezes at bay and meant we could enjoy the most of the weak sunshine – without the gusts it was pleasantly warm!

Southwold Pier had done a fantastic job – free of charge you get filled with a fantastic feeling of well-being. There was nothing we could find that was negative to say about it, and can honestly say it is a real tribute to what can be done to reinvigorate a pier for future generations to enjoy! Reluctantly back at the car, the map came out again.

"Um… we're going to have to go back south, it's only an hour or so to Felixstowe. It's not even noon yet, do you reckon we've got time to divert and see Felixstowe Pier?" ventured the silly woman behind the wheel.

"Well, it's do-able I suppose," replied the infinitely more sensible co-pilot.

"OK, we'll do it! Let's go!" And so we set off back out of the town to Felixstowe.

This was going to be one of those 'not quite sure what we'll find' kind of visits. There was conflicting information available as to whether the pier at Felixstowe was even open or not, as the owners had put in an application for demolition in 2004, and we'd discovered that it's not always wise to trust information on the internet as it can be horribly out of date. I'll also confess to only believing that Felixstowe was a busy container port (in fact it's the busiest and largest in the country) and didn't realise that actually it's an attractive and traditional seaside town too.

Just over an hour after leaving Southwold we stopped on the seafront at Felixstowe. There's not a hint of port here at all (or any other fortified liquor), it really is a pleasant place. There is a long stretch of sandy-with-a-hint-of-shingle beach, flat promenade and a sprinkling of beach huts. Lining the prom are well-kept floral beds, which today were hard to spot as families were now out in force enjoying seaside delights such as fish and chips and ice creams, and it was quite noisy as a result!

Before we arrived at the pier, we paused to admire a fantastic model of a Felixstowe F2 seaplane biplane from 1917, made from plants, and then to the pier. Things were looking up – there was a building here in red and white at the landward end of the pier which stretched forlornly out to sea. The building had 'The Pier' and 'Amusements' written on it – and it was open! If we weren't going to get a seaward end-of-the-pier kiss, at least we'd get an arcade one! It had a rather odd looped illumination on the top of it that looked rather like a stylised crayfish and a bit familiar. Then the penny dropped – we have a modern picture postcard at home with 'Save Britain's Piers!' on it that features Brighton's West Pier, Herne Bay, Hastings and Felixstowe. In the pictures it looks bleak and barren, concrete decking, dull blue railings, a row of these Mickey Mouse ear illuminations on poles and a solitary pigeon. Oh dear.

We walked to the other side of the entrance first to have a good look at the structure. Nope, they were still there... From this angle, in the sunshine and backed by a bright blue sky the pier really doesn't look too bad (apart from those lights!). It was time to go back and see how far we could go (so to speak... that's a whole new pier-based challenge and I don't want a criminal record, thank you!).

The amusement arcade would have been blacker than a black thing in the dark if it hadn't been for the most slot machines and games that I'd ever seen in one place illuminating the gloom. Above them were neon strip lights in every colour of the rainbow. It looked like a child had coloured it in with a box of felt-tip pens! But fortunately there was a way out – part of the deck at the back was still open for business. Although it was only about 7m (25') or so at least it was outside!

It was a bit depressing to be brutally honest. The 'decking' is concrete, the open area secured on top of the railings with building site barriers and scaffolding and the curious concrete-block assembly of a miniature go-kart track filling the space. We squeezed round the side and walked to the barrier. Festooned with messages we felt a bit threatened.

'Danger!'

'No Access!' And then the more intriguing 'Jumping or climbing on or off this pier is forbidden.' How, pray, does one jump ON to a pier? And has anyone tried?

We peered through the metal barrier. There wasn't really a lot more to see. On the surface of it, the pier doesn't look in bad condition. The rails aren't pretty but on the whole they're intact. The concrete surface won't catch fire at least, and looking over the edge, although some of the piles look a bit bashed in places, there's nothing hanging off or looking in peril of collapsing. We kissed in front of the gulls who took no notice whatsoever and went back to the seafront wondering why the pier seemed to be so unloved.

There is really little to tell about the history of poor Felixstowe Pier. It was built as the last of the trio of landing stages by the Coast Development Company for the Belle Steamers. Its simple design of cost effective hardwood by Rogers Brothers was popped into place and opened in August 1905. It was 805m (2,640') long, one of the longest in the country at the time and was just a railed promenade deck with a T-shaped landing jetty at the end. To spice things up a bit, a large pavilion was built at the landward end and a 3'6" gauge electric tramway from one end to the other provided transport for passengers and their luggage. It cost 1d for a one-way trip – doesn't seem much today but would have been quite an expense only the rich could afford back then.

The railway also brought lots of visitors to the town and things were looking rosy right up until the 1930s. Then war broke out and the pier was sectioned. Because the tramway had obviously been rendered unusable and the landing stage now obsolete because of the lack of visiting boats it was decided the sectioned end part should go. The Royal Engineers were called in and duly demolished it, leaving the pier just 137m (450') long. Nothing changed, nothing happened and everyone seemingly lost interest in the pier until the 1990s.

The 1996 plans for a £2.5 million rebuild would have seen the pier and landward buildings totally revamped to include a ten-pin bowling alley, roller skating rink, café, shops and a bar. The pier itself would be re-decked and furnished with new kiosks and landing stage to encourage the modern boating trade to come back. £70,000 was needed for immediate repairs but that money never materialised and the plans were shelved. In 1999 a charitable trust offered to take it on but by 2003 had been unable to raise enough money for a feasibility report such was local apathy for the rebuild. The pier was then allegedly given back to the original owners, Pier Amusements Ltd for the sum of £1 by the council. Pier Amusements promptly applied for a demolition order in 2004.

Fortunately for us (and the pier) that total lack of apathy surrounding its existence has meant the pier has survived. It crops up again as a perennial thorn in the side of the council in the town's regeneration plans of 2007 as a potential project. It is stated as being an important landmark for the town and in a prime area to be visited by tourists which (and any fool could have spotted this) makes it ripe for smartening up and renovating. The only heartening remark in the article is that if the current owners do not do something with the pier to regenerate it as an asset for the town, they (the council) will have to consider applying for a Compulsory Purchase Order and doing it themselves, but there is no time-scale given. Never mind, at least it has been realised that the town has a wasted asset here and are aware it needs something doing to save it in the near future. We look forward to coming back in the next few years to see what has happened, and (said in my best firm teacher's voice) I hope there is some improvement worth seeing!

Back to the car. Check time – 12.40 (blimey, that was a speedy visit!). Get out map. "Erm, Darling...?"

(Dubious reply) "Yes...?"

"There are only three more piers left on this side of the country to visit. Harwich is about an hour away. And Walton and Clacton are only another 20 miles after that. I reckon we could do them, no problem at all and then head for home. What do you think?"

(Long pause followed by deep, long-suffering sigh. And we're not even married yet!)

"Go on then. You've got the map. You're driving."

What a sensible man, not arguing with the driver even though she appears to be totally stark raving bonkers!

The driver has learnt a little lesson here. Just because it doesn't look very far on the map, and adding up those little numbers by the pretty red and yellow wiggly lines gives a do-able figure, it doesn't necessarily mean you will arrive at the destination in a sensible amount of time. Felixstowe to Harwich did not take 'about an hour' (and those twenty-odd miles to Walton and then Clacton wouldn't take 25 minutes either, such are the little wibbly country roads in this part of the world!). It took nearer an hour and a half to get to Harwich. We were still talking, which was a good sign, although conversational politeness was a bit thin on the ground!

Much like Felixstowe (whose huge and mysterious port could be seen just over the water), Harwich was a bit of a surprise. We navigated our way more by luck than judgement to the water's edge in the old town – I say by luck, but this was because since leaving Lowestoft we'd been sailing blind to all these extra piers. The maps, journey plans and information on the piers was all neatly tucked up in a folder marked 'Piers to Visit' at home. Ooops. The old part of the town just oozes history, and in fact the port of Harwich goes back hundreds of years, ideally sited as it is on the east coast and the estuaries of the rivers Stour and Orwell. There are lots of old and interesting buildings down on the water's edge too, and many of these are listed. The main one of these from where we were sitting was the Pier Hotel, which was rather grand, although fortunately not called the Grand Pier Hotel, as in our experience these have a nasty habit of catching fire!

We walked along the quay and onto the waterfront itself and the first thing we were faced with was a very lovely little ticket office, looking like a little Victorian ornamental birdcage, and felt encouraged to explore the little pier. Harwich is not one on the Piers Society website and we had uncovered its existence by accident while looking up other piers. As such, we weren't sure if it would fill our criteria, so were a bit worried. However, by the side of the ticket office there were two very informative notice-boards telling us about the history of the Ha'penny Pier and we happily stepped down onto its neat decking.

The pier is L-shaped, and we walked along the short bit first before turning right to walk parallel to the quay-side. There was no doubt in our minds now that this was in fact a rather lovely little pier, an overlooked gem that should definitely be added to the pier enthusiasts list! The long planked deck with understated simple black railings was very peaceful. Dotted along the length of the pier are wooden benches and single shade lamp posts, similarly painted black. It feels like it really is a part of the (normally) busy waterfront, and from the end of the pier we looked across the estuary where the skyline was dominated by huge shipping cranes – the port of Felixstowe! (See, I said it wasn't far!)

We leant against the railings and drank in the peace and quiet of the surroundings, watching the container ships across the water, the smaller vessels on this side of the river and the water lapping gently against the quayside. We also had a kiss. Unsurprisingly, lips felt like they were on the verge of chapping now. These were no mere pecks, after all, these were full-on pier kisses and we meant every lingering moment! As we searched our pockets for an elusive tin of lip balm, we read all about the history of this little pier, with which I will bore you now!

In 1845 it was decided that the area along the front of Harwich Quay should be developed so that steamships with lots of passengers could come and go with ease and bring in more income for the town. As is often the case today, back then the money couldn't be found to carry out these plans until the Harwich Corporation put forward a more viable scheme with funding. This was eventually passed and work began in 1852 with Peter Schuyler Bruff leading the work to build the pier and quay.

In 1853 the pier opened for business, 105m (343') long with a north-east arm halfway along it. It was initially called the Corporation Pier but soon became known as the Ha'penny Pier because that was the toll charged to walk along it. These tickets were bought from the Ticket Office which was originally a two-storey building without the bell-cage that can be seen today (this one was built just before 1900). The pier saw plenty of custom from the cross-channel ships and local steamers up until the newer Continental Pier (now called Trinity Pier) was built. The Ha'penny Pier even saw active service during World War I when it was used by the Royal Navy.

Unfortunately the pier caught fire in 1927 and was halved in length, leaving the odd elbow-shape that exists today. Since then life has continued very quietly until today. Now there is a foot ferry that goes over the estuary to Felixstowe from the pier and free guided tours of Old Harwich leave from here during the summer. Up until 1988 the pier was owned by Trinity House, since then it's been owned by the Harwich Haven Authority, but what a great job they've done, we both agreed it was worth visiting as we strolled back past the little tea room by the Ticket Office and back to the car.

(Nervous silence) "Er..." I started.

"Yes, I know. It's only fourteen miles to Walton-on-the-Naze and we could be there in twenty minutes. Go on then," came the weary reply.

I started the engine and we pulled away to wind our way through the lovely old streets of Harwich towards Walton-on-the-Naze.

Tracking the journey via the internet when I got home I found that it was actually fourteen and a half miles to Walton. In the other column it tells you how long it will take. Forty minutes? Surely not? But yes, it was probably nearer that, and it felt like it too! But here we were in what is allegedly England's friendliest town. Based on our visit here, we couldn't possibly comment, because there seemed to be a total absence of people on a Sunday afternoon, but I'm sure they really are lovely! We parked up on the hillside in a quiet street and ambled down to the direction of the pier – it's not difficult to find piers, head downhill to the coast, look left, look right, locate the pier. Simple as that! The same crafty technique worked here too, although we nearly fell over the cliff because our chosen road ended in railings, but below us was the enormous corrugated dark grey roof of Walton-on-the-Naze's pier.

Walton-on-the-Naze (the 'naze' bit comes from the Viking word 'ness', meaning a headland) on the north Essex coast has come a long way since the early tourists discovered it, with the boom really starting in 1829. A very astute philanthropist, distinguished civil engineer and manager of the Eastern Union Railway, one Peter Schuyler Bruff (later the constructor of Harwich Pier) was behind the building of the town's new pier, Pier Hotel and two large housing terraces. Now the third longest pier in the country, then it was a mere 45m (150') long for landing goods and passengers from London and Ipswich steamers. It was lengthened in 1848 to 91m (300'), but was fairly short-lived in this incarnation, washing away in a storm in 1880.

The railway had arrived in the town in 1869 which brought more visitors out of the smoke for some clean sea air. In 1895 it was decided Walton really needed to have a decent pier again to cater for these holiday-makers. The Walton-on-the-Naze Hotel and Pier Company (there's a natty short name that trips off the tongue) duly opened a replacement designed by J. Cochrane that was a heady 244m (800') long. Like Felixstowe Pier it had a nifty 3' 6" gauge electric tramway for goods and people. Several extensions followed, largely because the coastline here is susceptible to erosion by the wild North Sea waves and had suffered considerably within a short period of time, and the pier ended up at the current 792m (2,600') long.

As far as amusements for the visiting holidaymakers, they could enjoy a modest pavilion at the seaward end, an amusement arcade and the exotically named Seaspray Lounge. To add to these already heady delights, the pier also had a tent for theatre performances!

In 1935 the electric tramway was replaced with a pneumatic tyred battery car that ran between two wooden beams, but this was short-lived because of the outbreak of war. The pier was dutifully sectioned and holidaymakers stayed away, but the town made a valiant effort bringing the pier back to life once hostilities ceased, although the pier changed hands in 1937 and a fire in 1945 damaged the pier and the battery powered carriage. The breach was repaired and in 1948 the contractors put down a two-foot gauge railway track along the length so that a diesel engine could help lug materials to the end of the pier, but it was decided to keep this for pleasure rides, which it did until the 1970s.

Slowly people came back to their favourite haunts for summer holidays and once again Walton began to buzz with holidaymakers. This time they were of the budget variety because of the post-war austerity, but this led to the creation of some large caravan parks. These are still here today and are a testament to nearly seventy years of cheap and cheerful holidays! The pier continued to provide amusements for all of the family during this time, marred only by storms in 1978-9 which battered the pier so severely a 33m (108') section collapsed into the sea.

Today the pier is still owned by the New Walton Pier Company which has owned it since 1937, and they continue doing a rather fantastic job – why fix what isn't broken?! We'd made it down to the awesomely huge entrance to the pier by now. It's not the most attractive of pier pavilions, but blimey, it's big and because of the expanse of eye-catching paint, you can't really ignore it! Since 1946 the number of amusements inside this 'hangar' have gradually increased and today there are a staggering five acres of amusements all under one roof!

It's an odd experience and a bit draughty and echoey at first to go into such a big space filled with what is essentially a fairground. There are not just slot machines and grab-a-teddy type games, there are children's rides like the teacups (about as fast as I like to go...), dodgems, roundabouts and a test-your-strength machine. There's a bowling alley, waltzers, every fairground treat you can imagine interspersed with more arcade machines and all liberally sprinkled with fairground smells too – candyfloss, doughnuts, fish and chips, burgers! We suddenly realised that in our haste to visit all these piers in one day we had neglected to eat, but with gurgling stomachs that were threatening mutiny we honourably decided to carry on to the end of the (extremely long) pier first! We passed lots of families enjoying their cheap-and-cheerful day out on the pier and came out into the brisk sea breeze to tread the planks.

There's a lot of planking here, and although it's not in tip-top condition it has a certain weather-beaten appeal about it. There is an equally weather-beaten set of railings along one side of the pier and a rustic, textured wooden equivalent on the other. The pier not only feels blooming long when you're walking along it but it's pretty wide too. At one point you can spot where the old diesel engine would have run on rails along the pier, although long gone, the planks that have replaced where they were are longer than the others, a ghost from the past if you know where to look.

It's an interesting pier to walk along, not just because it's plain and weather-worn but because of the interesting curve towards the end. Towards the end of the pier are the fishermen. In the summer they hope to hook bass, garfish and sole, while in the winter hardy anglers have a chance to catch flounder and cod. An annual ticket to fish is reasonably priced and allows twenty-four hour access to the pier – a midnight walk on a winter's night along this pier's not for the fainthearted!

We thought we were approaching the end of the pier, marked with a lifeboat bobbing on the choppy sea, but as we got closer realised that this was just a pier mirage, experienced by foolhardy kissers who try and do ten piers in one weekend without adequate sustenance. Instead, we had reached the Walton and Frinton lifeboat station (thankfully both towns choosing to shorten their names, thus preserving the sanity of the RNLI!).

Amazingly there has been a lifeboat at the end of Walton Pier since 1900, but we were looking at the four-year-old wave break and new berth for the modern boat. The new facilities, opened in May 2005, cost £1 million to build and also have maintenance and storage facilities and are easily worth every donated penny.

We stumbled around the lifeboat station and were delighted, in our weakened state, to see the real end of the pier! The final stretch is around a very pleasing curve, and as the only people walking this far, propped ourselves up on the rails at the end and looked at each other. For a second I'm sure Jay looked like a bacon sandwich, but it may have been a hallucinatory image. I daren't ask him what I looked like... a sugary doughnut probably, but I'm sure that kiss was a bit *too* hungry to have been just powered by love!

We parted sheepishly and turned to walk all the way back, hopefully with the promise of a late lunch at the other end. We strolled around little huddles of fishermen and the occasional wind-blown couple venturing this far along the now very windy and chilly deck. We plunged back into the relative safety of the hangar, but not before we marvelled at the proliferation of multi-coloured beach huts that were clinging to the cliffs in terraces like rows of little wooden budgerigars. We'd never seen this many beach huts or ones so far from the sea, but guessed this was the legacy of Walton's popularity as a holiday destination, and was comforting to see.

In the hangar we picked our way to the Seaspray Diner, a nod to the old Seaspray Lounge from the 1930s. It had apparently been a very busy day on the pier, as food waste, burger cartons and sugar sachets littered the table along with a liberal sprinkling of salt. Fortunately we were too hungry to care and sat with a very hot bucket of coffee each and a polystyrene tray of chips. We added to the salt snow on the table top, polished off our snack and wearily set off back up the hill to the car. Whilst Walton's pier isn't a traditional old-fashioned promenading venue with fancy wrought iron or an air of gentility, it has a lot for a family wanting a cheap and cheerful day out at the seaside, which is what is built for. There are no pretentions here, just a good day out, and although we were shattered rather than invigorated by our walk at the seaside, Walton's pier continues to provide a well-received day of entertainment for everyone!

I can't remember who pushed who up the hill, but we made it somehow.

"Clacton?"

"Yup."

And off we went.

Clacton-on-Sea is in Essex. Much like Southend there is invariably a bit of a snort of laughter accompanying the name as they seem to be inextricably linked with cheap, brash holidays of the 60s and 70s, so it was another pleasant surprise to turn up and find another lovely seaside town. Living in a coastal holiday spot I know that people who live in one of these places have a moan about the youngsters visiting for drinking sprees, the noise, the litter, the after-hours punch-ups and the like. It's very easy to overlook all the good features of where you live – turn off your prejudices and see what's around you!

Parking up was a bit of a problem initially but we found a spot in a line of cars just off the seafront. I am not a fan of parallel parking and try to avoid doing it wherever possible (typical woman I hear you cry!), so after much manoeuvring, cussing under my breath and turning several shades of fetching scarlet we were finally parked up.

Clacton turns out to be a rather interesting place, and unlike the other seaside towns we had visited was considerably newer. Originally a tiny village, the town itself was founded and created by one Peter Schuyler Bruff. Remember him? The same man responsible for the first pier and buildings at Walton-on-the-Naze and Harwich Pier had a brainwave and overcame fierce opposition from the few locals to develop the area. He saw the potential of its proximity to London and how easy it would be to bring in hordes of holidaymakers by steamer so as well as being responsible for the original town being built, he also designed and had constructed one wooden pier which opened on the 18th July 1871.

With access by boat really the only main way into the new town, Bruff really had captured the potential of the place and there were plenty of steamers arriving from London, being operated by the Woolwich Steam Packet Company. The initial pier was designed with practicality in mind and was a straightforward wooden walkway just 146m long by 11m wide (480' by 36'). With an uninterrupted deck and no buildings at the entrance it soon became popular for promenading.

A branch line from London in 1882 brought yet more visitors, as did custom from the Belle steamers and by now Clacton was an established and thriving town, but it was obvious that the original pier was no longer suitable for all the extra traffic and requirements of the day-trippers and long-stay holidayers. A pier extension was started in 1890 and finished three years later, and it may have taken a while to complete but had some very daring features for the time. At 360m (1,180') in length now the pier had a polygonal pitch-pine pier head and a polygonal Regency-style pavilion with a concert hall at the seaward end with a simple entrance adorned with advertisements and offering refreshments. Looking at some fascinating old picture-postcards, amusements included 'Popular Concerts' at three and eight o'clock and also intriguingly offered 'hot and cold sea water'. The mind boggles!

With the turn of the century and changing demands from visitors, many new features were added over the next thirty years. In 1922 it was bought by Ernest Kingsman, who owned it for the next 49 years and was not slow in loading the pier with some impressive additions. A lifeboat house was built towards the end of the pier along with the Blue Lagoon dance hall; then a few years later the Ocean Theatre. In 1931 Ernest had the pier deck widened and the following year added the Crystal Casino and a large outdoor swimming pool, open-air stage and in a few years later the enormous 'Steel Stella' roller coaster. If modern amusements weren't your thing, there were a flight of broad steps leading down to the sea from half-way along the pier to allow instant access into the sea for bathers.

In the space of twenty years the pier had become unrecognisable, positively creaking with amusements, most of which were dwarfed by that enormous roller coaster! Unfortunately, sectioning for the war meant the casino and a children's theatre were demolished. Although the pier neck was repaired, these buildings were never replaced. A post-war concrete jetty was built at the end, allowing boats to continue visiting, and life continued fairly uneventfully until the 1970s, with dolphins and killer whales moving into the site of the swimming pool from 1971. I can't get the image of orca cruising around in a swimming pool out of my head, no matter how hard I try!

In 1973 a fire damaged the roller coaster, and photographs from after that date show a helter-skelter and Ferris wheel doing their best to fill the space. Serious storms with extraordinarily high tides in 1978 and 79 caused £100,000 worth of damage that took nearly a year to repair. Just as work was completed another severe storm the next year resulted in damage to the lifeboat house and Dolphinarium, and meant there had to be an emergency evacuation of the resident killer whale, dolphin, sea lions and penguins! Storms wreaked a bit more havoc in that well-known tempest of 1987, but the pier has weathered the lesser storms since and provides a fantastic six and a half acres of fun for the visitor!

We had parked on the edge of some rather super ornamental gardens – I might be wrong but they look Victorian in style and have floral beds, fountains and mature trees and are situated up above the promenade which gives fantastic views up and down the coast – and of the pier too, which looked monstrously huge! To get to the pier entrance we had to descend a regal flight of steps at the side of a very elegant bridge that arched over the pier approach road and gave yet another view of the entrance. Even this was grand – slightly curved and dotted with towers on both sides. There's something hard to resist about pier entrances like this, they draw you in!

To begin with, it felt like we had returned to Walton Pier, as the first area of the pier is filled with fairground rides and attractions under cover, which provides all-year, all-weather entertainment for people, important in our iffy climate! We walked through and emerged out into the fresh air and made our way towards the pier end. We passed the entrance to the modern-day version of the Dolphinarium, although modern viewpoints mean that rather than killer whales and dolphins, it houses fish of all kinds as a popular SeaQuarium instead. It's a novel addition to a pier and was one that was busy, even though it was getting a bit late on a Sunday afternoon.

We walked down the pleasantly wide and spacious pier – in the summer this space is utilised for fairground rides, but now we only had to negotiate the occasional globe-toped lamp post with a circular bench around the base. The railings on the pier aren't terribly ornate, but are painted a crisp white and have a slight wave-shaped curve to them. The lifeboat house is not as large as it used to be, but today's is a little cream and blue chalet style with a steep ramp down to the sea. We weren't sure if it's still in use – it does look a bit as though it's all locked up these days.

As we passed the multi-sided restaurant I turned to Jay.

'Have I fallen asleep and am walking along the pier with my eyes shut or is it going very dark?' I asked.

'Hmm, I knew it was getting late, but I'm sure it's not nightfall yet,' he replied.

We glanced around. It was getting incredibly overcast. Gloomy. Cold, and menacingly grey. We put on a spurt, it looked horribly like rain, and we were a long way from the safety of the covered amusements. At the end of the pier we could see the post-war jetty – it's still used today by the *Waverley* on her summer jaunts around the country. Looking out to sea we could see some twenty or so tree stumps rising out of the water, and knew we were looking at the beginning of a new wind farm some 7km away at Gunfleet Sands. When finished it would be home to forty-eight turbines, green energy for many years to come with any luck.

Safe in the knowledge that when we visit a pier the weather stays dry, we ignored the thickening clouds and kissed a tired but triumphant kiss. We'd done it! Ten piers in a weekend! We had aching feet and were distinctly tired but we were still talking (a good sign!) and had retained our sense of humour (even better!). We leant forward for another kiss. OW! What was going on? We were under attack and our run of good luck was at an end. Night had not fallen, it was a huge and quite impressive hail storm, and it was determined to turn us to pulp as we cowered at the end of the pier.

What started as a dignified walk back turned into a frantic run, punctuated with squeals as the hail got harder. It seemed an incredibly long way back to safety, but eventually we made it, very wet and out of breath with cold, scarlet faces from the stinging onslaught of the icy storm. The name 'Sunshine Coast' must have been having a day off...

We got back to the entrance at four o'clock. We could have been sat at home by now, instead we stood and watched torrents of vertical rain pour out of the sky relentlessly.

"We timed that right!" said Jay cheerfully. "Fancy a coffee?" (He says that a lot).

We dashed to our right and through the door of an invitingly steamed-up café at the front of the pier. The charming young girl was able to provide us with a much needed mug of coffee and managed to find a couple of Danish pastries that had seen better days after rooting around under the counter, but we really didn't care, we were defrosting and drying out in the fuggy interior. Eventually we looked around, and were delighted to see that the walls were covered with photographs of the pier in its heyday, which made for some interesting viewing.

It has certainly been a popular spot, and an aerial picture which I would think dated from the 1920s or 30s shows just how big the rectangular deck of the pier was. The swimming pool took up a quarter of that shape, people thronged the decks and two huge paddle steamers can be seen moored at the pier head. There are a wealth of picture postcards, railway posters and photographs of the pier all the way through its life which makes a fascinating pictorial history for the casual observer. We drained our mugs and realised thankfully that the rain had stopped, so we left the sanctuary of the café and headed back up the steps, through the gardens and collapsed into the car.

"Home then?" Jay queried.

"Ohhhhh yes!" I replied, and we set off on a long and wearisome five-hour drive back home, 256 miles away and punctuated by several coffee stops!

As we eventually stopped outside our house I ventured nervously,

"Do you fancy pencilling in a few pier visits next weekend then?"

A savage singular eyebrow shot skywards.

"That'd be a no then. Just thought I'd ask!"

CHAPTER 14

Over the Sea to Man! (Or - Steps to Stardom in Ramsey)

Not surprisingly it was a little while before we considered another pier trip, but I had been doing a little research and writing some letters and e-mails to see if I could find out whether one particular pier was open for visitors. At the time, the National Piers website had a list of 55 surviving piers, but it didn't state whether these were all open to visitors. We looked at our country map marked with locations of these 55 (and one or two others that we had discovered) and decided that sooner or later we would have to travel over the sea to the Isle of Man to see the pier at Ramsey. However, we felt it prudent to find out what the current state of the pier was, as conflicting news articles on the web veered between open and closed!

I ran off an email to the Chairman of the Friends of Queen's Pier, Ramsey outlining what we were doing and could we visit, and waited for a reply. The Manx people are a friendly bunch, and it wasn't long before I received an answer. Fantastically it came very quickly – we were very welcome to visit but would have to employ Photoshop techniques to get us on the far end of the pier as it was currently prohibited to let anyone walk along it. We felt disappointed, but read on. However, Chairman Fred suggested that we write to the Manx Department of Transport and ask permission as it would be a shame for Queen's to be the first pier where we'd been denied access!

So, nothing ventured, nothing gained we thought. A letter went and duly a letter in a very smart envelope came back. It was good news! Although we wouldn't be allowed access to the main body of the pier, the Department of Transport were happy to arrange for the pier gates to be unlocked for us and we could stand on the landward end of the pier for our kiss. Wow! Some logistical juggling ensued, with emails back and forth to Chairman Fred and the Director of Harbours who held the keys, sorting of ferry times and booking bed and breakfast accommodation. All successfully done, the May Bank Holiday weekend of 2009 saw us getting up at a ludicrously early time to drive up to Liverpool for a ferry trip over to the Isle of Man!

It felt quite exotic and adventurous boarding the Sea-Cat under the watchful gaze of the Liver Building and then sailing gently out of the river Mersey before the Captain applied full throttle, and with a mighty roar we headed out into the estuary towards our destination. Even on the Sea-Cat it takes four hours to get there, so we had plenty of time for various musings and observations. Incidentally, if we had been travelling by Victorian steamer it would have taken us five and a half hours – modern machinery hasn't cut that much time off the journey!

Ask the person next to you what they know about the Isle of Man, and, assuming you're not actually there, their reply will probably be 'Manx cats, the TT, a tax haven and the Laxey wheel'. As we bounced over the waves it struck us that we knew very little about our destination. It was in the Irish Sea. We managed to add Manx kippers, Loghtan sheep and the *Ellan Vannin* shipping tragedy to our list (although I have since found out that the name Ellan Vannin is the Manx name for the Isle of Man) but then we lapsed into shame-faced silence.

However, it would appear that the island had forgiven us and was keen to update our knowledge. As the ship pulled in to Douglas, the sun came out and we watched a dolphin make lazy arcs in the lapis sea just outside the harbour entrance. Magical! It's a word we would use an awful lot of times over the three days we planned to be there – we'd allowed a bit of time for sight-seeing too, and I think we'd have stayed longer if the constraints of work hadn't been there. 'Wow!' was another word and one I use far too many times, but the island has so many unexpected and beautiful features it takes your breath away.

It has electric trams! Horse drawn trams! Steam railways! Bijou post-war bus depots in every town (and it remains a closely guarded secret as to how they can accommodate so many vehicles somewhere the size of your front room!) and the most fantastic scenery that you'll ever see. In the centre of the island are the mountains and hills, dominated by the misty peak of Snaefell, which while we were there was swathed in shades of dour grey, mossy green and chestnut brown. Around the edges, the lush green scenery is embroidered with gorse and tumbles in a rush to the cliffs, sands and beaches before reaching the deep blue sea. We both fell instantly in love with the place, and even if it had been dull and wet it still would have ensnared us in its Manxy charms!

Douglas, the main town of the Isle of Man used to have a pier too, right in the centre of its promenade. It was started in January 1869 and was designed and built by John Dixon of London, and at 304m (1,000') long it cost £6,500. He had the 78 cast-iron piles and girders made in Southport. It was so exciting that the *Illustrated London News* ran an article on it just after it opened in September 1869 saying:

> '(It has) 78 cast iron piles which support, by pairs of columns,
> the wrought-iron girders, overlaid with a timber floor 17ft
> wide, but spreading to a width of 40ft at the seaward end.'

Known as the Douglas Iron Pier or the New Promenade Pier it also had a refreshment room at the end and on summer evenings a band would play. To get onto the pier you had to go through the entrance which had:

> 'An office, like a little Chinese pagoda, for collecting tolls,
> with handsome gates and a recording turnstile.'
> ILN, 18th September 1869

It would have cost 1d to walk along the pier, although you could also buy a monthly ticket for 1s 6d or an annual pass for 5 shillings! That's cheap by other pier standards which generally charged a 2d promenading toll.

It even inspired a poet, J.M Sutherland to write a lovely poem about it in July 1873 which describes an evening on the pier. Steamers would arrive at 8 p.m. and girls covered in flowers would turn up to promenade. I particularly like this verse:

> 'On summer eves musicians play,
> The people here all love romancing,

Which makes them animated, gay,
Tho' here is not permitted, dancing.'

('The Douglas Iron Pier' by J.M. Sutherland)

It says a lot about Victorian pier life and promenading rules and both articles are real snapshots of Victorian life and niceties. There's also a lovely postcard of 1890 which shows the pier relatively empty but the beach alongside is strewn with huge white sheets. The guesthouse owners would lay them out on the beach to dry once washed – at least you knew they were clean and aired, even if they may have acquired sea-life in the process!

Anyway, the pier didn't really last very long. In 1891 it was closed and the offered up for sale for £1,300. Other seaside towns looked at the possibility of relocating it in their resorts (notably Penarth and Abergele) but decided against it. A Manchester scrap dealer eventually began to dismantle it in 1894, and soon the pier was gone. There was an urban myth that it was rebuilt at Rhos-on-Sea near Colwyn Bay in 1895-6 but it was just that, a myth, based on an error published in a book from 1952!

I have digressed substantially and gone on about a pier that doesn't even exist (sorry, especially if you were expecting a brief chapter after the last one!) but while doing research for this book I have uncovered all sorts of other information and sometimes it has been a shame not to be able to include it. The Iron Pier at Douglas existed for such a short time, but was so highly thought of by people that I think it really needed to be mentioned, if only to remind people that once there were around one hundred glorious piers in this country and they all deserve remembering!

Back to the current journey and we had wound our way through little villages and seen picturesque views out to see (punctuated by many 'wow's) until we came over the final hill into Ramsey, where we'd managed to get a room, and we glimpsed the last remaining pier on the island that we had come to see. We made a lovely descent into Ramsey – one thing that makes a real impression is the peace and quiet everywhere. The Isle of Wight is feted for the fact it feels like it got stuck in the 1950s, and the same could be said about here, but there is a lovely sense of wide open space and tranquillity too here.

Ramsey is the second largest town on the island and has a lovely atmosphere; quiet streets and lovely old Regency and Victorian brick buildings. There is a large harbour which the River Sulby flows in to, an attractive red and white swing bridge and lots of evidence of things maritime. We found our guest house and introduced ourselves, then tiptoed out without waking the dog and had a long walk around the town. We found ourselves at the seafront which, like the town, was quiet and a touch neglected but very pleasant, and before I am accused of writing a tourist guide to the Isle of Man (although I'd be glad to if the job is available...!) we must mention the pier, because we had just encountered it and couldn't resist having a little look before our formal visit the next day.

Ramsey's pier was the second of just two built on the island and is today the only one surviving. It was commissioned by the Isle of Man Harbour Board, designed by Sir John Coode and then constructed by Head, Wrightson and Company of Stockton-on-Tees. The pier was built to a length of 683m (2,241') and 6.5m (21' 3") wide. The deck widened at five places along the length to accommodate seating and to allow for passing loops in the 3' gauge, horse-drawn tramway rails that ran the entire length of the pier, right up the centre. The tramway was originally used for running construction materials to the seaward end, something that Messrs. Head and Wrightson had also done at Herne Bay.

The Queen's Pier was officially opened on 22nd July 1886 by the Lord Bishop of Sodor and Man (wasn't the Island of Sodor where Thomas the tank Engine lived?) and was named in honour of Queen Victoria who, together with Prince Albert had come to the island in 1847. Unable to land in Douglas because of rough seas, the Royal Yacht came to Ramsey instead. Unfortunately the Queen was suffering from severe sea-sickness and stayed on board (you would have thought that was the last place she would have wanted to be!), but Prince Albert landed and enjoyed a visit. For 1886 it had cost quite a large amount of money – £45,000 for what was essentially just a landing stage, no wild entertainment included and definitely no dancing! There was a thriving steamer trade coming from Liverpool, Fleetwood, Belfast and the River Clyde, but they used Ramsey purely as a dropping-off and loading point, and as a result the town didn't develop a tourist industry in the same way as other seaside towns.

Two pretty little octagonal wooden kiosks were built by local Ramsey builder Edward Gawne at the landward end of the pier and a small tea room with restrooms were erected at the seaward end of the wooden decking. In 1899 a new two-level landing stage was added and the tramway was upgraded – now passengers and their luggage could be transported with protection from the elements in a new enclosed carriage.

The pier enjoyed many prosperous years, helped no doubt by more Royal visitors arriving in 1902. The visit of Edward VII and Queen Alexandra on August 25th shows the pier and entrance way thronging with people – it was lucky that His Majesty wore a white felt hat or he would never have been seen in the crowd of well-wishers! Queen's continued to stay busy right up until the outbreak of the First World War – 1914 saw more than 36,000 people arriving on the Isle of Man via the pier.

On 14th July 1920 the Manx people were preparing for more Royal visitors, this time King George V and Queen Mary. Once more the Royal Yacht *Victoria and Albert* with escorting battleships was heading for its planned berth at Douglas when rough seas intervened again, and for the third time, Ramsey welcomed regal visitors, giving rise to the name 'Royal Ramsey'. With such a sudden arrival there were no people watching when the royal couple made their way down the pier to a waiting car and off to Douglas, but the following day, Ramsey's townsfolk turned out in huge numbers an hour before the King and Queen were expected, cheered loudly and sang 'God save the King'. It should also be noted that the King '*was attired in an admiral's uniform and had side creases in his trousers*' – daring fellow!

Life was uneventful for the pier for many years after that – the tramway received another upgrade in 1937 when an 8hp petrol-driven Planet locomotive took over the journey along the planks. The addition of a fifteen-seater passenger car in 1950 accompanied some tweaking to the line, extending it somewhat along the pier. A dull, typically 1950's concrete entrance was thrown up in 1956, totally obscuring the little Victorian kiosks and turning an inviting entrance into something more austere.

The next forty years saw the decline of Queen's pier, despite another visit, this time from Elizabeth the Queen Mother on 4th July 1963, who rode down the pier behind the little locomotive in its carriage. By 1969 there were only around three thousand people arriving by steamer and in 1970 the last of the Isle of Man Steam Packet Company boats called in and all further services were suspended. The pier continued to stay open to visitors arriving on foot and for those wishing to fish from the structure, but nine years later the landing stage had to be fenced off because it had become structurally unsafe. The tramway ceased operation in 1981 and by 1990 the landing stage had broken away from the main body of the pier and was subsequently dismantled.

The following year the seaward café was destroyed by a fire, and despite a replacement shelter and toilets being installed, these were vandalised just days after opening. Worries about the structure of the main pier and the upset of the mindless vandalism sealed the pier's fate and it was closed. The Friends of Queen's Pier were formed in 1994 and have worked tirelessly to try and secure some future for the pier. Restoration then was estimated at between £2-4 million, while demolition would have cost just over £1 million, but the people of Ramsey have not let this become a reality. Some broken tie rods were replaced in 1996 and a structural report in 1999 found that structurally the pier was in better condition than thought, making a full refurbishment around £1.3 million. However, there has been much dillying and dallying from many quarters, and the pier remains in a stripped-down version of its old self, awaiting that magic go-ahead for restoration.

At first viewing the pier is breathtaking in its simplicity and length, rushing out across the glistening sands shrieking to dip its toes in the cold sea. It looks considerably longer than its 683m (2,241') as it proudly takes sixth position in the country's longest piers. Unfortunately it holds a similar position on a list from 2008 of piers that were most seriously at risk from collapse or demolition. We breathed in the fresh ozone-laden air of the evening as it playfully tugged at our coats and as we walked back into the town for an excellent evening meal and a well-deserved sleep, both declared we were looking forward to tomorrow.

The next day dawned chilly but bright and we set off for our high noon meeting. Did we mind a local reporter covering the story we were asked. Of course not we replied, thinking we knew no one on the Isle of Man, so we would be assured anonymity from the wider populace. How wrong we were...! There at twelve o'clock were three people to greet us – cheerful Chairman Fred, Adrian Darbyshire from the newspaper and our man-of-keys from the Harbour people. We were off!

The pebble-dashed 50's entrance really isn't the height of elegance, but it is fairly vandal-proof (especially at the sides where there are some very spiky pieces of metalwork!). While the blue main gates were unlocked, we read the plaques on either side, one commemorating the visit by King Edward VII and Queen Alexandra, the other the later visit by King George V and Queen Mary. Then... through those wrought-iron gates we preceded, stepping gingerly over numerous smashed pigeon eggs and grimy detritus. Up above us the wooden roof was broken in places and slate-grey pier pigeons cocked their heads at us below them as we passed. This guano besmirched cavern is also home to a rather forlorn remnant of one of the luggage trolleys from the pier's earlier days, and we squeezed around it and out through the gateway onto the thick metal latticework that bridged the gap between land and pier planking.

Fresh air! And looking through the pier-kisser proof railings, we could see a long way, if not quite *all* the way down the pier. From our vantage point the planking and railings looked solid enough, although it was obvious that parts of the structure had been tidied up to make it safe until some proper renovation can be carried out. Rusty tramway rails stretched down the centre of the decking and sat ready to go was another old luggage trolley, brown and oxidised to the tracks. And just through the barrier are the remaining bodies of the octagonal Victorian kiosks, painted green and white, roof- and window-less now.

We had our first pier kiss under close observation, then had to repeat it a few times so that Adrian and Fred could take some pictures. It's very hard to kiss when you're suffering from a fit of giggles and the wind is trying to blow your hair and coat into your mouth – we managed somehow! Satisfied with our collection of hastily snapped pictures through the rails we were ushered back through the gates and Queen's Pier was devoid of human company again.

Fred insisted we go down onto the sand and look at the pier from underneath, as we would get more of an idea of its construction and condition from there, and we followed him onto the damp sands. Once there we got a real sense of how big the pier really is. The rows of three cruciform columns, with the outer legs raked and diagonally braced, towered over us and stretched endlessly out to sea. Occasionally an extra pair stuck out where the seats were, and despite being a bit rusty in places, and spattered with barnacles and bunches of glossy black mussels (which Fred said make for good eating!), look in good solid condition.

The decking and railings are sadly not in such good repair, and with the sun now above us, it illuminated the places where the rotten decking had crumbled and the extended seating areas had in places fallen into the sea.

High above us the lamp standards, once topped with milky glass orbs now stood white, rust-streaked and headless, but still proud, holding onto the railings and keeping guard, with only the seagulls for company. It could have been a really melancholy visit, but there was something infectious about Fred's enthusiasm for getting the pier sorted out and up and running once more. In fact everyone we spoke to that had anything to do with the pier seemed positive about its future. As always, the main hurdle seems to be pale pink, rather than red, tape and a serious lack of funds with several zeros on the end. If we had a crystal ball we would tell all the pier owners what the winning lottery numbers were so that worthy projects like this one could leap that obstacle and make some decent progress. As yet, sadly we haven't acquired that magical piece of equipment, but I'm sure you'll know when we do!

We profusely thanked everyone for making it possible to have a kiss on the pier, even if we hadn't set foot onto proper decking, and vowed that we would come back in the future to see what progress had been made – we were sure it would, and that next time when we visited we could walk unhindered down the planked promenade deck. We said our farewells – Fred promised to send over the cuttings from the newspaper article and we left the seafront buoyed with enthusiasm for pier renovation and the likes of the Friends of Queen's Pier who are doing such sterling work!

We had the most wonderful time on the Isle of Man – we visited Peel and stood watching seals in the harbour, saw Ireland and Scotland from the fantastically pebbly beaches, where every stone is different and multicoloured. We drove around roads that felt very familiar because we had seen them on television during the TT races, and marvelled at the white-topped mare's tail waves and unspoilt scenery. Hospitality here is second-to-none too, from our lovely landlady Pat to the people in the restaurant and everyone we met connected with the pier – we will be back, whatever happens to the pier (and we hope something positive does soon!).

You might think that should be the end of our little Manx jaunt. So did we! The following Thursday our story was published in the esteemed journals of the fair Isle we'd visited. And then, my phone started to ring itself silly! We had forgotten about the powers of the internet, and the story had swiftly gone global. When we checked, it had been picked up in India, Vietnam, America, Germany... We were stunned. Our local papers rang and organised interviews, as did Burnham-on-Sea and Clevedon Piers. Several BBC radio stations asked for interviews and we even had a call from Radio Dublin, but they didn't call back. We were devastated... perhaps they had looked and realised we wouldn't be travelling over there after all! And so our path to global stardom had started... to be honest we were a bit bemused by all the fuss but decided that if people were interested in the story then we would encourage the attention – not for us, but because it would draw attention to every pier we visited and highlight the need for them to be saved and preserved for the future.

Burnham Pier

Deal Pier

Town Pier, Gravesend

Southend-on-Sea Pier

Southport Pier

St Anne's Pier, Lytham

Clevedon Pier

Paignton Pier

Bournemouth Pier

Weston-super-Mare Seaquarium

Cromer Pier

Southwold Pier

Walton-on-the-Naze Pier

Queen's Pier, Ramsey IOM

Colwyn Bay Pier

Beaumaris Pier

Bangor Garth Pier

Saltburn-by-the-Sea Pier

Totland Bay Pier

Birnbeck Pier, Weston-super-Mare

Hastings Pier

Eastbourne Pier

Bekonscot Pier

Worthing Pier

Bognor Pier

Brighton West Pier

Brighton Palace Pier

The Wedding Day

The Grand Pier, Weston-super-Mare ablaze

The Grand Pier, Weston-super-Mare - rebuilt and reopened

Wedding kiss on Brighton Palace Pier

W.O.W! (Or - Wonders of Wales – Colwyn Bay, Llandudno, Beaumaris, Bangor Garth and Aberystwyth)

Following two weeks of media frenzy, photos interviews and a teenage daughter mortified by us being called 'serial snoggers', we decided to get away incognito and unannounced for a five-pier weekend to North Wales. Dressed in Groucho Marx disguises, and under the assumed names of Pitt and Jolie, we eventually swept into the glorious curve that is Colwyn Bay. This beautiful stretch of coast was bathed in the sort of beaming sunlight that only occurs between torrential May squalls, promising stormy backdrops for photographs and threatening to see how fast we could run to dodge each outburst!

The North coast of Wales, running from Chester to Angelsey, although a bit bleak in places, has long been a popular holiday destination for the workers of Manchester and the industrial heartlands since the advent of the railways. There are flocks of static caravan parks like sheep grazing the gentle slopes. Nearer the water these become more regimented, resembling the exact tightly-packed estates people have come here to avoid. Further along the coast there are some more traditional resorts, and Colwyn Bay is one of these.

The Chester to Holyhead railway was laid down in 1844 and passed through the area on its way, but it wasn't until 1865 that the first house was built at Colwyn Bay. During the next thirty years the town increased rapidly in size to accommodate everyone that wanted to make sandcastles and breathe the salty fresh air. It was a very short time after this that the town acquired the pier that we had come to see.

As we burst out of another dastardly rainstorm which threatened to pound the car into the road we found ourselves on the promenade right next to the pier. The Victoria Pier is a stone's throw from the golden sandy beach, sprinkled with pleasing round grey pebbles, and a short distance from the town, reached by a quiet, wide promenade. Perhaps it was the silence of the morning, the lack of anybody on the beach or the fact that we had inadvertently both fallen hook, line and sinker in love with piers, but the sight that greeted us here on the beach stunned Jay into silence and moved me to tears.

Victoria (if I may be so bold as to call her by her first name) stands on the sands desolate and alone, a sad and sorry shadow of her former self. She was once a stunning beauty, but is now a mass of peeling paint, collapsed ironwork lattice, missing and rotten timbers and small gardens of wild vegetation sprouting in the neglected corners.

For all that, it cannot be said that this is an unattractive pier – it's just about complete, but in dire need of rescuing. This is the aged dowager duchess of piers, once the belle of the ball but now past her prime, tired and world-weary but still retaining her charms from long ago.

The main body of Colwyn Bay's pier, just 96m (316') long and 12m (40') wide, was designed by Mangnall and Littlewood of Manchester (whose assistant E.A. Sutherland had also worked on Blackpool South and Morecambe piers) and opened on the 1st of June 1900. It was not just a straight forward rectangle, but had circular balconies softening the corners and providing cosy seating out of the way of the main walking space. The decking was wooden and the wrought-iron railings as ornate as lace befitting a queen – each cream-painted panel a riot of swirls and intricate scrolls. To the right of the deck was a 'Moorish' style pavilion, which rather daringly for the time was illuminated by electric lights. The pavilion inside was as lavish as the outside, regal, grand and luxurious and seated 2,500. Visitors paid their toll to enter at the quaint polygonal kiosks, each topped with a roof resembling a pineapple and a lamp standard!

As the popularity of Colwyn Bay as a resort increased, so did that of the pier. People returning home after their holidays raved about the high standard of entertainment and fittings, so in 1903 an extra length of pier neck was added, running 229m (750') from the rear left corner of the pier out into the bay to provide a space for outdoor performances. Although the wrought-iron decorative rails are of the same pattern as the main section, seating areas were set out in little rectangular extensions beyond the decking, rather than circular. Sited where it was, this extra length of deck meant one could walk from the entrance straight down the left side of the pier all the way to the end unhindered.

During World War I, performances were put on for the wounded troops, sent to recover in the fresh sea breezes of the coastal resort. A new 'Bijou' (how I love that word!) theatre to seat 600 was built in 1917 to provide a venue for lighter entertainment. Sadly, the main pavilion was destroyed by a fire on the 27th March 1922 in a huge blaze that produced fierce flames and thick black clouds of smoke that look very similar to our recent one at Weston. Similarly there was nothing left of the pavilion but it was rebuilt at a cost of £45,000 and opened again the next year. This incarnation was smaller with dome-topped towers, what looked like a clapper-board frontage with white-framed windows and a glorious Dutch gable-style façade to the front. Sadly this lasted a mere ten years – another conflagration razed it to the ground, and shortly afterwards another fire reduced the Bijou theatre to ashes. The last (and present) pavilion was opened on the 18th May 1933, but sadly the theatre was never replaced.

As other seaside towns discovered, trade began to decline during the 1950s and the lack of visitors to Colwyn Bay meant the pavilion closed, and despite repairs in 1954 the pier was sold in 1968 to the First Leisure Company (Trusthouse Forte). They demolished the ornate entrance gates and sweet pineapple toll booths and replaced them with the rather oddly shaped 'towers' and Golden Goose arcade. This has been described as 'distressing' (not by us, I hasten to add!). It certainly makes you stop and wonder 'why?'

In 1976 the owners applied to demolish the pier but a fierce display from the locals, who raised a petition containing 4000 signatures, forced this application to be overturned. However, the fate of the pier was not looking any brighter or stable. In 1979 it was sold again, this time to Parker Leisure Holdings who converted the Dixieland Showbar into a disco and bar – this was successful and well received. By 1986 Victoria Pier was becoming a serious drain on the purse of anyone who owned her. Structural repairs to the seaward end cost a staggering £250,000. Another application for demolition was made the following year but was again refused.

Its life hanging by a thread, the pier was put up for sale again in 1989 and 1991. When it didn't sell, the pier was closed to the public completely. Mr and Mrs Paxman bought it in 1994 and lived on it while they carried out repairs and renovations. The pier was reopened to visitors in 1995 following repairs to the neck, but the pavilion was proving so expensive to repair that in 2003 the Paxmans advertised the pier for sale yet again.

Our poor old Victorian albatross was now owned by Steve Hunt, who wanted (and still wants) to see the pier renovated and opened as a viable business once again. However, Mr Hunt tried to obtain funding from other sources – as a private owner he's not eligible for Lottery funding. He invested his own money into repairs and filmed *Pier Pressure* with the BBC in 2008, which showed him trying to restore the pavilion to its Art Deco glory. The following year the Conwy County Council presented him with demands for alleged unpaid council tax amounting to over £5,000. Mr Hunt refuted this and refused to pay, resulting in the council declaring him bankrupt. Steve has been battling to overturn this judgement – the pier remains locked and untended, its future still uncertain, teetering continually between demolition and a plan to restore it. Steve Hunt is still fighting to clear his name and get the pier up and running – you have to admire his determination and passion, many lesser mortals would have given up by now.

It was a shame that we couldn't have met with Steve – but we had left very little time to set up a meeting. Hopefully we can help bring more awareness to his ongoing project and help him get the green flag to start his project again.

We walked along the promenade, simultaneously in awe of the detail on this pier and also aghast at the terrible state it was in, almost crossing our fingers in the vain hope it would stop the decay. We went to the main gates and peered through the barrier by the right-hand tower. It didn't look very cheery but at least the decking and railings here are in good condition and look cared for. We squeezed in to the gate as much as we could and had a sad kiss here. It would be a real coup if this pier were open when we came back in the future – the fingers stayed crossed!

Fortunately the tide was on the way out, enabling us to walk out along the sand and have a closer look at the state of the structure and stroll under the pier itself (one in the eye for all those health and safety executives out there – look! We're not wearing hard hats!). The main pier piles were pre-fabricated in Widnes and screwed into the seabed by steam-driven machinery. The main piles are individually numbered and the ones along the edges of the pier have lovely Corinthian tops, something we'd not seen as ornately before.

The ravages of the sea have taken their toll on this old metal-work unfortunately, areas were heavily corroded by rust and many of the supporting cross-bracing struts were hanging on by a thread or had snapped completely and were missing or dangling in grotesquely shaped pieces.

Looking up at the decking as we walked further along more and more of it was missing or obviously rotten. Some areas looked solid, but I'm not sure I would have wanted to try it out. It would be like playing a very real version of the BBC's *The Adventure Game* finale, where contestants had to walk across an invisible game-board. One false move and the 'evaporator' would get you... The wrought-iron railings seemed to be following the same pattern – some were hardly touched by rust, others totally corroded and contorted.

The dusting of silvery barnacles on her legs and the stunning curve of the bay towards Rhos was highlighted by the golden sunlight and a glowering bruise-coloured sky as we turned back. It was strikingly beautiful but only served to highlight the loneliness of this pier and her current position. We reluctantly left the pier and drove thoughtfully out of Colwyn Bay on to our next seaside town.

The threatening rain held off and seemed to evaporate in the strong sunlight – May flexing its muscles and hinting at summer warmth! We drove up and over the Little Orme and Craig y Don and stumbled suddenly into Llandudno – it was closer than we had realised! From this vantage point we could see the spectacular coastline for and aft, sheltered flat bays nestling between high craggy hills that looked like miniature volcanoes. To our right was the sea, today a patchwork of blue hues. To our left, the mountains, resplendent in an ever-changing cloak of moody colour, standing guard over the whole scene.

Llandudno is a particularly spectacular example of this scenery, with the Great Orme to the western end of the two-mile long sheltered Llandudno Bay. The beach is an enviable mixture of silver-gilt sand and pebbles, with picture-postcard views in all directions. Llandudno today is the largest resort in all of Wales, but it's another example of a town that was specifically built as a Victorian holiday destination which was helped by the arrival of a branch line of the railway in 1858. So successful was the resort that only six years later it was being called the 'Queen of the Welsh Resort'.

The graceful curve of the bay is mirrored by the wide sweeping promenade, lined with grand and stately Victorian hotels and guest houses set well back from the sea front. I can vaguely remember in the recesses of my memory travelling by train from Bedfordshire to Llandudno and spending the day on the beach, where I was terrified by the Red Arrows putting on a display. I was probably five or six at the time! I can also remember paddling in the sea, but not much else, although the memories are happy ones!

Llandudno is a resort with loads to do if you do fancy visiting. You could visit an underground Bronze Age mine, go dry slope skiing, take the longest cable-car lift in the country up the Great Orme from the Happy Valley ornamental gardens, stay in the bed and breakfast at the Great Orme lighthouse or watch Professor Codman's Wooden Headed Follies (that's Punch and Judy to you!). But wait! Probably the most important thing here is the pier, and the chances are you've already seen it on the big or small screen. It's such a good example of a Victorian pier, and full of attractive features that it has been used numerous times in films and for television programmes, and we found a smashing parking spot on the winding Great Orme Marine Drive that leaves the town but provides super views out across the bay and the pier.

Not only is the pier here an intriguing Y-shape, it has two entrances as well, and we galloped down the hill (in that kind of slightly out-of-control, where are the brakes style) to board at the original gate on Happy Valley Road. Apart from having to weave our way through lots of parked cars (where there would have originally been patiently waiting horses and carts), very little has changed here. The original stone gatehouse is still there – in the 1920s you could book motor tours from here, and buy your ticket, go through the turnstile and promenade along the pier.

Much like Clacton-on-Sea, Llandudno built its pier as soon as work started on the town itself in 1858 – despite having the railway to bring people and materials into town, sea was always going to be another way of increasing the tourist potential of the resort, and with piers being THE place to be seen it made perfect sense to get one installed as soon as possible.

However, this wasn't a state-of-the-art highly fashionable prom – it was 74m long (242'), had just sixteen piles and had been constructed by the St. George's Harbour and Railway Company. Fortunately (for the current visitors) a serious storm damaged the pier in 1875 which, coupled with the need for a longer structure to cope with an increasing number of steamers that currently could only call at high tide, meant that a new pier was on the cards.

Charles Henry Driver and James Brunlees (he of the pile jetting system, and engineer of numerous viaducts such as the Solway Firth and piers at Southend and Southport) drew up some new designs and Walter Macfarlane of Glasgow made it a reality. On 1st August 1877 the new 376m (1,234') pier opened complete with an 18m (60') unique Y-shaped pier head. There was an abundance of ornate ironwork, balustrades and railings, eight quaint square kiosks arranged in pairs along the length with three larger octagonal buildings at the pier head.

In 1884 the odd extension was added, running in from the right-hand side next to the Baths Hotel (later the Grand) and providing a second entrance to visitors from North Parade, as well as providing access to the Llandudno Pier Pavilion Theatre at this landward end. This pavilion is almost worthy of its own chapter, it was really quite incredible. Because the seaward end of the pier sundeck pavilion was struggling under the immense number of visitors, this new pavilion really needed to wow the crowds, and boy was it flamboyant! Looking like something from Kew Gardens it had three storeys, seating for two thousand people and a swimming pool in the basement! Sadly this had to be filled in again because water quality couldn't be resolved, and there was a tiny problem with the roof too. Originally totally glazed, the roof was destroyed in a winter storm in 1883 and had to be totally rebuilt, this time in lead. The original architects were dismissed. Ouch!

This behemoth eventually opened and proved to be a very popular venue, holding orchestral concerts and variety shows right up until the 1970s when people had pretty much been lured away from such delights by foreign hols and popular comedies on television. It was sold in 1983 for £10,000 to the Llandudno Pavilion Company who, in 1984 closed the pavilion, but the 'basement' remained open, where an amusement arcade and ghost train resided. However, this was cleared out and the enterprising Llandudno Dungeon experience installed. Consisting of a walk-through horror waxworks it was a well-visited attraction. Sadly, falling visitor numbers and rising costs led to the whole collection being sold to France in 1990. There were plans to restore the pavilion to a Covent Garden style of building, but nothing ever happened and the building became a haven for vandals. Eventually the inevitable happened and an arson attack destroyed the main structure in 1994. The site now remains a sad neglected ruin with ethereal pillars rising up from a tangle of weeds and rubble like a Greek ruin – investigation of old postcards and photographs makes me wonder if these could be the supporting columns of the first-floor balcony, in pairs and quite ornate. Unfortunately there doesn't appear to be any light at the end of the tunnel for this project either and this site will continue to be a neglected wildlife garden for some time yet.

The side extension and pavilion meant that the final length of the pier now topped 699m (2,295'), making it the fifth longest in the country. Trusthouse Forte bought it in 1968 – at least they didn't apply to have it demolished, instead leaving it alone apart from a bit of concrete strengthening the following year. And that is really all the history there is to report – many people still flock to the pier here and have a thoroughly fantastic time.

I try and describe the piers we visit to the best of my ability, but on this occasion I found an article that really takes the Welsh Cake and I have to hold my hands up to its descriptive capabilities. A British Tourist Authority report from 1975 says this about Llandudno Pier:

> 'It zooms out of the sea, all 427m (1,400') of it, in a spectacular Indian Gothic style rather like a Maharajah's palace floating on a lake. Cast iron, brackets of iron lacework, an outstandingly pretty balustrade like an enlarged fishnet, ogee roofs curling away to the sky all add up to a totally pleasurable experience.'

Wow! Not sure I can compete with that...

Llandudno Pier is gorgeous, and just a teensy bit quirky – the deck is wide and all the embellishments are painted blue and white, reflecting the sea and sky on a fantastic summer's day. And what embellishments! The railings are ornate wrought-iron work in a design that wouldn't be out of place in Morocco and are topped-and-tailed with blue rails. The kiosks are similarly painted and we had never seen so many different things for sale, each kiosk having its own theme. Personalised ducks, herbal treatments, an entire kiosk with personalised football-themed things, a similar one with frogs, seaside sweeties, slippers etc. Originally there were just the eight little kiosks along the pier, but the extension beside the hotel is now also full of them!

The pier deck is otherwise uncluttered, with discreet lamp-standards painted black and mounted on the deck railings and the occasional wooden bench tucked in here and there. We were glad of the kiosks to shelter around as the wind was really quite strong by now. In between kiosks we stuffed our hands in our pockets and trotted on to the next one, but we enjoyed watching the gulls swoop and glide on the wind, then occasionally apply the brakes and hang in the air motionless against the gusts.

At the pier head the huge space is tastefully filled with buildings, including the wonderful flying-saucer shaped restaurant (see, I said I was no good at descriptions!), its roof gleaming silver in the bright sunshine and smartly resplendent in the same sky-blue and white livery that we could see everywhere else.

At the very end of the pier is a concrete jetty providing a little rectangular haven for fishermen – it also meant we could peer over the edge and look at the piles, thickly covered in barnacles with a light rust dusting at the top but standing firm! It was a stunning place to have a kiss, lips salty with sea spray, chilled slightly by the sea breeze and with the impressive geological striations of the Great Orme highlighted with mossy green behind us. It is always nice to see so many people enjoying a pier, whether they are fishing, out with the family or just ambling to the end, admiring the view and going for a coffee! Today there were plenty of anglers at the pier head, lots of families and the occasional elderly promenader bowling up and down the pier, propelled by the frisky breeze.

We circled the buildings here and headed back up the other side, impressed by the tidiness of the kiosks and planking. Yes, if we were going to be picky there was a bit of flaky paintwork and a touch of rust streaking, but you can't keep a pier totally perfect, as the caustic nature of the salty sea spray gets into everything and starts its damage incredibly quickly. As we got to the 'newer' extension to North Parade, we found we had even more things to look at. The Grand Hotel is just that, and looms in an imposing wedge-shaped castle over the pier.

This extension is now home to lots of rides and amusements for the younger members of the family, including a huge wavy slide, a bouncy castle and crazy golf. There are more kiosks and a very interesting little book cabin where we bought some postcards and looked at pictures of the pier from its past. We got talking to the lady behind the counter and she very kindly donated a print of the pier in the 1920s to help write this chapter, which has come in very handy! It was suggested we might like a personalised pair of slippers or a duck (neighbouring kiosks!) but we resisted the temptation and walked back under strings of bunting to the main promenade once more. It would have been lovely to spend a few days here and explore properly, but such is the transient nature of a pier kisser – it was back to the car and off to our next destination!

Anglesey is the little island at the top of Wales, separated from the mainland by the Menai Straits, that is often overlooked but is steeped in history and stunning scenery. Anglesey, or Ynys Mon, a much more beautiful name is the sixth largest island of the British Isles, bigger even than the Isle of Man. There have been people here since the Neolithic era, and virtually every raiding party that followed decided to stay here. Nowadays it is also home to red squirrels, a nuclear power station, choughs (that's a bird not something naughty) and a large ferry terminal.

We weren't here for any of those, although it would be fantastic to see some red squirrels, they will have to wait for another day. We were heading for Beaumaris and were lucky that our route took us over Thomas Telford's beautiful Menai Straits suspension bridge and the equally beautiful Straits themselves, the road following along the waterside for a while, in and out of the trees before we arrived at the beautiful town of Beaumaris. A delightful mix of new, old and 'blimey, how old?', it boasts an antique gaol, a courthouse of equally senior years and a medieval castle begun in Edward I's reign. It's also a popular centre for yachting, carrying on where millennia of other boatmen have landed and set sail.

To encourage the Victorian lovers of fresh air and the sublime, dramatic scenery of Snowdonia viewed from across the water, Frederick Foster's initial simple pier of wooden piles and iron girders served as a landing jetty to these visitors from 1846 for nearly thirty years. A wild storm necessitated a rebuild in 1872, and this was lengthened to 173m (570') in 1895. A small pavilion was added at the seaward end, probably to provide refreshments and a little baggage line was installed with manually operated luggage trucks and mineral wagons to carry the bags but it did the job! Sadly this fell into disuse during the First World War as the fit and able men were conscripted and visitor numbers tailed off.

The steamer traffic from Bangor, Llandudno and Liverpool resumed after the war and the holidaymakers enjoyed day-trips out to other resorts and the nearby Puffin Island until the late 1940s. A lack of maintenance and steady demise of the steamer trade during the following years meant that the T-shaped landing stage had to be demolished, but in the 1960s local yachtswoman and lifeboat secretary Mary Burton made a sizeable private donation to ensure that the main body of the pier was preserved for future generations to enjoy. The work was duly carried out and further repairs have been carried out as required by the local council, leaving this interesting little pier available for boat trips and sea fishing trips as well as some pretty good crab fishing from the pier head while enjoying an ice cream from the kiosk at the entrance!

Whereas Llandudno had been a study of blues, the sky over Snowdonia was now a fascinating palette of greys, lit from the west by golden searchlight beams of light, which made for some fantastic effects on the water. The wind was still strong, causing the waters of the Menai Straits to form choppy white-toped wavelets that slapped crossly onto the pale pebbly beach and noisily up the side of the pier. A myriad assortment of little craft bobbed up and down, tossing their heads against the restraint of mooring lines, adding to the rushing watery noises that filled the air – it was so quiet we almost expected to see a Viking longship appear from the open seas, such is the ancient, unspoilt air of this place.

We ventured past the little kiosk at the pier's entrance and walked along the first part of the pier, here of solid stone construction and topped by a modern fancy red-brick paved walkway. To our left was the local lifeboat station, and I think I'm right in saying this is the busiest one in Wales. It's probably the only one with its own swimming pool as well, which is situated behind it! Well, it *looks* like a swimming pool! Rectangular, blue lined, full of water and a nice turquoise painted surround – and it doesn't actually say anywhere what it is, so it was necessary to use our imaginations...! Neat silvery modern railings run the length of the pier and there are those little touches that really make this a pier – a handful of black ornate Victorian style lamp posts on the solid section of the pier, a lone blue telescope to keep a look out for invaders (possibly grey squirrels on rafts) and a rubbish bin (very important).

For such a neat little pier it feels very spacious, thanks to the uncluttered wooden decking. Over to the right-hand side are extensions like wooden outriggers on a catamaran, and we wondered if there had either been a plan to make this pier wider that had not seen completion, or maybe that was something that would be happening in the near future. Although it means I can't waffle on inanely about the architectural delights of Beaumaris Pier (yes I heard you breathing a sigh of relief, I'll get you back later) the unhindered walkway and unadulterated simple lines of this pier are refreshing against the wild and rugged scenery.

At the compact pier head there are metal steps down to the water for ease of boat-boarding and what looks like a rather utilitarian dark wood 'bus-shelter' pavilion at first glance. Looking again, the top fascia has possibly been made with a nod to a pre-war rural railway station, with Romanesque windows for extra light (I'm bigging them up. They're arched top windows, OK?). Outside there are some more bins, some lifejackets and some more wooden benches, painted red to complement the little bits of red on the shelter.

While partaking of a little pier-based intimacy (i.e. a kiss) we couldn't help but notice that the thundery slate-black sky that had been looming up behind the mountains was now revealing itself to be a deluge of Biblical proportions, pouring in spectral hissing curtains across the other side of the water. With the painful memories of Clacton still vivid in our minds, we made our polite excuses and hastened back down the pier at a mean pace, into the main street of the town and into the welcome arms of an open establishment that upon closer examination appeared to have got stuck in the 1950s. This is a statement and in no way intended to be rude – it was very pleasant and provided us with much needed food and drink so that we could hot-foot it back to the car for the next leg of our journey. Back at said car it was apparent that the weather was playing a particularly nasty trick on us – it was still gloriously sunny and dry on this side of the water and the tempest had been whisked off along the coast towards the open sea!

It might have seemed like a huge task to visit four piers in one day, especially so far from home, but once that initial distance to Colwyn Bay had been covered, we had in fact only had to travel about forty miles to see all of them and now had a mere six miles between here and Bangor to traverse (I know we'd been here before, but this time it was *thoroughly* researched and passed by the co-pilot first!). As we drove back along the road to the suspension bridge, I suddenly screeched to a halt in a lay-by and leapt out of the car, camera in hand.

"What's up?" asked my long-suffering co-pilot.

"Look! There's the pier!"

And there, reaching two-thirds across the choppy flinty waters of the Straits was Garth Pier, the ninth longest pier in Britain, although it is dwarfed somewhat by the impressive scenery behind it!

I took some pictures and we continued on our way back over the bridge and into Bangor. It's one of the smallest cities in Britain, tucked into the foothills of Bangor Mountain and with a popular university that doubles the population of this attractive and historical place called by one daily periodical the Athens of Wales (without the lovely warm sunshine though!). We passed some of the university buildings as we headed for the pier and pulled up in the very reasonably priced car park right outside the gates.

Described as one of the three best surviving Victorian piers in the country Garth Pier has changed very little since it was begun in 1893, other than now being a bit shorter, which is quite refreshing. We headed to the elaborate wrought-iron entrance gates and octagonal kiosks resplendent under silver-painted onion-shaped domes.

The gates which were sadly topped with wreaths of old barbed wire across the top are very ornate, with a pair of shields and Victorian globe gas lights. They are also weighed down with notices – no less than four banning dogs and four advertising the existence and delights of the café, but there are also three awards displayed here including the British Construction Industry Small Project Award, justly deserved for rescuing the pier from total dereliction and returning it to its former glory.

Although commended for being such an original Victorian pier, this was not by luck. The pier was originally designed by J.J. Webster of Westminster, took three years to complete and cost £14,475. Mostly built of steel with screw piles and cast-iron columns, the wooden deck with widened sections extended 472m (1,550') into the Straits and had a pontoon landing stage at the pier head with steps to the jetty and foreshore. The wider sections accommodated some attractive polygonal kiosks and the rest of the deck was adorned with ornamental lamps and handrails and had a 3' gauge baggage railway added after its opening in 1896.

A busy steamer service regularly called at the pier from the Isle of Man, Liverpool and Blackpool, and it's not until you look at pictures of the piers in their heyday does it become apparent how big the boats were – they dwarfed the piers! Unfortunately in 1914 cargo steamer *Christiana* slipped her ropes and collided with the pier, taking out a section and damaging the end. The Royal Engineers affected a temporary gangway repair until some proper work was carried out in 1921 but it also meant the end for the baggage railway too. A photograph taken after the incident shows a neat break with the decking curving spectacularly down on either side of the break like an inventive roller-coaster! It was also found that the piles were really badly corroded – the use of steel rather than wrought iron meant this had happened much faster than usual for a pier, and they were repaired at great cost.

With high maintenance costs and the same old problem of dropping visitor numbers, Garth Pier was closed in 1971 when it became too unsafe. The local Afton Borough Council wanted to demolish it, but Bangor City Council objected and bought it for a token 1p in 1975. They managed to secure Grade II listed status for it and then set about securing funding from various sources including sponsored plaques before work started in November 1982. Using hollow steel sections to repair parts of the pier it was re-opened finally on 7th May 1988 by the Marquis of Anglesey, and bits of the old pier that had to be removed were donated to the Anglesey Sea Zoo (sounds so much better than the Sealife Centre!) for use in the tank for pier-dwelling fish!

We dropped our money into the honesty box at the gate and prommed onto the main deck of the pier arm-in-arm. We found a large board covered with sponsorship plaques, neatly arranged in alphabetical order and larger plaques commemorating those involved in the restoration and opening ceremony. The pier deck is pleasingly wide and airy – there might not be traditional flashing lights and amusements here, but there is plenty of fresh air and more of those stunning views of mountains and Anglesey's wooded slopes!

The little kiosks along the length of the pier contain all sorts of different attractions – tourist information and an education centre, little nick-nacks and woodcrafts. The kiosks themselves are rather interesting, with miniature Gothic-style trefoil-topped windows and very steeply pitched silvery roofs. There are plaque adorned benches against some of the elegantly curving silver fish-net railings and some other solitary seats positioned on the wider balconies providing a place to admire the view in the tranquil atmosphere this pier affords.

The end of the pier was particularly attractive, ringed with lantern-topped cast-iron lamp-standards, the silver railings reflecting the sunlight as it bounced off the continually glowering skies! The much-advertised tea-rooms were here too in a fourteen-sided pavilion topped with a fabulous burnished silver roof shaped like an upside down flower, a shape mirrored by two much smaller rounded shelters with seats at each corner of the pier head. Here in the corners, the decking was extended out over the water as elegant rounded balconies, and we avoided the screaming children learning to ride their streamer-bedecked bicycles in the wider space in order to have our last kiss of the day (wasn't there a notice saying 'no cycling' at the entrance?! Where's a bouncer when you need one!). But wait! What's this? In the quiet corner we'd been heading to where a young couple already engaged in a kiss – was this allowed? Should we have taken out carte blanche end-of-the-pier kissing rights? What was the world coming to, shouldn't be allowed... We settled for a kiss on the rounded balcony instead, sheltered from the wind and bicycles, which in hindsight was a far superior place than a shelter, and had a much better view too!

Here at the end of the pier we could look also down onto the jetty – the original one went when the *Christiana* collided with the pier in 1914, and it meant the pier was slightly shortened. We'd just walked 457m (1,500') instead of 472m (1,550'), but the metalwork stairway and six levels of platforms mean that anglers can still come and fish whatever the state of the tide – in fact although the pier closes at 9 p.m. in the summer, it offers tickets for night fishing too. The lower levels are liberally garlanded in more barbed wire – perhaps this was to stop people jumping *on* to the pier after all, obviously more of a problem than we'd ever realised! We stood on the other balcony and looked back up the pier. We could see the structure of the pier from here, the columns sceptre-like and linked with diagonal cross bracing in pretty good condition, evidence of a restoration job well-done twenty years previously.

Still warmly clasping hands we began the long walk back to the gates, past the mandatory coin-operated blue telescope and a shrieking small child that had parted company from her bike yet again. Despite keeping a keen eye turned to the waters for the feather waders on the mudflats that were mentioned in the window of the education centre, we failed to see any fishermen thus adorned. They don't sound a terribly practical form of attire for an angler, but perhaps they provide a good form of camouflage…

We'd had a fantastic day – the rain had miraculously steered clear of us and we had experienced four piers that were not only very different as far as style went but also with regards to their fortune, and it gave us lots to talk about as we relaxed over dinner in a comfortable restaurant that evening.

Despite more heavy rain in the night, the next day started off clear and bright and we set off on one of the most scenic drives of our whole adventure, eighty-four miles up into the mountains of Snowdonia where I continually said 'Wow!' at the views. Trawsfynydd power station stood in a misty, pastel-painted landscape like a scene from a futuristic sci-fi film as we started our descent towards Dolgellau which took us through the bosky gloamings of the Coed-y-Brenin Forest Park. From Dolgellau there was considerable winding of the road and more downward gradients, through Machynlleth before dropping down into Aberystwyth and the last Welsh pier on our list.

Aberystwyth – an historical market town of 'only' fifty pubs, which with a university population of nearly nine thousand means Friday and Saturday nights out must be quite crowded! It's an extremely well-filled town, and it needs to be because Aberystwyth is pretty isolated – it's nearly two hours to get to the next major town on roads that aren't bad in the summer but pretty scary in winter conditions. As well as the first purpose-built pleasure pier in Wales, Aber has a castle and the longest electric cliff railway in Britain that takes visitors to the top of Constitution Hill where they can see the stunning views from a camera obscura.

The Cambrian Railway first came to Aberystwyth in the 1860s from Machynlleth to transform the town into a booming tourist spot and oldest health resort in Wales. While the railway branch line was being built, the

Aberystwyth Pier Promenade Company cunningly commissioned a pier designed by Eugenius Birch, the great Victorian pier designer. I often wonder if that was his real name or what people called him when they saw the finished pier, but until I get my time-machine (paid for with a lottery win from that crystal ball that's first on my wish list), we'll never know! Whether it was design or purpose (and I suspect the latter), both the railway and the Royal Pier opened on the same day, Good Friday 1865. Some seven thousand people paid a toll to go on the new pier which had cost £13,600, was 292m (958') long and had been put up to Birch's plans by contractors J.E. Dowson.

A diabolical storm just months later in January 1866 saw a 30m (100') seaward section of the pier completely washed away. Because it had not been open for very long the owners could not afford to replace the neck and it was only rebuilt in 1872 once it had been sold to new owners. A new narrower section 70m (230') was installed, along with a gallery and refreshment room up top. By now Aberystwyth was the 'Biarritz of Wales' and experiencing a Victorian tourist boom. The seafront was now lined with tall buildings, set well back on the wide promenade to avoid the ferocity of the Irish Sea.

In 1896 some new bits of the substructure were added, with wrought-iron rod braces, cast-iron piles and columns concreted into the rock. Eugenius Birch liked to build his piers using cast-iron piles, despite opinion erring towards wrought-iron constructions. He believed, obviously knowing what would happen to many of his piers, that if one were to be struck by a boat, wrought iron would buckle and bend causing a large area of damage that was also expensive to renew. By using cast iron, the struck section would shatter, minimising the area (and therefore the cost!) of the section to replace. What a canny man!

A stunning new pavilion was also built at the landward end in the same year. Designed by Londoner George Croydon Marks (best known for his partnership with 'Mr Lightbulb' Thomas Edison) the Glass Pavilion was built by the Bourne Engineering and Electrical Company and cost £1,000. The beautiful arch-roofed building had three aisles covered with glass-domed roofs that were supported and decorated in the popular Gothic style of the time. It held three thousand people and was opened on 26th July 1896, appropriately enough for a pier with Royal in its title by Alexandra, the Princess of Wales.

The night of Friday 14th January, 1938 brought a really monster of a storm. Wind speeds were estimated at being around 90 mph (140 km/h) and by the morning it had destroyed or damaged virtually every single building along the promenade. Not surprisingly 61m (200') of the pier was swept away, although other damage was minimum which was a relief. Apparently on a calm day it is possible to swim around the end of the pier as it stands today and look down to see the old columns still lying where they were felled on the sea bed below. Following the storm, the pier was closed for the duration of the Second World War as it was seen as a security risk.

By the 1970s the pier neck was in such awful condition that it was considered unsafe for public use and was subsequently closed. The Don Leisure Group bought the Royal Pier in 1979 and in 1986 spent the huge sum (for then) of £250,000 to improve and repair the remaining 91m (300'). The following year a new restaurant and snooker hall were opened and the pier has remained pretty much the same up until today, with the odd modern 'improvement' here and there. There was planning permission granted in 1986 to build a new pier alongside the old one, but thankfully this was never acted upon and Aberystwyth has been left with a (short) remnant of a Eugenius Birch pier and a stunning Victorian pavilion.

Today, just in case you are not sure where you are, or have attention deficit disorder, the Royal Pier has everything the modern holidaymaker (or student) could wish for, all appropriately labelled. There's the Pier Brasserie, Inn on the Pier (a pub), the Pier Pavilion (for snooker, pool and refreshments) and Pier Pressure (a feeling we know well...) which is a nightclub. There's also Pizza Royal (pizzas!) and an ice-cream parlour, making a wide range of different flavours on the premises. Having someone with an extraordinarily sweet tooth in the car, we tried to find a parking space and make for the pier as quickly as possible.

For a Sunday morning the place seemed to be incredibly busy. A pink chicken ran past us, followed by a fairy. We managed to find a spot not too far from the sea front and walked through the side streets admiring the towering Victorian and Edwardian buildings that today have a distinctly studenty feel to them. Three Minnie Mouses (or should that be Minnie Mice?) with pink ears bounced off us and giggled their way down the hill. Shaking our heads to dispel this unnerving vision we were distracted by the aroma of coffee from an inviting café as we passed, and we found ourselves inexplicably pulled in. A large latte and a teacake the size of a saucer smothered with golden butter seemed to do the trick, we were having no more hallucinations, so we stepped back into the street for the very short walk to the pier. A cowboy wearing a pink hat edged in marabou flashed by. We looked at each other worriedly.

We can be a bit slow on the uptake sometimes. Emerging onto Marine Terrace a jogging river of pink assailed our vision. Ah, it's a charity fun-run! It was tricky negotiating first a horde of runners then all the spectators, but we were soon on the promenade and right outside the pier entrance.

From under the tonnage of neon signs and new entrance we could still see the old Glass Pavilion and original roof shape – despite the fact that this pier is not overly huge and is buried by modern add-ons, there is still the essence of the original buildings and grandeur. From the side, we could see the roof shape more clearly, and also the original Eugenius Birch pier legs (the thicker legs in groups of four with lower cross-bracing are his. Well, not *his* legs, but the pier legs he designed...). The newer, thinner section is easy to spot too, this part of the pier still unused by people, although the performing starlings pause for breath here before roosting, giving the plain metal barriers a kind of avian feathered pipe-cleaner look.

It was a shame we hadn't visited Aberystwyth in the colder months, as it is well known for its starling displays as the sun goes down. These huge gatherings of birds at sunset in the autumn and winter are known as murmurations, massed aerial acrobatics in clouds of tens of thousands of birds that create fantastic shapes in the air. We were lucky enough to have seen small murmurations over the Somerset Levels, but never the huge swirling shapes that are often filmed for television. The birds are gathering in groups (which is safer against hawk attacks) before an invisible signal is given and the birds suddenly disappear – in this case under the pier onto the girders, in Somerset into the trees. Once roosted they snuggle together for warmth during the colder nights – the whirring clouds of birds a prelude to surviving the night en masse.

Further to the right of the pier on the prominent hill we could just make out an odd cabin near the top – this is Constitution Hill and the shed for the cliff railway. Just above it is a kind of pagoda-style tower which we deduced was the camera obscura. The geology here is stunning too, and today it was set off by yellow gorse, highlighting the convoluted layers of strata in the rocks. In a nature vs man battle of the impressive, the town buildings start at the bottom of the hill and follow the curve of the bay around to where we stood – mostly five-storey, proud architectural styles, highlighted with different pastel shades of paint. It was a close call, but I think perhaps here man gets the point... although if we come back and have another, longer visit the vote may go the other way!

We went back to the entrance and stepped inside, our eyes taking a moment to adjust to the gloom – we were in the amusement arcade! We wandered around the machines, spotting the same old favourites that we had seen in many a pier arcade. Then, there at the back, quiet on a Sunday morning was an air hockey table, beckoning to us. Words were not necessary – we freed our hands from pockets and got in the crouching starting position, tension tangible in the air. Go! Five minutes of hysterical giggling, mad flailing and football terrace cheers (and boos) later, the game was over. I had been trounced (again).

"Another game? I think I've got another pound."

"Oh yes please!"

And off it goes again. I love the quick-fire silliness of air hockey, and the way it makes your face muscles ache for ages afterwards from all the laughing... brilliant! We had a couple of goes on the penny falls and then had our kiss at the far end of the arcade.

Back outside we had a look at the underside of the pier. The tide was going out and the old legs were clear to see now amongst the rocky shoreline. On the opposite side I found some steps, went down and picked my way over the heavily striated, ripply rocks to stand under the pier, but stopped short – a large starry smooth hound (think dogfish!) had been washed up there, over 70cm (2') long and sadly dead, but still beautiful. I ran my fingers cautiously over its cream-coloured skin, dappled with chocolate spots, feeling the fearsome rasp against my hand as I went against the nap. Further under the pier I looked at the fine-boned girders and bracing, sturdy enough to have stood the pounding from waves and storms for more than one hundred and forty years. A small noise made me look round – and there struggling to get out of a rock pool was a pigeon, only just fully fledged and probably taken its first flight from under the pier's girders. Looking up, two anxious pigeon faces looked down at me. Being essentially a bunny and tree hugger I couldn't leave it there. Yes, I know it's a pigeon and people die from infections carried by them, but it's not my call to decide whether another creature must die. I picked it up out of the water and miraculously found a dry fleece hat on a rock nearby.

"It's your lucky day mate – I hope black's your colour!" I told the bird as I popped it into the hat and tucked it onto the concrete ledge well away from the tide line. At least I gave it a chance – and got a good look at some classic engineering in the process!

Back on the promenade, the charity fun run was still in full swing. A group of plump women bounced past in pink tutus and we popped through the gap left in their wake to walk back through the town, the last time we would visit Wales on our quest to kiss on all the piers in the country. This time round... I just know we'll come back to them all again!

CHAPTER 16

It's Soooo Bracing – and Frothy and Gorgeous!
(Skegness, Cleethorpes and Saltburn)

Following our Welsh jaunt we had another little flurry of interviews and photographs – it has to be said it was quite fun, although some photographers have a funny idea of posing a picture, including getting Jay to pick me up with one hand and still look cheerful! This time we were snapped on Clevedon Pier, where Linda Strong the Pier Mistress offered us a plaque on the pier, which was a generous and very touching offer.

At the next available weekend, near the end of June we made yet another early morning getaway for the north-east and the final few on this side of the country. Slowly and surely areas of the map were being cleared – once this weekend was over we had only the South Coast piers to see, although there was still a lot of travelling involved! We had picked a weekend with some fantastic weather – clear blue skies and blazing sunshine, so we were hoping there would be a light breeze at the coast to keep the searing heat at bay!

The trip was uneventful (well, I did hit a very unfortunate magpie on the road to Lincoln– I apologised profusely but he did fly straight out in front of the car) and we arrived at Skegness, cheerful, colourful and, to quote the jolly fisherman who has skipped along the beach in the advertising posters for the resort since 1908, 'SO bracing!' As we got out of the car at the back of a wild log flume ride, we nearly fell over in the heat – not quite so bracing today, in fact it was positively tropical! Everywhere was buzzing with people. Children in flip-flops carrying huge inflatables, tattooed dads in football shorts, bare chests already shrimp pink (that's going to sting in the morning!), gaggles of adolescents loudly showing off to similar groups of the opposite sex – there's something fun about a seaside town at full swing on a summer's day!

We walked along the road towards the pier entrance, past the pleasure beach (there's a big rattly roller coaster here), casinos, traditional and branded fast-food establishments, hotels, cafes and everything else you would expect from a traditional seaside town! Along the bustling front there's little evidence of the town's Victorian origins, but as I later researched the resort and its pier I found a real wealth of information and some wonderful newspaper articles from the Victorian period to provide an insight into what Skeggy used to be like.

Originally a little port, Skegness had a population of less than 400 during the 1850s, some of whom were fishermen while the others farmed the very fertile lands locally. The local gentry would come to the sandy beaches to 'sea-bathe', but it wasn't until the advent of the railway in 1872 that hordes of people come here, including the hoi-polloi – working class day-trippers! All the trappings of a town had to be provided for the inevitable holidaymakers – hotels, guest houses, a promenade and tea-rooms were soon being built, and in 1876 the Earl of Scarborough (who had helped bring the railway to the village) was behind the forming of the Skegness Pier Company to get a state-of-the-art pier built too.

A competition was held, with a £50 prize for the winning design, and Messrs. Clarke and Pickwell of Hull were the victors from the forty-four entrants. Head, Wrightson and Co., the builders of Ramsey Pier were called upon to construct the new design and work began in 1880. This has to be the only pier I have come across (unless there's an article I've missed) that was breached by an accident before it was even complete! *The Hull Packet and East Riding Times* on Friday November 26th, 1880 reported that on the night of the 19th November a large vessel, presumably already overturned, had collided with the pier, resulting in some of the piles being knocked in and destroyed. Fortunately it didn't seem to hold up the construction too badly, for on the 4th June 1881, or thereabouts, the pier was opened.

I say 'thereabouts', because generally it is thought that the pier was opened on the 4th June by Prince Alfred, the Duke of Edinburgh. However, there is actually no evidence of this and it seems to be yet another urban myth – you would have thought that a Royal visit would have warranted a mention in the local paper, but this was not the case. In fact, it appears that the pier opened without any ceremony at all in the week preceding 10th June as the *Lincolnshire Chronicle* of that week said that 'on Saturday the Grand Iron Pier was opened to the public'. The confusion appears to have happened because the Duke of Edinburgh did visit Skegness at short notice in the same week to inspect the Coastguards' houses and landed at the pier. It was so unexpected that there were only a few people there to greet him, although by word of mouth this had grown to about a thousand by the time he reached the pier gates (which must have been pretty much the entire population of the town in those days), but he certainly didn't open the pier!

Now open (at a cost of about £20,000) it was the fourth longest pier in the country back then, stretching 554m (1,817') out 'into the German Ocean' as it was reported at the time. The pier was nearly 8m wide (25') with four wider bays to accommodate seating, although there was also continuous cast-iron seating with decorative shields on the backs that ran up both sides of the pier. Apparently the southern handrail of the pier also incorporated the gas main for the pier. I hope the metalwork was solid as gentlemen were partial to a smoke back then!

At the front of the pier the Gothic-arched toll booth (and two little similarly styled kiosks that sold traditional seaside treats like winkles and sweets, although hopefully not in the same little paper cone) were both made of dark pine and were reached by a flight of eight sweeping balustraded steps that wouldn't have looked out of place at the front of a big grand house. The Victorians were really hot on symbolic representation, and these steps were to emphasise that the pier was of elevated status as it had to be reached by climbing up to get to the entrance, and all the visitors back then would certainly have got that hint!

At the seaward end was a T-shaped pier head with an Oregon pitch-pine landing stage on the northern side initially, but moved to the south when it was realised there was greater protection from the elements here! The 68m (222') by 37m (122') area was not only used by visiting ships but also was home to a 700-seater Indian style pavilion theatre and concert hall.

Along the length of the pier were ornate wrought-ironwork railings that curved round into seats and each seatback was further decorated with a little shield, more very elegant Victorian handiwork.

The very first chartered steamers arrived the following year – the Skegness Steam Boat Company had been started especially to bring visitors to the new town and to take them on visits out to the Lynn Well lightship, Norfolk and in particular to Hunstanton, for only a few miles away was the Royal residence of Sandringham, and the Victorians were inveterately ardent Royal-watchers who flocked to Skegness just to go on this trip! Considering that the town relied on the railway or steamers to bring its visitors it is amazing to think that just eight years after it opened there were over 20,000 people treading the Jarrah-wood decking on just one single August day! These steamer visits continued until 1910 when sandbanks in The Wash made the trips longer (because of navigating around the hidden sand bars) and far more dangerous.

Apart from trips to spy on royalty, the day-trippers could expect to be entertained by bands and entertainments in the concert hall, diving displays from a 24m (80') diving board (these were extremely popular right into the 1890s) and the delightfully intriguing confetti battles (what? How? Who? And more importantly, why?!). All this fun meant there needed to be more places to slake your thirst, so new refreshment rooms were built in the south-west corner.

Apart from a small fire in the saloon in 1895 that was quickly extinguished, life was jolly (and bracing) for Skegness Pier. Those dodgy sandbanks meant that the steamers could no longer go on their trips up and down the coast, and the landing stage was removed when it became unsafe – although there was talk of having a new one constructed, the company could not find the money, and the pier remained without a safe place for ships to moor. The motor schooner *Europa* had other ideas however, for one fateful night in 1919 following a furious north-eastern gale her anchor chains snapped and she was dashed into the pier. People had been watching the vessel from the pier but thought (along with the Captain) that the ship was safe and would be blown in the other direction – they were soon running for safety as the *Europa* crashed through the pier, the action of the waves causing her to rip a 46m (150') section clean out of the structure. Because the water here is so shallow at low tide, there are some spectacular postcards illustrating this accident, showing the bowsprit of the *Europa* still cleaving the pier in two the next day. It was estimated that it would cost £4000 to repair the pier, and £1000 to repair the ship, with litigation and lawsuits abounding as the finger of blame was pointed at her captain.

A 'temporary' structure filled the void left by the schooner, but a permanent repair wasn't made until 1939 when nearly £4,000 was spent on restoration of the breach and modernisation of the entrance. This included two entrances either side of a new large concrete Art Deco arch with shops on both sides and a glass-covered canopy over this section to provide weather protection. Having completed all these improvements, the pier was then declared a restricted zone due to the outbreak of war. Planks were removed so that enemies would fall between the gaps if they tried to use the pier for landing and it wasn't until 1948 when the pier had a further £24,000 spent repairing the war years' neglect. The glass canopy was extended further back along the deck and a cinema, amusement arcade and shops added to the entertainment already found at the landward end of the pier.

The post-war years were free from incident and the pier continued to be a highly popular venue for visitors, many who came from the first Butlin's camp in the town, open since 1936. The famous east coast storms and tides of 1953 caused minor damage and flooded the entrance, but when the sun shone, people could be seen lolling about in regimental rows of deckchairs up and down the length of the pier, working on a tan rather than taking gentle exercise in the sea breezes! In 1971 the owners had a real revamp and demolished everything at the entrance, replacing it with a purpose-built arcade housing cafeterias, shops and the amusement arcades. In hindsight, they probably regretted doing this, for the structures they removed were all listed buildings, and the council weren't happy. Now in serious financial dire straits, the owners sold the pier to Mr Robin Mitchell and breathed a huge sigh of relief!

However, it was not long before the hand of fate dealt another nasty blow to Skegness Pier, one from which it would never recover. On the 11th January 1978 high tides battered the east coast, made considerably worse by gale-force northerly winds. There were reports of sheets of glass from the arcade being peeled off by the wind, and with waves crashing over the top of the sea wall, a flood warning was issued. Workmen carrying out renovation work on the pier ran for their lives when they felt the structure beneath them begin to sway and the sea claimed another victory as it wrenched a huge section of girders, decking and ironwork out of the pier.

Just 115m (377′) of decking remained on the landward part of the pier – out to sea like a beached oil-rig sat the huge theatre and shelters, the space between them now a mess of twisted girders and shattered wood.

The marooned end of the pier was left deserted, home only to flocks of roosting starlings, until in October 1985 it constituted such a risk to shipping that work began on dismantling it. Unfortunately, during this work a fire began and what little was left of the old structure was swiftly reduced to nothing. Two workmen were rescued by the local lifeboat and plans to exhibit parts of the old theatre were dashed. In a bid to keep visitors coming to the pier, the deck was widened at the shoreward end and extensions built around it and the old railing and bench combination taken away to be replaced with plain railings that were painted blue. Skegness now had what was essentially a funfair on decking, but it had the desired effect and people kept coming.

By the 1990s tastes were changing, and now with more of a sense of pride for times gone by the pier was celebrating its history rather than trying to keep pace with flash modern amusements. The side extensions were removed, revealing the original Victorian framework and piles topped with decorated capitals. The railings were painted red and a ten-pin bowling alley was added to the landward amusements, and although the pier was trying hard, it was still a shadow of its former self.

In January 2000 however, the pier was returned to something the Victorians would have been very proud of following a £5 million redevelopment plan under the watchful eye of two of Mr Mitchell's children, who now owned the pier – back came decorative panelled railings, wooden benches with wrought-iron arms and legs and some Victorian-style streetlamps. Iron archways were erected over the steps up from the beach, and into these were incorporated some of the original little seat-back shields from the original seating on the pier. Although the pier is very much in different era sections now (70s at the front, 40s and 50s amusements in the middle and an original Victorian flavour out on deck), it has managed to remain unpretentious, providing varied entertainment for whoever cared to visit over the years, and perhaps this has been the key to its success.

We were delighted to spot a lovely fountain-cum-statue of the Jolly Fisherman skipping along just in front of the clock tower as we turned down Tower Esplanade to the beach and the pier – the entrance to the pier isn't exactly hard to miss, and with all the amusements around it's also easy to see why some call the town 'Skegvegas'.

Inside, we picked our way through the cacophony of arcade games and slot machines, past a ball pool and entrance to bowling and ice-skating downstairs! As we emerged into dazzling daylight outside we could also see the pretty ironwork archways leading onto the pier from the beach. Here too is a snack stall like no other – a maroon coloured tram going to Hunstanton, offering doughnuts, snacks and toasted sandwiches on the journey – what a lovely touch!

The outside area of the pier is a real delight and it's not hard to see why the decked section won an award. The silver railings aren't the most ornate in the world, but the bottom section with curling foliage and starry flowers is rather pretty. The black lamp posts are simple, and stand guard along the length of the pier – coupled with the planking that has been laid vertically (as opposed to going cross-wise), gives a fantastic optical illusion that the pier stretches off into the distance much further than it actually does! At the landward end there were some children's rides and a fearsome bungee gyroscope affair, making good use of the side extension space.

Skegness Pier was delightfully busy. We are often asked what it is that draws people to a pier – we still don't know, but here where there are no end-of-the-pier amusements, flashing lights or novelties we found lots of people just content to walk all the way along to the end and back. Just because it's there! We did the same – at the end the tide was out, but the beach was full of happy faces, sandcastles, donkey rides and there in the distance two large wind farms lazily turning in the haze on the horizon. These are the fifty-seven turbines of the Lynn and Inner Dowsing Offshore wind farms, and despite rumours to the contrary were not put there to generate power for Skeggy's amusements and numerous light bulbs, although it wouldn't be a surprise if they had been! There on the sand below us was also confirmation of where we were and what people thought of the place – 'SKEGVEGAS 2009' was written large and proud for all to see!

At the end of the pier it also transpired that Skegness really *is* bracing! A brisk, chilly wind induced a ripple of goose pimples as we decided to go for our surreptitious kiss... but we stopped short. There were another couple locked in a passionate embrace! Has word of pier kissing really become a global phenomenon? (More worryingly, were we responsible?!) Hmmm... we turned our back on them and had one too!

As we walked back up the pier, the feel-good factor really made itself evident here and it was obvious why, despite its constant ribbing by comedians, Skegness has been a popular resort for over one hundred years. The beach is huge, the sky wide and crystal blue and despite a nippy edge to the sea breeze, the air is very refreshing. The pier continues to be a real asset to the town, and everyone from tiny tots to elderly folk were enjoying the delights of the seaside there.

As we approached the pavilion we could see that the entrance (or is it the exit *from* the amusements?) has also had elaborate ironwork panels in the same design as the pier railings added as an adornment to the glass-topped porch. These little touches make what would otherwise be a plain and unremarkable pier deck just that bit more special and attractive. We walked under the arch next to the tram café and down onto the hot, soft sands of the beach to explore the Victorian pillars of this pier. Due to longshore drift (bet you wished you'd listened in Geography lessons now!) the sands have gradually crept up on the ironwork here, and the decorated tops of the piles are just about keeping their heads above the mini dunes at the landward end. The rest of the pier doesn't exactly soar majestically above the sands either, but it does stretch out elegantly towards the sea and give a glimpse of what it would have looked like when it was first constructed.

Walking back to the car was as much of a delight as visiting the pier, hearing excited screams of people on the rides, waving back at children on the land-train and watching little jiggling bodies on the back of the eternally glum-faced donkeys as they gave rides on the warming sands. Climbing back into the saddle we prepared to head north – we'd had another delightful kiss on our fortieth pier! Forty already! Blimey...

The journey to Cleethorpes was deliciously hot – we were extremely glad of having a new car with icy air conditioning as we trundled the forty miles up the coast to see Pier 39, although for us it was Pier 41. Confused? Welcome to *our* world!

Cleethorpes nestles just under the protective feet of Grimsby and is a seaside town that isn't – it's technically on the estuary of the River Humber, which just like Weston-super-Mare means that despite having a sandy beach, when the tide goes out there's rather a lot of sticky brown mud left behind! Cleethorpes is another north-eastern town that had been a village for hundreds of years – in the 1820s there were just 284 residents and it really only took off on the back of the sea air and bathing fashion, which also included drinking vast amounts of various ghastly mineral waters. The railway linked Cleethorpes to the industrial towns of Yorkshire and the boom began.

And of course, you can't have a seaside town that has a railway running into it without the fashionable accessory of a pier! Piers were such a Victorian status symbol that when plans for a pier at Cleethorpes were first proposed in 1866, the *London Gazette* ran a story about it. The Cleethorpes Promenade Pier Company commissioned a pier and the Manchester, Sheffield and Lincolnshire Railway became financial backers for the project, which cost around £8,000. Head Wrightson of Stockton, those super pier builders we have come across before (and who must have had plenty of piers stockpiled in a warehouse just in case a desperate coastal town wanted one) brought along some iron piles and a timber deck, and Cleethorpes Pier, all 366m (1,200') of it, opened on the August Bank Holiday of 1873. The useful partnership between the railway and the pier meant visitors were deposited right in the heart of the resort and pointed towards the pier and amusements. Initially the railway company, later known more familiarly as the LNER, leased the pier for £450 a year before buying it in 1904 for the princely sum of £11,250. Interestingly the promenade along the side of the beach wasn't built until 1885, which must have meant a sandy stroll for the day-trippers!

An angular pavilion was added at the seaward end three years later, a typically Victorian design that sadly lasted only fifteen years until it was destroyed by a fire. Its barrel-roofed replacement was built midway along the pier to the right of the main deck, and shops and a café were also built at the entrance. Interestingly this rounded roofed building, (think Oriental with a hint of Art Nouveau) was built without any form of heating at all – even allowing for thick woollen undergarments and ladies' multi-layered dresses it was deemed too cold to be used in anything other than the summer months, and it wasn't until 1923 that central heating was added.

Cleethorpes Borough Council bought it back in 1936 and the pier was subsequently sectioned during World War II. Unfortunately the breached section was never re-joined and eventually it was demolished, leaving the pier a more diminutive 102m (335') long – salvage from this part of the pier was apparently used to construct the new stands at the Filbert Street Football Stadium in Leicester. Grimsby and Cleethorpes were heavily bombed during the war (in excess of seven hundred bombing raids were carried out) with the towns being seen as sneaky easy targets. Despite this, the pier survived (although even today the occasional bomb has been found in the mud along the coastline) and carried on providing entertainment unhindered until the 1960s.

By 1968 the pier was looking a bit tired and a £50,000 modernisation programme meant there was now a gleaming six-hundred seat concert theatre and a new café and bar for the delight of holidaymakers, making it one of the most up-to-date venues on the east coast. The concert hall held a diverse range of events from the traditional and expected end-of-the-pier shows and pantomimes to wrestling, coin and stamp fairs, dance festivals and bingo – something for everyone! However, declining numbers of visitors over the next decade meant that in 1981 the council reluctantly sold the pier to Funworld of Skegness for £55,000 – if anyone could re-ignite the appeal of a seaside attraction, they could.

Poor old Cleethorpes Pier struggled though, and in 1983 it was offered back to the council who politely declined, saying it needed £200,000 worth of work doing on it to make it a viable concern. Two more years of uncertainty went by, until it was bought by Mark Meyer, who then invested £300,000 in revamping the pier and unveiling it, like a newly emerged butterfly, as Pier 39 nightclub in September of the same year.

For those waiting to boogie there was a shelter outside the pavilion and the whole pier was widened – this can be seen clearly today, the more modern piles are distinctly different from the originals. Whitegate Leisure then took it over as a concern in 1989, spending in excess of £500,000 on the pavilion and shelter – however, the pier changed hands again in 2005 when the new Waterfront Bar was opened by the National Piers Society Honourable Vice-Secretary, Tim Mickelburgh. A year later, and the pier was sold *again*, this time to local businessman Kash Pungi, who spent another £500,000 on having new supporting legs installed (with all that dancing and nightlife going on upstairs it's not surprising it needed new legs again!). The new supports took five months to put in place and used over forty tonnes of steel. I'm not the world's best mathematician (in fact me and numbers have a very distant relationship), but I think that's around £1.3 million spent to improve the pier in twenty years. We were expecting to see something impressive for this amount of dosh, that's for sure!

The sun was still belting down when we emerged from the car some two and a half thousand miles from the North Pole and nearly ten thousand miles from the South Pole. Cleethorpes sits on the Greenwich Meridian and these are handy distances for the polar explorer blown off course by a freak wind – fortunately our destination was much closer to hand, along a well-kept and interesting promenade. The pavement was decorated with a red and yellow Greek-key design pattern (and a trail of enigmatic yellow duck prints...) and the child in me attempted to walk along the patterns until I was pulled clear of certain death under the wheels of numerous cyclists, prams, skateboards and tots on scooters by my glamorous assistant. Was everyone on wheels? We hadn't seen anyone walking yet, and were relieved to see a legion of bareback horse riders appear noisily down the road as we dodged more wheels.

We passed well-groomed sea-front gardens (sadly going out of fashion in many seafront towns these days as councils have to cut spending) and a land train sped past us, curiously disguised by layers of camouflage netting – we were feeling very much at home amid these somewhat random happenings! We gazed seaward across the warm inviting sands, sprinkled with afternoon sun bathers, children industriously building sandcastles and burying siblings, and past donkeys standing ever patiently (as only donkeys can) towards the pier. We both remarked how attractive it looked, and sauntered a touch faster to get to it!

A little further along the trail of duck feet we paused in the shade to gaze at the innovative cascades and fountain, looking all the more like something from *Alice in Wonderland* for the large dose of washing-up liquid that someone had tipped into them – but it didn't matter, bubbles are beautiful! We turned to walk behind a very neat and imaginative crazy golf course, and were amazed to find *another* pier! An immaculately turned out model of Pier 39 sat as the obstacle on one of the holes – perhaps it should be labelled Pier 38 ½?

We dropped down to the seafront, passed throngs of wheeled visitors (roller-skates, pushchairs, wheelchairs and motorbikes this time) most of whom were becoming acquainted with the contents of the numerous bars in the immediate area. We crossed the road and found ourselves at the entrance to the pier, a plastic-y archway onto a steep decked ramp – sadly the cheery image of what the pier would be like faded here as the reality of worn-out woodwork and fittings became apparent despite the amount spent over the years. Metal hoops decked with simple white lights tried to lighten the atmosphere as we tentatively made our way onto the pier, parts of the decking flexing and bouncing unnervingly underfoot and there were an awful lot of loose or broken planks too.

The pier-side railings, black and initially plain are actually quite stunningly Art Deco (and unlike anything we've seen on another pier), although much of it was hidden by ghastly municipal concrete benches or piles of junk from the pavilion. 'Pier 39' nightclub (with much of its signage faded and missing) is also past its prime, the north-east side peeling and tatty, a lot of rotten woodwork and peeling paint. Always looking for a positive, we did spot two particularly handsome pigeons under the roof line who posed for a picture! In all honesty, what we saw hadn't happened overnight and it was a bit of a shock to find a pier open to the public that was in such a state despite having had so much money spent on it.

Once at the end we saw more of the same and decided it was best to stare intently out to sea (or kiss protractedly with our eyes shut!) and forgot about the pier for a minute as we studied the skyline – shipping of all shapes and sizes graced the horizon (for that is where the sea had vanished to – it's like being in Weston again!) and there was even an oil rig. To our right, a curious circular island rather like a fort... we now know that there are two of these man-made islands. They are the Humber Forts (Haile Sand Fort and Bull Sand Fort) and we had probably been looking at Haile Sand. They were built in 1914 to protect the estuary from the German fleet, and the 18m (59') high by 25m (82') diameter constructions were completed five years later. That must have been one heck of a construction job, for the North Sea is not the most forgiving of environments to live next to or work with – they can't have been comfortable places to be posted either, and there would have been two hundred soldiers at a time on each fort!

After our kiss we strolled back, looking at the surrounding beach life – jingling donkeys, funfair rides and the busy prom while we sidestepped wind-blown cider cans and twanging planks. We met a journalist from the local paper at the front of the pier and gave her an interview (which we've never seen...) and in hindsight, we've now learnt to be more tactful about places we're visiting. I'm sorry to say that we weren't terribly complimentary about the pier. I think we were still in shock. In retrospect, we did find nice things about Cleethorpes Pier – the Art Deco railings, the glorious blue and white paint scheme and the barrel-shaped roof of the pavilion is very easy on the eye.

We slunk away under the pier afterwards, thinking we would probably have to add Cleethorpes to Deal in our list of places we'll never be allowed back to. And there on the warm (very soft) sands on the north side of the pier, are some very attractive, decorative piles. There are an incredible number of different iron-work legs and pipes under there – the south side has the newer, plainer ones, and some faux arches to copy the shapes on the other side. A bit like peering under Granny's skirts and finding she's got bionic legs. We high-tailed it back to the car before we were spotted and run out of town – perhaps we could redress the balance in Saltburn by the Sea, far enough up the coast where our faces weren't known!

We holed up in a motel in Grimsby, the Thelma and Louise of the pier kissing world and hid from the posses of angry Cleethorpes residents, setting off the next glorious morning for the journey up-country to the most northerly English pier at Saltburn by the Sea. It was one of those fabulous quiet summer mornings that promised brilliant blue skies and searing hot sun later in the day – and it didn't disappoint!

We chose to eschew the faster motorway route to Saltburn in favour of the more coastal road via Bridlington, Scarborough and Whitby and it was a superb choice. The sky was a vibrant aquamarine blue, the temperature steadily rising and the scenery breathtaking. As we drove north the hills became more frequent and the gradients more spectacular – it's the automobile equivalent to a roller coaster theme park. Unfortunately the car let us down with its tiddly engine, and while we flew like a bird on the downhills, the uphills necessitated some frantic down-shifting and jettisoning unneeded luggage to get us back to the top for the next exciting descent!

Saltburn was not a disappointment either, first scaling the huge Huntcliff Nab switchback of a hill and squealing as we drove down the other side towards the original hamlet of Old Saltburn, a bijou collection of fisherman's cottages and pub nestling beside Skelton Beck. It is a breathtakingly beautiful spot, and extremely popular on such a hot summer's day. Looking northward there is little of the 'modern' Saltburn to be seen, other than the pier beckoning us onward. We always get a little frisson of excitement when we first spot a pier that we are visiting (and I now realise that I sound like a total pier geek saying something like that again– how sad!) and despite the lure of parking up by Skelton Beck and running onto the sand without a care in the world we pressed on – another interview, another pier and another kiss!

We found ourselves on Marine Parade, a grand road that sits on top of the cliff tops and is the Victorian heart of 'modern' Saltburn. We found a spot to park on Amber Street, one of the original 'jewel' named streets and marvelled at the panoramic views from the cliff tops.

Back in 1856 Saltburn consisted of the one row of houses and the Ship Inn down by Skelton Beck, life being dominated by the vagaries of the wild North Sea. Quaker and entrepreneur Henry Pease was walking one day along the coastal path and, inspired by the beauty of the area, had a prophetic vision of building a town on the top of the headland. During the 1860s his dream became a reality – as many houses as possible had sea views, and these were so important a covenant was placed on Britannia Terrace (now Marine Parade) that any trees planted there were not allowed to exceed 1'6" (that's not even 50cm high) above the footpath! His grid system of roads were named after gemstones and Saltburn by the Sea quickly became a haven for wealthy industrialists during the summer, and as a breath of fresh air for the workers of Teesside to escape to, all aided by the railway.

Although there were steamers visiting the new town, a pier was soon on the agenda. A structure was commissioned by the Saltburn Pier Company in early 1867, designed by Mr John Anderson (who also had invested in property in the town) and by December construction was underway. Built of iron trestles supporting a wooden deck, the pier cost £7,500 and was 457m (1,500') long, with a landing stage for steamers at the seaward end and two little octagonal kiosks at the entrance to collect tolls from the Victorian promenading public. Opening in May 1869 it was an amazing success with over 50,000 visitors recorded during the first six months. Steamers were soon in regular operation from up and down the coastline, visitors were entertained with a brass band at the pier head and by 1873 gas lighting illuminated the length of the pier and a saloon had been added to the pier head. Another addition to the seafront was that of the Cliff Hoist. To aid the passage of ladies in crinolines up and down the formidable 37m (120') high cliff to the pier, Mr Anderson built a wonderfully Heath-Robinson contraption in 1870 that was essentially a wooden cage lowered up and down the cliff face by rope from a wooden tower that looked rather like a wicker lighthouse. I would imagine the sales of smelling salts increased hugely too!

It wasn't long before Mother Nature decided to intervene in the success of the pier, and in the winter of 1875 an enormous storm and tidal surge tore the seaward 91m (300') end of the pier away. Along with it went the profits of the pier company – coupled with an economic downturn the Pier Company went bust and the pier and cliff hoist were sold at auction in 1880 for just £800.

Although the pier's length wasn't reinstated, it was repaired by new owners the Saltburn Improvement Company who also widened the pier head, added windshields and incorporated a bandstand and tea rooms. The Cliff Hoist was surveyed and found to be dangerously rotten and was promptly demolished. Knowing that a replacement was essential to the success of the pier, Sir Richard Tangye's company were commissioned to design a funicular railway along the lines (if you'll excuse the pun) of the two at Scarborough. The completed cliff railway opened in 1884, with two ten-person cars ornamented with stained glass windows travelling up and down the 71% incline for a modest fee. To complement the new railway, the two original kiosks were replaced with two buildings more in keeping with the new designs, one being used as a cloakroom, the other as a café.

In 1900 another storm damaged the pier but it remained operational until a ship collided with the structure in 1924, wiping out a 64m (210') section and marooning the bandstand at the far end. In 1929 repairs were started and the full length of the pier re-opened the following year. A new theatre had also been built at the landward end to cater for dances, shows and meetings and the pier continued successfully until 1938 when the local council purchased it and it was duly disabled for the war. With steel and materials at a premium after the war it wasn't until 1952 that the pier was restored to former glory and re-opened to the public once more, seeing over 25,000 visitors in the first month alone! Seeing figures like this no matter what year a pier is opened to the public just goes to show what a place they have in the hearts of people and how a pier can irresistibly continue to draw people to it.

Sadly it was only a year later that the pier was to be closed again – a severe storm left the framework of the pier badly twisted and the repairs cost £23,000 to put right. These repairs took five years to complete and no sooner had the pier opened than it suffered more damage to the seaward end. In 1961 more unusually fierce storms twisted twenty piles, and this awful fate was repeated during the early 1970s, leaving the pier in a precarious state. While emergency plans were being drawn up to save the pier, yet another tempest struck, reducing the length of the pier to 335m (1,100') as more of the structure was washed away. Exasperated, the council applied for an Order to have the pier demolished. As we'd seen before, it takes a lot more than that to keep one of these fine ladies down!

A public enquiry declared that thirteen of the trestles should be removed and the rest of the pier restored. The pier restoration took five years and in June 1978 the remaining 207m (681') were opened to the public once again. The entrance buildings were similarly restored, with further work being carried out in the 1990s and then a huge restoration project, funded by National Lottery grants saw a major conservation carried out. Work was done to strengthen the iron trestles underneath the pier and an inclined path provided easier access. Officially re-opened to the public in 2001, we were visiting the new Pier of the Year for 2009!

We decided not to take the Cliff railway down to the seafront, instead following the zigzag path down the cliff face, tastefully adorned with cultivated areas sporting maritime plants, ornamental grasses and large ammonites to highlight the geological importance of this area where huge deposits of fossils lie embedded in the rocks close by. The sea breeze had been refreshing at the top of the cliff, and now as we wound our way downwards, we were struck by the heat reflected from the land in this sheltered spot! At the bottom, we turned and looked back up the cliff and were rewarded with the sight of the little cliff railway sliding down (and up!) to the little station next to where we stood.

The sand was soft and warm, the sun skin-bakingly hot, the sky blue and the sea improbably bluer, and here we were in a little spot of England where time was standing still and the creations of the modern world seemed a million miles away – heaven indeed! The promenade was pleasantly busy and the wood-framed buildings held the tantalising aromas of candy floss, hot sugary doughnuts, and the salt-and-vinegar sharpness of fish and chips, overlaid with a hint of coffee. We drifted away on an olfactory high for several seconds before coming back to earth and promising ourselves a visit once we'd been to the end of the pier and back.

We slipped onto the pier via a side gate and stepped onto the neat solid planking confidently. Although relatively new, everything about the pier has been tastefully done in keeping with its history. The railings are monochrome and gently curved, an impressive wide inclined, uncluttered deck leading out to sea. Once on the level section of the deck it broadened twice to accommodate bays with seats before widening at the seaward end where we watched a flurry of surfers catching the waves and riding them back to the wide beach. We snuck a discreet kiss at the end, knowing full well that two of the other people standing there gazing over the railings were the journalist and photographer we had come there to meet!

We had a very pleasant interview on the end of the pier and collectively watched some two dozen people surfing on the beautifully crafted waves under the glorious heat of the sun. Saltburn is apparently a well-known spot for surfers and on a day like today it was really easy to see what the temptation of this spot is – I could easily have leapt over the end of the pier into the sea, so it was just as well we had business to attend to! We waxed positive over Saltburn and had some fantastic pictures taken a little further back along the pier. This time odd poses worked – we knelt down and the photographer lay flat on the decking, something that elicited strange looks from passers-by! We were grilled by some elderly promenaders, who loved the story and wished us well with the rest of our journey. On such a scorching day we could quite easily have spent more time in Saltburn, but sadly we both had work beckoning on Monday, so we bid our sad farewells and headed back along the spacious pier. There was still time left to jump onto the hot, silky sand and have a look under the pier and admire the fantastic restoration work that's been done here.

We left the beach and pier and bought a ticket for the cliff lift, and waited for the little red and white carriage to make its way down to us. This is the oldest remaining water balanced lift left in Britain, with 4500 litre (1,000 gallon) water tanks in each car, and able to take 10-12 people in each car. Distinctly more civilised than the wicker man of old, the Saltburn cliff lift has changed very little since it opened in 1884. I am relieved to say it is regularly maintained and has required very little updating over the years. An electrically operated water pump was added in 1924, aluminium cars replaced the wooden ones in 1979 and an hydraulic braking system and replacement winding wheel were installed in 1998, a real testament to Victorian engineering.

Being a complete coward when it comes to going in planes, up lifts etc., I was a bit apprehensive before boarding, but I am still alive and can report that the little lift is remarkably smooth and swift and has lovely little stained glass windows too.

The view is incomparable and we were sorry the ride was over so quickly, but we stood at the top and watched the cars going up and down for a little while before we reluctantly bid farewell to Saltburn and headed back to Amber Street feeling that it was not just the streets of Saltburn that were jewelled, but the pier and the scenery and the cliff lift... I think we liked it!

CHAPTER 17

The Long and Short of It
(Hythe, Southampton, Southsea Clarence and Southsea South Parade)

It had been a couple of months since we had last been exploring piers and we felt that we needed to get out and about in some bracing maritime air again. Heading into the deep south meant we could carry out familial visits in the area, thus earning much needed Brownie points, and we'd also been asked to give Radio Solent a ring when we were in the area, so the morning of August 1st saw us doing a radio interview before setting off for Hampshire's piers at Hythe, Southampton and Southsea (What a superstar lifestyle we lead!).

We arrived in the gorgeous Sleepy Hollow town of Hythe, snuggled between the New Forest and Southampton Water in very un-summery weather. The day was grey, damp and chilly, visibility not great and the drizzle of the instantly clothing-drenching kind. Our plan, such as it was, meant catching the ferry to Southampton (giving us a sea bird's eye view of the Royal Pier there, then back in time for tea. The following day we'd head further along the coast to Southsea's piers then home. It wasn't looking like being a great weekend with the land being as wet as the sea, but we'd give it our best shot!

Hythe was still asleep when we arrived at eleven o'clock, and we approached the pier through the shore-end gates and station buildings, decorated with floral tubs and making us feel we'd stepped back in time. We bought our ticket and stepped onto the planks that pointed out a very, very long way into the distance where we would catch the ferry. We could have taken the train and stayed dry but we walked – what were we thinking?! As with all the piers we had visited, Hythe is unique. It is in the *Guinness Book of Records* for having the oldest, continuously operating pier train in the world, running since 1922 and it's the seventh longest pier in the country, reaching out 640m (2,100ft) into the deep-water channel of Southampton Water.

The wooden planks, made of ekki (or red ironwood, especially resistant to decay and termites. Not that I'd expect to encounter a termite over Southampton Water, and especially not on such a rotten day as today!) shone silkily in the drizzle, the light picking out the sponsored plank inscriptions really nicely. Ekki costs about 10p per 1cm, so selling planks in this way raises valuable funds for the upkeep of this considerably lengthy structure. We started out reading the planks as we walked and picked up on all the details of the pier as we went too, a sort of pier library if you will.

Despite its solid construction below decks (I hope!), the sheer length of Hythe Pier manages to give an impression of a fragile and almost temporary construction. It's only 4.9m (16 feet) wide, but this incorporates a narrow gauge railway, footpath and cycle path (also part of a local and European coastal path!). It is *not* a gangplank!

Before the pier was built, landing a ferry boat from Southampton on Hythe's waterfront was a tricky business – passengers complained about getting wet and muddy and it was a fair old walk up the sloping mudlands to the main shore. In 1874 the first order to make a pier here was drawn up, and the plans incorporated a narrow gauge tramway to run the length. However, work on building the pier didn't start within the two-year stipulated time-span and so permission lapsed. Further plans and companies were drawn up, but it wasn't until 1878 that work actually started, with the intention of running steam ferry boats to Southampton.

Designed by Mr James Wright and built by the same people that had constructed Bournemouth Pier, Bergheim and Company of London, the pier cost around £7,700 to construct. Held up on cast-iron screw piles, wrought-iron girders strengthened by various bracing supported pine joists and planks, running from end to end (this also gives the impression of incredible length, even if it is just an optical illusion!). Over the years the decking has been replaced by oak and ekki planking for strength and durability.

The pier was opened officially by the Mayor of Southampton, on 1st January 1881, who arrived by launch from the Royal Pier at Southampton. Despite plans for a tramway, this wasn't included in the finished design and luggage was transported back and forth on two-wheeled hand carts, but after several years of use it was found that the wheels were causing too much damage to the planking, so it was back to the drawing board for a better way of shifting trunks and luggage to the ferry.

The ferry service was originally provided by two steam boats *Frederica* and *Louisa* but in 1889 James Percy (a descendent of the Earl of Northumberland, who was also known as 'Harry the Hotspur') commissioned a paddle steamer specifically for the ferry service, and in honour of his ancestor named it *Hotspur*. Percy's homage remains to this day, as every boat that has been used for this ferry service has retained the name *Hotspur* in its title (although current services are often provided by a catamaran ferry boat called *Great Expectations*). We travelled on board *Great Expectations* but passed *Hotspur IV* used for relief services, moored at the end of the pier.

The hand-pushed carts were replaced by a hand-pushed tramway in 1909. Tracks for the cart were sunk into the planks; and luggage, goods and even a few passengers were pushed by a porter up and down the length of the pier. Four little wooden shelters were also erected along the length of the pier to provide much needed protection from the wind and rain, which can howl up and down Southampton Water quite ferociously in the winter! It wasn't until 1918 and the end of World War I that it a decision was made to replace the tramway with an electric railway on the south side of the pier. Supplied by an electrified 'third rail', the gauge remained at 2 feet wide and began running sometime during July 1922, although surprisingly there was no official opening ceremony or mention in the local papers.

Instead of a muscular porter, locomotion was provided by three four-wheeled engines purchased from the Ministry of Munitions at Avonmouth Mustard Gas Works near Bristol. Originally battery powered, they were converted to run from the third rail, and pulled two custom-made carriages at a time. Accessed by sliding doors, each carriage had wooden slat seats and state of the art electric lighting too! The engine also pulled a luggage truck and supplied the ferry boats with fuel oil by way of a tank truck. This gorgeous little set-up has remained pretty much unchanged since 1922. The third-rail remains on the seaward side of the track and the fenced-off track has remained to the south of the pier. Livery has altered somewhat over the years, from green, to green and cream, then blue and cream and red and white. Today the locos and carriages are back in dark green, and you can experience what it would have been like to step onto the little electric train back in 1922.

The pier hasn't come this far without its share of incidents, however. In 1885 a schooner struck the pier partway along, an accident that required major repairs. Following repairs and despite war and many years of service, the pier remained unscathed until November 1st 2003, when dredger MV *Donald Redford* collided with the mid-section of the pier, tearing a 45m (150') hole in the centre and damaging two more spans. Despite severing the electric rail and blowing the main transformer, a major disaster was narrowly missed. Just minutes before the accident the train had arrived back at the shoreward end, full of football fans returning from Southampton. The master of the dredger received an eight-month prison sentence for what was essentially drink driving, and the pier was amazingly out of action for only six weeks, reopening on January 7th 2004 thanks to the hard work of contractor Dudley-Barnes Marine and the pier maintenance crews.

As we walked along the pier on this dreary day, only a plaque marks the spot of this last collision and there is little evidence that any disaster has occurred at all. The railings are delightfully uneven and the little train swept past us with a rattle and hum as it carried a few travellers to the ferry terminal at the end of the pier. As we neared the quaint station we were approached by a couple of people and quizzed as to whether we were the pier kissers they had heard on the radio that morning! We asked what gave it away and they said that not many people would be walking along taking pictures of the railway line, piles and railings quite as intensively as I had been! We happily posed for a picture, which was published in the Hythe *Herald* the following month – thank you Tony Pokusinski for sitting it out in the drizzle and taking such a lovely picture, give that man a warming mug of cocoa!

We jumped on the impatiently waiting ferry and headed, with *Great Expectations* across Southampton Water to see our next pier. Always expectant we watched the end of Hythe Pier slip away into the mist and got a real sense of quite how long and reedily thin it is when seen from the water. Heading towards Southampton you can still see plenty of interesting maritime sights – today we were lucky to see *Bladerunner One*, a ship especially designed for shipping wind turbine blades to off-shore wind farms from its base on the Isle of Wight (but sadly not captained by Rutger Hauer, the Dutch actor and star of the film of the same name). However, it was dwarfed somewhat, and so were we, by the enormous edifice that is the cruise liner *Independence of the Seas.* Launched in April 2008 she has 15 decks and is 154,407 tons. That's BIG. There's accommodation for 4,370 passengers and 1,360 crew and if surfing, climbing and whirlpool saunas are your thing then this is the ship for you, more like a floating city than cruise liner! We crept past, as unnoticed as a little woodlouse past a giant redwood as we came in sight of our next destination, Southampton's Royal Pier.

In all honesty, if you didn't know what you were looking at you may be mistaken for thinking that Southampton's once splendid pier was little more than an abandoned jetty, used for storing junk and little more. Sadly this is extremely close to the truth, and it's worth delving into the archives to see what this pier used to look like in its heyday. It's an unusual shape, Y-shaped at the head with an extra large sticky-out bit on the eastern side before the head, giving an enormous surface area for buildings and pier furniture.

Southampton port has always been extremely busy – when the Royal Pier was built it was to cater for the huge numbers of steamers bringing visitors and day trippers to and from the city. The 274m (900') pier was constructed from wood by William Betts and the then Princess Victoria (soon to be Mrs Queen Vic) opened the pier on July 8th 1833 with her mother the Duchess of Kent. It cost £25,000 and incorporated a wider pier head at 45 degrees to the main neck and a pair of tollbooths at the entrance. Southampton railway station opened in 1840 and meant that there were more visitors wanting to use the pier. They were taken back and forth by horse-drawn omnibus right on to the pier where steamer traffic from France and the Isle of Wight called regularly.

In 1864 a floating pontoon and bridge were incorporated leading onto the pier in order for the newfangled steam locomotives to deposit their customers right at the dockside, where up to ten steamers at any one time could berth. In 1871 a station was built on the pier as well, on top of a new extension piece below the pier-head. A pavilion, round and almost Turkish in style was built in 1894 hosting dancing, concerts, exhibitions and roller-skating. Those Victorians certainly knew how to have a wild time!

Sadly the heyday of the pier as an entertainment venue was over by the outbreak of World War I and following the war the track and station had so badly deteriorated that they were closed in 1921. For somewhere that witnessed so many great ocean liners coming in and out next door (including the maiden voyage of the ill-fated *Titanic* in 1912) this could have meant the death knell for the pier. It wasn't all bad news though, as boat traffic such as the Red Funnel ferries continued to flourish and the pier was still well used, with the pavilion being extended the following year. The original gatehouse had been grand but typically Victorian, with a clock tower looking remarkably like a crown. Following continued brisk business the gatehouse was demolished and replaced with its current flamboyant Taj Mahal construction opened in 1930, and it was outside this incongruous building that we now found ourselves. I say incongruous only because today it is marooned like an exotic island in a sea of continuous, seething traffic heading on and off the Isle of Wight ferries next door and the busy road just metres away. I wonder how many people pause on their journey to admire this beautiful remnant of a once grand and thriving pier?

The six cast-iron heraldic lions bearing the arms of Southampton dotted around the roof were recycled from the earlier gatehouse, and Edward Cooper Poole spared no quarter in his designs of what was described as a wedding cake! With an enormous pineapple on the top and Corinthian columns all around, inside the hall extended right up into the domed roof – a really grand entrance for your day afloat! We spent a while looking around what is now Kuti's Royal Thai Pier restaurant, and the very pleasant staff allowed us to be as nosey as we liked (it's not often we're given that amount of freedom!). Even today, beautifully and sympathetically decorated, this is a very grand building and must have made those visitors paying a toll to walk on the pier very excited! Today the restaurant affords very good views over the remnants of the pier, from the veranda or the upper floor of the building, although it's not exactly the sort of view you'd want to see as it's not the most attractive pier nowadays.

The demise of the pier and pavilion really began from World War II when they were closed as it was deemed too great a target for the German bombers, being on the edge of the docks. Fortunately the pier wasn't hit and reopened in 1947 with the pavilion being extended and used as a ballroom from 1963 at a cost of £100,000. When the ballroom company ceased trading in 1979 the pier was closed too as it was deemed to be financially unviable to keep the whole property open. The gatehouse became a restaurant in 1986, but any plans for renovating and re-opening the pier were dashed the following year when a huge fire completely destroyed the pavilion and bandstand at the pier head. Another inferno in 1992 consumed most of the pier neck and damaged the conservatory at the back of the gatehouse. Since then there has been very little progress as far as saving the pier is concerned, it's just a forlorn heap of old timber in the water, like an unloved grebe's nest. As we looked out over it from the back of Kuti's (which is as close as we could get because the structure is so dangerous) and had a very sad kiss, we mused over what could be done for the skeleton now.

Used as a storage facility where there is still enough decking, the pier's piles appear to be quite solid (and there are many of them) but aerial views show the decking gone or burnt through in many places and the railings rusted and held together with barbed wire. At the time of me writing this there were huge redevelopment plans afoot, mainly proposing that the pier be demolished and rebuilt, along with houses, shops, bars and restaurants along its length, but the curse of the pier redevelopment seems imminent again, with no one being prepared to foot the bill or take the risk.

We walked back to the Hythe ferry terminal, pausing to look back at the old pier – what would the future hold? Re-development? Demolition? Or just a further unloved decline, marked by gradual collapse into the sea? We really hoped it would be re-development, but only time would tell. Good luck Royal Pier – and Southampton Council, get on with it, the pier won't hang around for ever!

Back on the little friendly ferry to Hythe, we gazed sadly into the water, feeling a little down at the thought of another lost pier. We were cheered up by a group of large silvery sea bass swimming close to the harbour wall and sticking their heads up out of the water, taunting the glum fishermen further down the wall who were peering intently into the water there and seeing nothing! The *Great Expectations* made the trip back to Hythe pier quickly and uneventfully. The rain had stopped and back at the pier-head station we paused to look at the little train – should we travel back in style? We had a little debate about this while a bemused railway chap looked on pityingly. Had we used up enough calories walking the length of the pier earlier?

Oh, why not! We boarded the little time-warp machine and rattled out of the station, swaying gently above the sea back to the quiet floral bedecked station and the car. Back in 1949 we hoped tomorrow would be brighter and more optimistic – we were off to Southsea, playground of my youth!

Sunday did indeed dawn bright, warm and sunny – totally opposite to yesterday's incessant drizzle and we set off for Portsmouth and Southsea in a cheerful and optimistic mood. As a teenager I would often catch the train (an ancient diesel multiple-unit with thick bouncy sprung seats and carriage doors that went clunk) from Eastleigh to Portsmouth Harbour and then either wander around Portsmouth and Southsea or catch the ferry over to the Isle of Wight and spend a day on the beach. Not perhaps your usual teenager behaviour, but I've always liked to buck the trend! Jay also has links with Portsmouth, having done some fire-proofing work inside the impressive Spinnaker Tower that now dominates the skyline of this interesting and historic city.

Old Portsmouth is really where you could spend days and days and days exploring. Here is the dockyard, HMS *Victory*, HMS *Warrior* and the *Mary Rose*, the old city walls and fortifications, a fantastic piece of coastline where you can sit and watch the busy maritime traffic weaving in and out of the Napoleonic Spitbank forts in the channel, and of course, neighbouring Southsea with just as much to offer! I could write a book on the history and sights of this area, but I'll rein my enthusiasm in a tad and concentrate on the piers. That's what we were here for after all!

Clarence Pier and South Parade Pier are technically in Southsea, not Portsmouth, but the two districts sit comfortably side-by-side on the Solent and I recommend parking near the ports and Old Portsmouth and enjoy the walk along the coastline. We parked amid the impressive floral displays near Southsea's Clarence Pier on a very busy, bustling day, even at nine o'clock in the morning and headed towards the seafront, breathing in the tang of the sea and the candyfloss. For breakfast? Now that's something even I've never tried, although I can list chilli con carne on toast and cold curry among things I would have!

As we made our way towards the pier, Jay stopped and pointed at a signpost.

"Victoria Pier? Is that on our list?" he queried.

"Er, no," I hesitantly replied, frantically looking through my paperwork.

"There are just the two piers here, one in front of us and the other further along the coastline to our left. And neither are called Victoria!" I stated defiantly.

We decided to set off in the direction of Old Portsmouth to find out about this mysterious apparition. It wouldn't be the first time we'd found another pier not on the list! On a day like this it was really pleasant walking along the sea front, and I dare say we needed the exercise. The beach is mostly shingle along this part of the coast, so the waves elicit a delightful swish-and-suck as they make landfall. Compared with the water quality back in the 80s (dire and murky, you wouldn't want to fall off a ferry), I couldn't believe quite how clear and vivid the teal water was now, although I still don't think I'd take the plunge here today! We went inland and found ourselves inside the walls and then picked up the signs for Victoria Pier again. We had to slip back through the walls at the Sally Port (remains of Henry VIII's Tudor fortifications and not some exotic lady of the night), and there, just off the promenade was a little pier.

"That's not a pier, it's a jetty!" exclaimed husband-to-be in a disgusted tone.

"Well, hang on," I said defensively (more for the pier than my own integrity!) "It's on legs. There are people fishing and walking along it. It's got lighting on it. Why isn't it a pier? I think it is!"

"Hmmm..." replied the strong and silent one. "Let's see."

We knuckled down for an in-depth investigation and a pier-based disagreement that may end up with handbags at dawn. Bring it on!

Under closer inspection, Victoria Pier is a simply built kinda gal, with three black Victorian-style lamp standards along its length. The sides are edged with basic metal railings, nothing fancy and decorative here, and underfoot, good solid concrete. At the seaward end, the pier turns at right-angles to the right, where there's some rusty grille decking underfoot and steps going down to the water. Tall navigation lights mark the end of the structure (it's a pier!) and while we were there deliberating, found it to be well used by modern-day promenaders and a couple of fishermen. Under our feet it looked like the piles were reinforced concrete, badly weathered in places, revealing the ironwork inside.

Jay still didn't feel it was a pier. I did. We agreed to disagree (I haven't told him that I'm including it here in the book!) and still had a kiss, although my partner-in-pecking was very reluctant, mumbling something that may have sounded like "But it's not a pier!" As I released him from a headlock and unlocked him from the railings, we headed back along the promenade to our original destination, Clarence Pier.

In retrospect, it's been really difficult to find out much information about Victoria Pier (cue Jay cheering), BUT there is reference to it being a popular promenading spot for the locals not long after it opened (a point to me, I feel!). Opened on 16th May 1842 and reached by a little passageway through the old Sally Port walls, Victoria Pier was originally wooden, and named after Queen Victoria – she must have been delighted! It was to provide a boarding point for passengers sailing to the Isle of Wight by steam packet, the water being consistently deep at this point in the channel. It had originally been intended to call the pier King William Pier but Victoria became queen before the pier had been completed, prompting a swift name change!

Shareholders were also very excited by the opening, with thirty of them retiring to the local George Inn where they enjoyed 'dinner and wines of the finest quality'. Having a landing point here was nothing new. Victoria Pier had been built on the site of Powder Bridge, a jetty that allowed gunpowder to be loaded directly from a magazine in the Tudor Square Tower onto ships. Later it was renamed the Beef Stage when the use of the tower changed to that of meat storage! The pier was kept busy with several boats calling every day, and by 1847 passengers were conveyed between the newly opened railway station and the pier by omnibus for onward travel to the very popular destination of the Island (Queen Victoria's residence at Osborne House helped to boost the tourism trade immensely!). Originally the pier was decked with wooden planking, and there are reports of the locals soon taking to the planks to enjoy a (short) promenade along the pier. I have also found that there was another pier built a bit further along the same piece of coastline, stretching some 381m (1,249') into the water and called Royal Albert Pier, opening on 1st June 1847 at a cost of £1,200 but there is little else to relate other than it became part of the Portsmouth Harbour railway station at a later date.

The wooden Victoria Pier was severely damaged in a monstrous storm in 1913. Classed as 'the worst storm for fifty years' it ripped up the decking, carried away the landing stage at the pier head and completely demolished the entrance, leaving very little of the original structure behind. Rebuilt, the pier disappears from newspaper reports until fairly recently, when people have fallen off it and it has become a popular spot for fishing for pollock, mackerel, garfish, wrasse and bream. It was also a popular spot for bathers until the 1970s as a water outfall from the Portsmouth power station made the sea here warm all year round!

Nearly at Clarence Pier and agreeing to disagree over Victoria, we were presented by yet another very different pier! If you didn't know what it was, I really don't think it would cross your mind that you were over the sea and above the waves at all! Clarence Pier runs parallel to the shore, so doesn't go out into the water very far. Nowadays it is decked with concrete and covered with a very popular fun fair and amusements, but if we could go back to 1861 we would have seen a very different construction, and one that would have been more recognisable as a pier, although sideways on in a 'moored' position!

Opened by the Prince and Princess of Wales of the day, and originally known as Southsea Pier, it was quickly a popular destination for boat traffic, accommodating two steamers at a time mooring parallel to the shore. From 1866 to 1873 the pier was served directly by a tramline from the railway station which boosted popularity prompting a fantastic octagonal two-storey pavilion to be built, in glorious Victorian extravagance complete with colonnades and arches. The Prince of Wales (later King Edward VII) came back to the pier in August 1882 to open it and Clarence Pier remained a popular promenade spot and departure point for the Island and beyond. The Prince of Wales made an appearance again in 1896, causing some damage, but fortunately this wasn't the future King of England, instead a steamer of the same name that rammed the pier sideways!

With more boats wanting to use the pier and more demand from the public, a concrete extension was added in 1905 and a café sundeck and concourse hall added in 1932. Old postcards show a busy, teeming spot with a superb crazy wooden big dipper and the pavilion still doing a roaring trade. Wartime brought a particular danger from the air raids. Portsmouth was and still is a hugely important naval base and therefore became a major target for the German bombers, although at least with its sideways nature Clarence Pier wouldn't be sectioned! Huge swathes of Portsmouth were completely razed to the ground during raids, and on 10th January 1941 there occurred the largest raid of the war. Sadly bombs fell on Clarence Pier and it was completely destroyed.

Unable to do anything to repair or rebuild the pier during the war, the beach here was used to build 'Beetle' floats, which were hollow concrete floats to support floating roadways used in the run-up to D-Day. Local opinion at this time was that there were so many vessels in this stretch of water that it looked like you could walk to the Isle of Wight without getting your feet wet! Eventually in 1953 the first pile was driven in to create a new pier, and although it took six years to finish, Clarence Pier (still built sideways) was officially opened on 1st June 1961, exactly one hundred years to the day that the original pier had opened.

The new pier was graced with a striking 18m (60') round tower drawing the eye to the amusement arcade and restaurants below. Behind this frontage the funfair was reinstated, complete with rollercoaster and traditional amusements, and really very little has changed since then. We approached from the Portsmouth end of the pier, and to be honest it does look rather intimidating – a sort of prison camp on legs, with some noticeable security fencing and barbed wire and the building slab-sided and grey. It's only the Skyways roller coaster rattling over the top that shows it's something a bit different. Well, that and the words 'Clarence Pier' in rather large letters on the side!

Inside the barriers, it's a bit like a fairground that's stuck in the 1960s – lots of candy floss, doughnuts and cheap amusements along with dodgems, roundabouts and restaurants. There are also a handful of more modern rides which we'll call 'spin and spew' just so you get some idea of what there is, and of course, the roller coaster. I'm sure when I was at school it was called the Wild Mouse, and there was always someone (who knew someone, who had a friend of a friend) whose cousin had broken their neck/back or died on this very roller coaster as they fell from the top bend in a drunken haze. Ah, those were the days! Looking at it now it looks so basic and tame, very rattly and not very wild at all. I still wouldn't go on it mind, and despite Jay's gentle teasings, I declined the obvious lure of this seaside temptress, elbowed him sharply and looked at what else the pier had to offer!

It's easy to forget this is a pier, partly because of the concrete decking and the fact that the amusements are really sandwiched in so that there's not really an obvious view of the sea (unless you're up on the roller coaster!), but if you spot some letter-sized slots in the floor you could get down on your knees and peer through, because you'll get a little view of the water through these (I know, I tried!). At the far end of the amusements we watched people squealing on the log flume and going green on a ride that looked a bit like the rocking pirate ship. We found a gap and squeezed as far to the back as we could for our kiss, unnoticed by the holidaymakers and trying not to look furtive. Have you ever noticed that the harder you try to look innocent, the guiltier you get? After we had done the deed and had a Southsea snog, we then headed round to the front to have a look at the 50's styling.

The entrance facade is very noticeable, not just because of its holiday-camp uniform bright blue and yellow paintwork but also for the unusual tower, once an amusement arcade and café, now put to alternative use. It looks a *little* like an American diner somewhere on a dusty highway! On the ground floor is the Golden Horseshoe amusement arcade and various fast food concessions including (and here I got very excited) one of the last Wimpy burger restaurants in the country. I think it must just be nostalgia that caused the excitement – descending on a town in my teens having been brought up in the wilds of the countryside, burgers and fast foods were a real novelty to me, and I have to confess that during those initial bilious months of my first pregnancy the Wimpy chicken burger was all I could eat! No wonder the poor girl's like she is!

We paused for a coffee at the appropriately named Coffee Cup café under the tower before heading back on to the promenade to walk further along the coast to Southsea's second pier, glancing back at the front of the pier – it should look dated and kitsch but has managed just to look unusual, bright and cheery!

We didn't get very far past Clarence Pier before we stopped again, this time to watch the hovercraft service from the Isle of Wight roar up onto the beach in a blast of wind, spray and shot-blasting sand. It's the longest running hovercraft service in the world and the fastest way to zip across the Solent. There's something very thrilling and scary almost about this rubber-skirted dragon whirling up right in front of you, and quite unlike anything else you can experience at a ferry port!

We watched the hovercraft depart, scraped the sand from our faces (it does leave you with lovely soft skin!) then carried on along the wide pavement, past very English bowling greens and the amazing construction that is Henry VIII's Southsea Castle. This part of Southsea is so much quieter and genteel than the area around Clarence Pier and there are lots of chances here to relax and unwind, savouring the sights, smells and sounds around you. We carried on past the D-Day museum and coaches disgorging their (mostly polyester-clad) eager clients before we got to the Pyramids Sports Centre, a quirky and stunning piece of modern architecture housing swimming pools, flumes and various other ways to tone and hone your body!

Finally we were back on the seafront, a wide shingle slant of beach sliding down into the brilliant blue sea, where a roll on-roll off Red Funnel ferry slid past under the wise-eyed gaze of the elderly day-trippers sat in a beach shelter. On the opposite side of the road were some glorious floral displays so redolent of pre- and post-war Britain when *everyone* had a seaside holiday in this country and appreciated the simpler pleasures in life!

And there, at the end of this wide promenade, under simple fairy lights and grand dark-blue lamp standards sporting two very pretty lights was the gleaming pier – shining silver and bright, tempting and alluring in the summer sunshine!

We cranked up our pace and fairly sped along the remainder of the promenade to get to the pier. Were we *that* desperate for another kiss? There's no keeping us down! The entrance rather lets the grandness of this pier down a little – it's there, but it just seems to have been swamped a little by the addition of a modern canopy strung between two older and more imperial pineapple-topped kiosks. On the opposite side of the road stands a beautiful, but sadly derelict Edwardian mansion, Savoy Court. It is a perfect example of what the Edwardian architect was trying to achieve – perfect lines, proportion and organisation and was built in 1905 as private apartments for retired naval officers but later incorporated a café and ballroom and a disco/nightclub.

The pier originally pre-dated Savoy Court and was designed by R. Gale of Blackburn and built by those expert constructors Head Wrightson and Co from Stockton-on-Tees (also responsible for Ramsgate, St. Leonards, Herne Bay, Skegness, Cleethorpes and Queens on the Isle of Man – they knew what they were doing when it came to running up a seaside pier!). Work started in 1875 and involved a steam hammer mounted on a barge that was used for driving the piles into the seabed. It was opened on July 26th

1879 by Prince Edward of Saxe-Weimar, the General Officer Commanding of the Southern District of the British Army (short, natty titles were not really fashionable then!). It operated successfully with up to four steamers an hour calling at the jetties at the end of the pier until a serious fire on July 19th 1904 necessitated a complete rebuild.

The burnt-out structure was purchased by Portsmouth Corporation and a new pier was designed by local entrepreneur G. E. Smith as predominantly a pleasure pier rather than a landing jetty and was operational on August 12th 1908. The pier was 183m (600') long and used a new, innovative material for the decking instead of wood – concrete!

The rest of the pier structure was fairly standard – cast-iron screw piles, cast-iron columns braced by iron railway rails and latticed girders to provide bracing strength. On top of the basic pier at the landward end there was a large pavilion. It had two large halls, one used as a theatre for 1200 people, the other was a café by day and a dance hall by night. There were wind screens along the length of the pier, a common feature when people would spend all day on the pier in a quintessentially stripy deckchair and didn't fancy being blasted by a marine gale! Behind the main pavilion was a smaller building with a bar and lounge. The pier then narrowed before opening out again for the landing stage and bandstand, which had seating all around it. This provided musical entertainment not only for those seating close by but also for those waiting to board the next steamer.

Up until World War II the pier thrived as Portsmouth and Southsea had continued to expand and also become popular seaside resorts. In 1939 the inevitable sectioning occurred, with the military commissioning the seaward end as a depot. Unusually the landward pavilion stayed open to the public for dancing, except during July and August in 1940 when it was felt there was a real threat of German invasion, and in 1944 when it was used as part of the preparations for D-Day. Breach fixed and having escaped any damage from the bombing the pier continued to provide popular holiday entertainment for holidaymakers.

In 1967, just after another change of ownership there was a fire that destroyed much of the main pavilion, it was subsequently removed and rebuilt, the new incarnation offering more bars and contemporary entertainment. On June 11th 1974 the director Ken Russell was filming the rock opera *Tommy* in the theatre. It's thought a spotlight set light to some curtains, and it wasn't long before the blaze was out of control (if you watch the 'Holiday Camp scene', there are some scenes where smoke can be seen drifting in front of the camera – it's a real fire!). Over one hundred firemen battled the blaze, but a combination of strong winds and dry timber meant they had a real fight on their hands and the fire continued well into the night. Russell, never one to miss an opportunity, filmed the ensuing blaze and used a shot of the pavilion ablaze in the scenes of the destruction of Tommy's holiday camp. This time it wasn't just the pavilion that had been destroyed, as much of the underlying infrastructure also needed replacing.

Another rebuild took place, costing in excess of £500,000 with the deck replaced on castellated steel beams and the pavilion built as a faithful copy of the previous one – a real phoenix rising up from the ashes! The new pavilion incorporated two large entertainment areas, arcade and cafeteria and a covered walkway on the Portsmouth side. In February 2000 there was yet another fire at the end of the main building, which saw the bar destroyed. The buildings at the end of the pier were subsequently demolished and replaced by outdoor fairground rides. Some remedial work was also carried out in 2001 and 2002 on renewing cross-bracing on the pier supports and main support girders at a cost of around £100,000. There have been a number of changes of owner over the years too, and it looked like it was a bit unloved on our visit, another pier that looked gorgeous from a distance but could do with a serious visit from Mr P and his paintbrush (I'm sure he'd give a competitive quote under the circumstances, and he does a brilliant job!).

We climbed the front steps between the pineapples and decided that we needed sustenance and a hot liquid beverage before taking in the rest of the pier's delights (more likely the reason behind that uncharacteristic rush to the get here!). A hot cup of coffee and a tray of lukewarm cheesy chips later and we stepped out of the café and onto the broad concrete walkway to walk up the pier for a cheesy-chips-and-coffee kiss, not the best combination if you're going to up close and personal, which might be why it doesn't appear as a flavouring for lip balm...

The railings are a shiny silver to match the roof and curve pleasingly outwards. As we'd seen elsewhere the railings make up the back of seating that stretched most of the way round, also in silver, but where there were no benches we could see the decorative floral patterned wrought-iron panels. Sadly the rails, benches and panels have all seen better days and there was a lot of corrosion and rot evident with some bits missing completely. Once we got to the end of the pavilion the large open space was peppered with rides and attractions – a crazy golf course, hook-a-duck, swing boats, a bouncy castle and some intriguing kayaks that go round and round a small water circuit a bit like giant drainpipes.

We made our way to the end of the pier and went through a little wrought-iron gate (also painted silver) and down some steps onto the old landing stage. It is set lower than the level of the main pier and decked in wooden planking and metal grids and we found it to be an awful lot quieter than the main pier too, perhaps because its lower position insulates it from the world upstairs! We celebrated our end of the pier kiss surrounded by fishermen, fishing debris and old seaweed, and more psychedelically by an over-cheerful green octopus that bobbed and waved at us with a tentacle over the top of his bouncy fun castle on the main pier – very random and just a touch unsettling!

We strolled back up the steps and round the back of the Krazy Kayaks, before making our way towards the covered walkway. Looking from the outside to just be a corridor to the front of the pier, once inside we'd gone down Alice's rabbit hole to the best bit of the pier! Inside the unremarkable blue doors we found an antiques market in full swing – and discovered it's the only pier with a working barber on it too! There are swanky gold pillars, a draped fabric ceiling and a light airy feel that was a very pleasant surprise. We lingered over old books and trinkets for ages, emerging refreshed and revitalised at the front of the pier once again (although without a new hairdo), mindful of the pier's parting shot – 'please leave these facilities in a quiet and orderly manner' says the sign on the door, so we went out one behind the other, didn't push and left the facilities behind us!

Back on the promenade, we both decided that the silver siren was in need of a big makeover, but in fairness, the pier is still a popular venue, enjoyed by young and old alike, so hopefully she'll get the facelift she needs very soon – with that fantastic view and sparkly silver pavilion roof it would really make the difference. As we walked back past all the amazing sights Southsea had to offer, we paused and giggled at one that hadn't been there on the way to the pier. There on the shingle beach catching the rays, skirts hoisted thigh-high were two elderly beach babes, not a day under eighty, each of them! The biggest mystery of all is how they managed to get that far out onto the pebbly beach with their wheeled walking frames... worthy of a caption competition, surely?!

It had been yet another weekend of interesting piers, and depending on your viewpoint, one more than expected, but it's always worth trying to persuade one's recalcitrant love that you are on a structure you think is a pier, even if it's only to have another kiss!

CHAPTER 18

A Pierfectly Wonderful Weekend
(Or - Isle of Wight Wonders!)

Inspired by our Hampshire travels, we decided it was high time to take the plunge and venture overseas again – strangely going to the Isle of Wight feels as exotic and distant as going to the Isle of Man, requiring real military planning to co-ordinate and book the ferry. In reality it's just a couple of clicks on the wonderful world wide web and we were booked, but maybe I have an overactive imagination!

And so, just a couple of weeks since we had last visited, we were parked next to Southampton Pier's fantastic gatehouse once more, this time waiting, bright-eyed and bushy-tailed (well, we would be after a coffee) for the Red Funnel Ferry over the Solent to Cowes at silly o'clock in the morning. As the ferry pulled out we got a really good look at Royal Pier from the deck, and it really was a sad sight. The rot and decay was really visible here, and it was easy to pick out the circle of charred ash and timber where the pavilion had once been. Propped on the side was a rusted embarkation tunnel, propped up near holes in the concrete, nesting gulls and scrubby plant life. From this viewpoint, the future doesn't look very rosy at all, but we felt it should be restored – it would be an excellent tourist attraction as a viewpoint for watching shipping go in and out of the harbour.

As the ship made its way into the busy shipping channel we were joined at the side by a black dog that I swear was a relative of Boogie, the dog with more character than a Hollywood blockbuster, as found amongst the pages of *500 Mile Walkies* and other excellent tomes by Mark Wallington. The Boogie lookalike stuck his head over the side and calculated whether it was possible to leap on a passing cormorant without getting wet, decided it was too much like hard work and just barked furiously at it instead!

We got a ferry's-eye view of Hythe Pier again too (leaving the ferry bobbing precariously in our wake), but then the drizzle came back and we headed inside – we wanted a pier-filled weekend, not Solent induced exposure! Being a reasonably small island and easily reached from many south coast ports, the Isle of Wight was a popular place to visit by boat. As seaside holidays became increasingly popular, it was an exotic, unspoilt place to go to. However, it was also a tricky place to try and get ashore from your launch, and in some places richer voyagers had to be carried away from the water on the shoulders of a porter. Nowadays there are umpteen different ways to get to there – light aircraft, hovercraft, SeaCat, vehicular ferry or private yacht (and probably even bathtub if you were so inclined) to various different ports. Although we were docking at Cowes, we were going to be starting our island pier-kissing with a short journey to Ryde, the birthplace of British piers.

Until the ferry docks, I have you as a captive reader for a few more minutes – just long enough for a history lesson! In many articles and in most people's minds, piers are classed as being Victorian inventions, when in actual fact Ryde Pier was built in 1814, predating Victoria as monarch by twenty-three years. In that period of time there was King William IV, King George IV and preceding him, King George III (he of the madness and very long film), who reigned until 1820. If you cast your mind back to the Weymouth piers, he was also the pioneer of seaside holidays and drinking funny water, so in many ways it seems apt that the first pleasure pier was built during his reign in order to boost the tourist industry on the island. As we've just now docked at East Cowes, I shall spare you any more, although you do now need to jump in the back of the car so that we can disembark and carry on our journey!

I could spend pages waxing lyrical about the Isle of Wight, but I'll save you the sentiment, but will just say that I LOVE IT! Some people say that the Island got stuck in the 1950s, but when you look at the geography of the place, it would be very difficult to modernise and expand too much, and so the place does have a certain unspoilt, old-world quality. Please don't use the phrase olde-worlde, twee or quaint or I'll have to do something unpleasant to you – and to any sceptics, I suggest you go and visit. Leave your preconceptions, watch and trappings of the hectic daily life behind and relax and soak up island life (I should also mention that it's impossible to drive at pace here, there are enough speed cameras to populate a large city, and if you get up to 40 mph there'll be a bend, a set of traffic lights and a flock of cyclists to slow you down again!). For example, coming ashore at East Cowes, home of Queen Vic's retreat, Osborne House, the town gives all the impression of being a massive town as on the mainland. Leave the ferry terminal, drive up the road... and, oh! You're on a leafy winding lane! And such are the delights of the place. With nowhere being very far away, the journey to Ryde took around twenty minutes, and would have taken less, but I was looking out for red squirrels. I saw one, but sadly it was pancake-shaped and flat on the road surface – I'll keep looking!

Everywhere on the Island is quiet and full of amazing views, interesting architecture, historical knick-knacks, captivating beauty and unique quirkiness – Ryde has a postcard museum, a castle that's really a house, an ice-hockey team, five carnivals a year (one reputed to be the oldest in Britain) and a hovercraft station! It also has a delightful few streets full of antiques shops and cafés, and as you descend the hill, burst out onto a lovely promenade, decorated with flowers, edged by an interesting mix of buildings and ornate, decorative street lamps (were ugly buildings outlawed here?).

It's a wide entrance 'apron' from the impressive seafront, with pedestrian and car visitors going up the left-hand side of the pier and the railway sweeping in from the right before all running parallel out to sea. Ryde pier is the fourth longest in the country, unique in being three piers in one and also the oldest – it is also still used for its original purpose today, and there aren't many that have managed to continue as a viably commercial enterprise for so many years! The vehicular and pedestrian section is wide wooden decking that runs with the length of the pier. There's a painted pedestrian walkway to the right of this section and cars go on the seaward side – this seems a bit hairy in theory, but seems OK as long as you all keep your wits about you! Having given you all those juicy 'unique' selling points, we'll need to tell you more about this Grand Aunt of all piers!

Ryde was one of the places where posh visitors had to be carried ashore and then traipse across the half a mile sand to shore, and it was proposed in 1810 that an Act be put before Parliament for a pier in order to attract rich and fashionable visitors who could come ashore in comfort – much better than wet sand in your crinolines! The Parliamentary Act was passed in 1812 and a simple pier was designed by John Kent of Southampton. The foundation stone was laid on 29th June 1813 and opened on 26th July 1814. To begin with the pier was essentially a 3.6m (12') wide wooden jetty that ran 530m (1,740') out to sea.

This newfangled pier idea proved a fantastic hit (and as we've seen was copied extensively around the country very quickly!) and in 1824 it was extended to 622m (2,040'), then in 1833 to 686m (2,250') as visiting shipping became more frequent and also bigger and of deeper draught. Pedestrians and horse-drawn transport still shared the decking to the pier head, which was also extended in 1824 to accommodate visitors but had to be extended again in the 1850s. As with all piers there were tolls to use it, so passengers embarking or disembarking would have to pay 3d each, those wishing to ride a horse up and down the pier had to pay 4d and it was one shilling to take a four-wheeled carriage (quite a sum in those days) onto the pier. For those wishing to show off their best clothes and make a statement amongst the rich and influential, it cost 2d to promenade – the Georgian equivalent of a platform ticket!

By the 1860s it was obvious that a separate pier was going to be needed for increased luggage-carrying back and forth, as the popularity of the pier and the Isle of Wight increased, so a second pier was constructed parallel to the first, and a railed, horse-drawn tramway installed on it. This opened on 29th August 1864 and early postcards show this tramway, complete with trams and luggage carts and small wooden ticket booths at the pier head, simple plain railings and gas lamps (although these weren't installed along the length of the pier until March 1872 (I love the detective skills needed to try and pinpoint when these old photographs were taken!). The pier entrance was upgraded and remodelled in 1868 looking more like a Victorian park entrance than a pier, with octagonal buildings linked by turnstiles and gates and interspersed with Doric columns – very grand, but all part of the promenading experience!

Promenading on Ryde Pier wasn't just about showing off your finery in public, there were also plenty of things to see and do. The bay and water surrounding the pier were always teeming with fishing boats and pleasure craft, from steamers down to rowing boats. There were swimming platforms and slipways along the side of the pier and at the pier head, refreshment stalls and rooms (fancy a hot drink of Oxo anyone?!), slot machines and a weighing machine and benches and shelters along the length. Other diversions included the fantastic opportunity to watch torpedo experiments being carried out! On 27th August 1874 people watched one such experiment carried out from the *Oberon*, which blew up a mine moored just 24m (80') away from it. The local newspaper reported that torpedo successfully exploded the mine and caused 'devastation among fishes scarcely as great as the previous experiment' and that things on board the ship were disarranged but only a few plates broken. Two sheep and seven rabbits were also uninjured. Hmm... the mind boggles!

It wasn't long before the horse-drawn tramway was felt to be outdated and not suited for purpose. Work began on a third pier in 1877 to provide a direct rail link onto the pier. This option wasn't without its sceptics and various options were bandied about before settling on a proper railway. The steam railway was jointly owned by the London and Brighton and South Coast Railway Company and the London and South West Railway and would provide connecting transport with their steamer services back to Portsmouth. Further track from St. John's Road to Ventnor and Cowes was owned by the Isle of Wight Railway and the Isle of Wight Central Railway, and the rail pier opened on 12th July 1880. It had a scissors crossover to allow access to all platforms and once off the pier, the railway descended into a tunnel under the town and off to other island delights!

In 1885 it was felt that the tramway pier needed updating too – proposals for a steam or gas powered tramway floundered when gravel-filled carriages run onto the pier to test whether it could cope with the extra weight caused the piles to start sinking into the mud! An electric tramway was poo-pooed as being a ridiculous concept that would never work, but was eventually installed as a third-rail system, which opened in 1886 and ran quite successfully until 1927 when it was replaced by petrol-driven transport that lasted until 1969.

Work also started at around the same time to replace the old wooden piles along the length of the pier with smart new cast-iron ones, but at the shoreward end engineers ran into trouble from an unusual source. When they ran into difficulties driving the new piles into the mud, excavation uncovered several large tree trunks some 3m (10') below the surface. With similar trunks having been found further along the coast (and the Victorians being very interested in ancient history at this point), it was thought that they had once been part of an prehistoric forest, from a time preceding the sea's breaching of the River Solent or from when the sea was much further away!

In 1895 a concert pavilion was opened at the pier head and the head was remodelled in concrete in the 1930s. During World War II the pier was modified for use by the military, which made good any adaptations and the pier continued providing an access point to the island after the war. The pavilion became a ballroom but owing to the poor condition of the pier-head structure, had to be demolished in 1971. If you look over the edge of the modern car park extension today (not that far over! No need to have someone hold your ankles!) you can see some of the old original decaying piles.

Following nationalisation of the railways in 1948 and the sweeping Beeching cuts of the 60s, the section of line between Shanklin and Ventnor was closed in April 1966 and then steam services were withdrawn from the pier on 17th September of the same year. The whole railway line was shut in the December. However, the death knell that had seen the demise of many other little railways across the country at the same time was not to sound here. The pier-head station was rebuilt and the line upgraded and given a third-rail electrical supply. Following improvements, the tunnel under Ryde was now 23cm (10") too low for conventional locomotives and carriages to be used so when it reopened in March 1967, 1920's and 30's rolling stock from the London underground was used! This overground underground element has proved a unique selling point (and tourist attraction) for this little railway, and although gradually replaced by more 'modern' 1960's stock, remains essentially the same.

In 1969 the tramway pier – due to structural conditions and changing requirements – was finally closed and the structure partly removed, leaving the disused pier between the railway and promenade piers. This has proven to be really useful and was used as a temporary diversion route for pedestrians (obviously with some decking put back on) after a ship crashed into the western side of the pier in 1974. The whole pier was granted Grade II listed status in 1976 and a five-year re-planking programme was finished in December of that year. In 1980 a modern waiting area was built, using some of the original buildings but essentially replacing the original Victorian waiting rooms which had now served their purpose.

Having been up and running for nearly two hundred years, I'm really aware that there's an incredible amount of history that I haven't mentioned, even though I'd love to – I think that may be yet *another* book if that was the case, but I apologise if there's something you were hoping to read and I've not included it! I do think it's worth mentioning Ryde's other pier though. Just a few hundred metres to the east and opened in 1864, the Victoria Pier was built in order to promote the Stokes Bay Pier and Railway Company who operated a rival ferry running from Gosport (opposite Portsmouth).

It quickly became a pleasure pier and had public swimming baths at the pier head and a swimming platform at the landward end in 1875. By 1885 the 'ozone iodised' baths (strongly recommended for gout, rheumatism and liver complaints, and probably totally disgusting!) had become extremely popular, frequented by more than a thousand people in just nine months. However, by the outbreak of World War I, Victoria Pier had become increasingly derelict and unloved and was considered such a hazard that in 1916, an order for its demolition was granted by the Government, and by 1920 it was gone. For some years afterwards it was possible to see the remains of the rotten piles at very low tide, but now it seems that even these traces of this Victorian pier have been consigned to memory alone.

And so, after that extremely potted history of such an interesting pier, we carried on walking along Ryde Pier, enjoying the wide open nature of the pedestrian decking and looking to our right to the old tramway pier and, further away, the railway where the quaint London underground trains echoingly rattled their way back and forth. The old tramway pier really doesn't seem that wide when viewed today. It affords a good view of the piles of rail and tram piers, the former solid and well braced, the latter looking very spindly in comparison, with spider-web cross bracing and an unhealthy dose of corrosion all over. The railway pier has standard functional railings, but the pedestrian and vehicular pier has some stunning ornate wrought-ironwork railings along the complete length, Victorian ovals and curls and painted a sombre black throughout – this is a business pier not a jolly 'kiss-me-quick' frivolity!

The shelters and benches that are spotted at occasional points along the considerable length are also worth getting run over to have a closer look at. Very Victorian in style and simply painted in black and white, it's the wrought-iron sea serpents that support the roof that are totally gorgeous and oozing style and quality workmanship. As I delved into various sources for research on this pier, I discovered that the Historic Ryde Society use this serpent as their logo, and have called him Cyril.

Once on the pier head we looked back along the old tramway – it looks much wider end on, and sadly the iron-work is more corroded here than at the landward end. It's a bit of a mishmash here – no neat planking and Edwardian refreshments and slot-machines, instead, lots of car-parking, street furniture and directions to the railway station ferry and catamaran services.

The pavilion building with its two discreet domes is white and functional, the railway station looks a bit ramshackle from the pier, wooden shingles and a bit of plywood and a mossy asbestos-sheeting roof. All said and done, it has to be remembered that this IS a fully-functioning commercial pier, with the amusements these days limited to a stiff walk up the deck and watching proceedings out at sea (or the trains or hovercrafts, which come ashore next to the landward end of the pier). There is a concession at the entrance to the pier, nattily called Platform Fun, which sells gifts, souvenirs, papers and refreshments for the excited traveller, but long gone are the Oxo stalls and ice-cream sellers of the past. We did wonder if it wasn't lacking a bit in this department, the pier appearing a little bleak and empty apart from rushing commuters and travellers, but if you know about the history it's still a fascinating destination – how about some information boards along the length that celebrate the history of the pier?

We wove our way between the parked cars (are there many piers with a car park at the end? Or speed humps, for that matter!), found a quiet corner near the berthed catamaran for a sheltered, and if I'm honest, a deeply passionate kiss – apologies for any passengers on the SeaCat who were unable to get away from that sight! (Do you know who we are?!) On our way back we marvelled again at the Cyrils on the shelters and the remaining piles and struts from the old pavilion ballroom extension, demolished in 1971. Despite the slightly gloomy weather, the sea here was still a wonderful petrol-green, the temperature mild and the pier really busy, a testament to the clear-thinking entrepreneurs who decided Ryde should have a pier to preserve the dignity of those rich visitors back in the early 1800s.

We made our way back over the wide esplanade and up Union Street to the car, pausing to look in antique shop windows and the Donald McGill postcard museum (he of the very popular saucy postcards produced from 1904-1962), before setting off for Seaview. Seaview? I hear you cry, but there's no pier there! Well, having established myself as being contentious when it comes to defining piers, and being the one who's had to do research for this jolly jaunt, I wanted to have a look round the island at old pier sites and at structures that *might*, if you squint and had an open mind, be classed as piers.

Seaview is only three miles away from Ryde, and an absolutely gorgeous Edwardian maritime town with views out across the Solent. Back in 1870 the population had grown to a heady three thousand, and the local squire wanted to develop the place into a fashionable resort, so decided to build a (principally) promenading pier. Finished in 1881, the Seaview pier was nearly 5m (15') wide and 305m (1,000') long, but of a construction that we've not come across before. For Seaview was a chain pier, essentially a suspension bridge to nowhere, and there were only two others in the country at Brighton and Leith, Scotland. Frank Caws, son of a local landowner, was an engineer and designed the four towers, from which hung the deck on tensioned cables. At the pier head was a pavilion and a crane, at the shore end a piermaster's building and a waiting room.

By the end of the year over 16,000 people had used the pier, including the Prince and Princess of Wales, who came to admire the beauty of it (and hopefully weren't worried about the way it swayed as you walked along it!). It really was a stunning piece of architecture, the towers more like ornate pylons, with the swag of chains between and approached by a wide driveway and two little squat gatehouses. The pier was not visited as much as people had hoped, but still turned a profit, with the pier head being expanded a couple of times and electric lights added in 1905. The pier company bought its own steamer in 1914, but with the outbreak of World War One the ship was commissioned for war work and steamers never returned to the pier. A visitor in 1930 had to pay a 3d toll to walk along it and described it as 'unique and undeniably handsome'.

After World War II it was seriously in need of repair but still regarded as being the centrepiece of the beach, but despite being listed as a building of special architectural and historical interest in November 1950, the following month saw the worst storms for forty-five years. On 28th December 1950

6m (20') high waves and 70 mph winds battered the coast and the pier. The poor pier could not withstand the onslaught and was totally destroyed. Today the town of Seaview looks out over the rocky beach from a sweet seafront road edged with a little wall, and sadly no remnant of the chain pier other than old postcards and holiday memories, but it's a lovely place to stop, stretch your legs and savour refreshments from one of the Island's many cafes!

Just four and a bit miles away from Seaview, Bembridge had a 'real' pier built in 1878, narrow and 76m (250') long, to provide access to and from the paddle steamers and boats that brought passengers into the newly dredged harbour. Sadly, services lessened after World War One when most people chose to use the Ryde ferry and railway rather than Bembridge which was now inaccessible unless the tide was high. By 1924 the ferry service had ceased and just four years later, the pier was demolished.

However, Bembridge also has a lifeboat pier, which is open to the public three days a week (see, there's the pleasure and tourism element!). With a lifeboat based here since 1867, the pier and all-weather station was built in 1922 by the RNLI, also 76m (250') long that stretched into deeper water, avoiding shallow ledges and meant that the lifeboat could be launched whatever the state of the tide. It was so efficient that lifeboat stations at Ryde, Brightstone and Brooke were shut. In 2008 the Bembridge lifeboats (there are two!) were launched 57 times and rescued 69 people – over half of these call-outs took place in the dark. As we arrived at the lovely sheltered harbour and made our way towards the lifeboat station, it became clear that all was not as it should be! The old lifeboat station, a curved-roof hen shed with a launching ramp wasn't exactly as we'd been expecting to see it – instead, there was a lovely new concrete jetty, ending with a platform on stilts where work was being carried out on building a brand new, sparkling lifeboat station fit for the twenty-first century and beyond.

Unfortunately the original pier, built from concrete was no longer strong enough to carry the larger modern 28-tonne Tyne class lifeboat. The facilities for the lifeboat-men are not really large enough and concrete rot has meant that there is a real risk of the pier, slipway and lifeboat house falling into the sea during the next winter storm. After launching (appropriate use of the word) a £10 million campaign, the old pier was demolished and work begun on the new station, which would take the Bembridge lifeboat (updated to a bigger, wider and heavier Tamar class boat) and crew into the twenty-first century. I'm not sure if I've become addicted to piers or kisses (and I'm not going to make my mind up *just* yet) but I was a bit disappointed not to be able to explore another pier and have another marine-inspired kiss, but never mind – it's another pier to aim to come back to on our revisit tour in the future!

Back at the car and trundling at a quite frankly pedestrian pace down winding lanes overhanging with lush hedgerows and bordered by thatched cottages, we ended up at Sandown, pausing just long enough to throw our luggage into the guesthouse, before hitting the road again. We were perfectly aware that Sandown has a fantastic pier that we still needed to explore, but we chose to eschew its delights and journey further across the island to the site of another of the Island's piers, sadly now missing.

Our port of call was Ventnor, and the journey there a twisting, turning, roller-coaster along the little roads – it's only six miles but everywhere you go here is relatively close and yet still feels like an adventure to get there! Ventnor was a Victorian resort and nestles into the protective side of St. Boniface Down, the highest point on the island. There are breathtaking views out to sea as the road starts to zigzag down into the town – we were hard heroes from the mainland and chose to park part-way down the hill and walk the rest, taking in the subtropical warmth this spot basks in, created by its sheltered position – great if you're an orchid! It is worth the walk though, down past the gorgeous Winter Gardens (fine Art Deco design from the late 1930s) and past Cascade Gardens (a Victorian rockery with attitude) where the natural spring water runs down through attractive landscaping under the viaduct down to the sea.

There at the bottom of the hill in the relatively new Ventnor Haven, is a new pier, that of the Fishery, where you can buy crab, shellfish, sea bass, lobster – in fact whatever the owner has caught and landed that day – heaven! Also at the bottom of the hill is a novelty paddling pool, containing a raised Isle of Wight that provides entertainment for the children in the summer. Nowadays there is an attractive circular bandstand (that looks a bit like a windmill wearing a skirt) where the entrance to Ventnor Pier used to be. There have been several incarnations of pier here (and indeed on more than one site), with the original idea to have two in the town, although something has conspired against the town every time one has been completed. The Western Pier was in use before it was finished (at 79m or 260' long) and steamers berthed at high tide. However, the PS *Chancellor* berthed one day as the tide was falling, subsequently grounded and she flooded on the next tide. The Western Pier ceased to be used...

The Eastern Pier was finished by March 1864 and longer than intended (I'm not sure how that happens...) but a series of huge storms that winter, something Ventnor is prone to, destroyed both piers. That'll be back to the drawing board then?

A replacement Western Pier opened on 5th August 1872 and was 61m (200') long. Work continued and it grew to 146m (478') but without a pier head because money ran out! Work was finally finished in July of 1881, but in November of that year a very violent storm hit and 12m (40') of the pier neck and the brand new pier head were swept away. You would have thought that to have a pier that took ten years to build and then be destroyed after only ten weeks being open would have deterred the Ventnorians, but no! Despite some grumbling about the total folly of building another pier, the construction of pier number three began in late 1885 and was open by July 1887. It had a horseshoe-shaped pier head (apparently for luck), and was an impressive 198m (650') long.

A survey in 1948 condemned all but a few piles, but the Ministry of Defence agreed to pay 90% of this having used it during war time, and so the council stumped up the remaining £15,000 and the pier was rebuilt, all bright and shining, 208m (683') long, welded steel and glass shelters glittering in the sun. The pier in this incarnation managed to last relatively unscathed, but winter storms, fewer tourists during the 1970s and no money for repairs saw the landing stage eventually demolished in 1975 and the pier eventually closed in 1981.

A fire in 1985 destroyed much of the shore end of the pier and there ensued a squabble over compensation and how much re-building would cost. By 1988 this had risen to over £800,000 and in 1993 it was decided that the pier would have to go and it was demolished at a cost of nearly £250,000. Ventnor Pier didn't go without a fight though, as the rig used to take it apart broke free during a storm and everyone on board had to be rescued by helicopter.

So far, apart from the Fishery, there are no plans for a new pier here in Ventnor, and we noticed that the Fishery is A) very short, B) protected by a nice new rip-rap harbour, safe from the storms and C) is solidly perched on concrete legs! I'm convinced this is another pier but my generally genial travelling companion wasn't feeling very well and wasn't up for another tedious debate. There's one that we'll have to leave for another day. We looked at the spot where the ill-fated piers had been and he asked if I minded that we go to look for a chemists to purchase some pain-relieving medication. Asked so nicely, I didn't push for a kiss at the Fishery. I know what would have happened if we had, it wouldn't have just been a kiss... Oy! No giggling at the back! I would have demanded seafood too! Honestly, you can't get the type of reader you used to!

We ambled back up the hill, found an obliging chemist and drove back to Sandown, where we had an assignation on the pier – only this time it was with newspaper reporter for the *Isle of Wight County Press*, Emily Pearce. Sandown Bay is quite breezy but apparently a fairly sheltered spot. To the east are high chalk cliffs, to the west high sandy cliffs, and the pier sits snugly in between these, right in the middle of a fantastic beach, pale smooth sand speckled with families and holidaymakers. Along the prom it's not a promising start, as we negotiated a few hordes of screaming youths – and even the deckchairs have hoodies...

From the beach, the Sandown's Culver Pier looks quite spidery, spindly and insubstantial in the middle, like the child of Dali and a 70's rock album sleeve. The fragile central legs carry the neck up to a boating jetty of very different character, a solid, squat concrete construction standing in the blue-green water. There also seemed to be a few interesting things on the deck that warranted further exploration! There has been a pier at Sandown since 1879, some nineteen years since the idea was first mooted. The Sandown Pier Company had built a pier just 110m (360') long (engineered by W. Binne) before running out of money, but at least Victorian promenaders had somewhere to go! The Sandown Pier Extension Company took over ownership in 1887, under the auspices of Richard Webster, whose father had done much to develop the town as a tourist resort.

By 1895 the pier had been extended to 267m (875'), complete with a domed pavilion. Amid much flag waving, bedecked decking and a regatta, the pier opened again on 17th September 1895. Bathing was allowed at the pier head and there were always a flotilla of bathing machines in use, something that inspired Lewis Carroll to mention when he wrote *The Hunting of the Snark*. Paddle steamers also visited regularly, and did so until the First World War. During the war, Richard Webster, Lord Alvestone, died and the council bought the pier for £2,500. The pavilion was then enlarged and the Sandown Prize Band, one of the best in the country, often played here. Bathing machines were only used as changing cubicles now and the continental method of using bathing tents was being adopted instead!

In 1933 a new thousand-seat theatre pavilion was built at the pier-head end, which opened on 23rd October 1934 by Admiral of the Fleet Lord Jellicoe. Used as a ballroom, trade was brisk, provided by many steamers including the PS *Sandown* from 1934. I managed to find a picture of this lovely (and quite large ship) at the pier head in August 1939, a picture of tranquillity and happiness – but in only months, things would be very different for both the pier and the paddle steamer. In 1940 the pier was sectioned and partly demolished. The PS *Sandown* commissioned as a minesweeper with the 10th Minesweeping Flotilla. She was later one of the ships used in the evacuation from Dunkirk and saved around 3000 men's lives.

Following sectioning and wartime neglect, the pier needed some post-war TLC, especially the landing stage. In 1954 the landing stage was redeveloped in its current two-deck incarnation from concrete, something durable that meant ships could moor no matter what the state of the tide. Bucket and spade holidays were hugely popular after the war and Sandown often held the English sunshine record! This meant that the town and pier were well frequented and business was brisk. It also received royal visitors in 1965 when Queen Elizabeth II, Prince Philip and Lord Louis Mountbatten toured the island, and boarded the Royal Barge moored at the end of the pier.

In 1968 the pier needed some serious maintenance. The pier-head pavilion had suffered some fire damage and was subsequently pulled down, with a new pavilion built at the landward end, meaning theatre goers no longer had to brave the elements to watch a show, especially in winter! Work started in 1971 on replacing the iron piles at the landward end with concrete ones, and Lord Mountbatten (who was also the Lord Lieutenant of the Isle of Wight) reopened the pier on 22nd July 1973. The theatre was now the largest on the island, and up until its sad closure twenty-six years later hosted many famous faces on the stage. In 1986 the pier was bought by Sandown Pier Limited, who leased the theatre to the council for a ten-year period after carrying out nearly half a million pounds of refurbishment work to it. On the August Bank Holiday in 1989 the theatre suffered a serious fire, causing £2 million worth of damage. The theatre opened again on 18th June

1990, although the landward end was back in business within thirty hours of the blaze!

Now still popular, visited by pleasure boats and a haven for fishermen (and spider crabs underneath) we were heading to explore the delights of Culver Pier and we reached it by way of some gorgeous formal planted beds, round the front of the Royal Pier Hotel (I'd watch that if I were you, hotels with that name have a habit of catching fire!), and down some steps to the entrance. It's a fairly standard pier entrance – advertising the delights inside. Could we really expect a whole day's fun in one? Would we be tempted by Lost Island crazy golf? There was only one way to find out, and with an hour to kill until our meeting (difficult to believe it was only noon), in we went!

Once inside, it's obvious that the exterior has been hiding some very interesting features. Sandown has an extremely grand arcade, rich colours behind the flashing lights of machines and tasteful glass chandeliers (no, I'm not joking! Typically Venetian in style with glass droplets, they are really very pretty!). There are loads of games here, a café, bowling alley and a kids' adventure land... and The Lost Island crazy golf. In 1995 I was lucky enough to win a competition to become part of a team and play *The Crystal Maze* from the original television series, before it was dismantled. The Aztec Zone there and The Lost Island crazy golf were incredibly similar! It was a real stroke of genius to construct this on a pier – creepy (albeit fibreglass) rocks adorned with skulls and plants, and with a real sense of adventure. I've never played crazy golf, but was beginning to feel the urge to take it up now!

Suddenly we were at some glass doors, leading to the narrowest part of the pier neck. Instead of exiting straight outside to a blasting gale we found ourselves on a ramp sloping down to the wooden decking and screened from the wind and rain (not that it was wet today). From the outside, this bit of the pier looks like Portacabins on stilts – inside we were treated to stunning sea views and airy arcade-style games with mammoth crane grab-a-toy units, another gap and then a café, lengthways on one side of the pier with seating on the other. It all looked very cheerful – doughnuts from 'the last remaining full-sized donut machine on the Isle of Wight. See it here!' We did! But we still didn't have one. The café is colonnaded like an old-fashioned fairground stall, and it was even surrounded by those colourful little lights that you'd find on the hoopla or dizzy rides. Surrounded by red, white and blue décor with a hint of sunny yellow, you can sit and dip a chip in your fried egg while down below you watch grandma (skirt sensibly tucked in her knickers) as she helps a small child build a sandcastle on the tawny sands.

As you may have guessed, we'd needed to stop for a bite to eat, and it's a brilliant spot to look at a classic beach scene – windbreaks, deckchairs and a few pebbles (ideal for providing decorating materials for that sandcastle), old and new hotels and some stylish blue and cream apartments next to beach huts and sandy cliffs. Lunch over, coffee downed, we headed out of this mini-fairground into the fresh air. This last part of the pier has plenty of seating (all in different styles, such as a high-back plastic sofa) and is protected from the worst of the wind by high Perspex wind-breaks, with all the classical things we were hoping to see on a pier. Strings of fairy lights? Check! Dodgems? Check! A train for the children? Check! Seaside snacks loaded with sugar and calories? Check! It was looking very good! There are even Donald McGill inspired cheeky photo opportunity stick-your-head-through boards scattered along the length.

At the pier head the structure widens again – here are more amusements, a snake tunnel slide, a fairground rocket ride, a real helter-skelter and *sniff* a water-shoot machine with firemen, just like there had been at the end of Weston's Grand Pier before the fire. And the pier doesn't stop there either! From the helter-skelter you can go down onto the concrete fishing and boating jetty, three-sided like a miniature harbour and on umpteen concrete legs. If I hadn't already known that this part of the coast can suffer terribly in the winter from storms, I'd have said it was slightly over-egging the pudding to have quite so many piles, but here the pier head looked ready to cope with anything the English Channel could throw at it, and I do wonder if it helps to protect the rest of the pier too.

There had been so many things to look at I hadn't done my usual notes on what railings, lamps etc looked like – that would have to wait, we needed to have a kiss! Looking out over the super-clear sea to the horizon, where a multitude of huge tankers and container ships plodded back and forth on their serious business we snuggled up and kissed for the 48th official time. Still magical and toe tingling. I don't *think* that's the result of all that coffee! We then trotted back to the front of the pier, although this time I *did* look at the railings (basic sky blue and white rails with some standard chain-link so you don't fall through) and the lighting (tall, sky blue with a little white globe on top, joined by links of white fairy lights), and anything else I'd missed (decking goes along the length of the pier, there are barnacles on its legs too!) before we burst out into the sunlight and sat on a bench waiting for the reporter.

After a pleasant interview with Emily, and the news that a photographer would meet us at Yarmouth Pier the next day, we headed back to the guesthouse. It had been a very early start, a packed morning and a lot to take in, and Jay admitted again that he didn't feel well, so I left him there and headed off for a bit of exploring on my own. It was the world-famous garlic festival and I was tempted, but didn't feel like visiting alone, so carried on driving until I came to Carisbrooke Castle, a stunning old motte-and-bailey castle, with a working donkey wheel, museum and Edwardian-style garden. I happily spent several hours there walking the walls and exploring the buildings, before I headed back to see how Mr Poorly was feeling.

Much refreshed by his afternoon nap, we planned what we would do for the evening. It's a testament to the compact nature of the Island that we managed to see quite so many places in just one day – five pier-based destinations (and technically all before lunch!) and a castle, and we now felt we deserved to see Sandown in a bit more detail, find somewhere to eat and have a walk along the beach, seeing as the day had finally improved and the sun was making an appearance just before it set!

Mostly Victorian, the original residents were responsible for laying out the neat esplanade and gardens, various parks, and for building some superb houses and villas. We walked past a little art gallery where we paused to critique the pictures, and admired and laughed out loud at some originals by Simon Drew (he of the pen and ink drawings and punning captions. Perhaps that should be pun and ink drawings...).

After a top-class Indian meal (sorry, didn't write the name down and I'm notoriously appalling with names) and some amusing entertainment from various hen nights and stag dos going along the road in fancy dress and undress, we made our way down to the esplanade and beach. We found the pier again and walked along past it, hand in hand on the sand as the sun slipped slowly and elegantly down below the horizon, a spectacular blaze of oranges and reds lighting up the sky and calm sea. We watched a pied wagtail hopping around catching sand fleas and coveted the beach huts, eccentrically painted, decorated with driftwood and wittily named. Feeling very loved up, we turned towards the sea and pier, as the lights magically came on all along its length, the pinky-purple neons, red curly lettering and white bulbs creating a firework display of shattered reflections on the wet, undulating sand. We didn't need to be *on* the pier to share a kiss this evening; we leant in towards each other sharing body heat as the twinkling silver stars speckled the velvet night sky and...

The next day dawned fresh and bright, hinting at what might come later but not yet having made up its mind. We emerged from our servants' quarters and had breakfast in an enormous dining room, overlooking a small garden full of gnomes before checking out and journeying to the other end of the island (something which took all of 40 minutes, being only 19 miles away). Today would (hopefully) see us visiting Yarmouth and Totland Bay piers, with a little time for sightseeing before our ferry home in the late afternoon. Buoyed up by the appearance of more sunshine, we drove into historic Yarmouth in cheerful mood. The town, on the banks of the River Yar has Saxon origins, with overtones of Norman history and Tudor influence. Henry VIII had Yarmouth Castle built on the harbour's edge in 1547 as the sneaky French had sacked the busy port twice, and he wasn't going to let them do it again!

From 1858 the Brockenhurst to Lymington Railway had opened and this meant there was a greater demand on boat traffic from Lymington to Yarmouth – this sounds like a job for a pier building company! The Yar Pier Order was passed in 1874 and a wooden pier for shipping use was designed by Denham and Yarvey and opened by the Mayor of Yarmouth on 19th July 1876. It was 209m (685') long and of simple shape – nothing fancy here! – and acted as a terminal for paddle steamers owned by the London and South West Railway Company. Shortly after opening, 46m (150') of pier were demolished by the wayward *Prince Leopold* who smashed through it on a bright, sunny day after apparently breaking free of her moorings. In 1877 the local boatmen staged a protest at having lost earnings since the pier opened (previously they had taken visitors back and forth over the Solent privately, now it was organised through the pier), and they tore down the pier gates as a mark of their annoyance.

In February 1891 the Yarmouth Town Trust took over administration of the pier and improved access by knocking down several buildings on the western side of Bank Street, thus creating Pier Square. The pier continued to be a huge success with purpose-built steamers providing a regular ferry route from Lymington to Yarmouth, and Sir Winston Churchill was among its many travellers in 1910. Another disaster occurred in 1909, when a 60-

ton barge, the *Shamrock*, on its way to Weymouth during a gale, crashed broadside into the pier; 15m (50') of pier neck was destroyed and the ship's owner refused to pay any compensation, saying that the accident was 'an act of God'. It was patched up, and the pier saw service in World War One as a jetty for Navy vessels, but by 1916 was in need of repair and the Town trust paid the £250 needed to do this.

In 1927 a pavilion was built at the shoreward end to house a waiting room and some office space at a cost of £2000, and the life of the pier continued prosperously until 1931. By now the rise of private car ownership had increased and people wanted to use their vehicles for getting to the Island. Although suitable for boats and pedestrians, Yarmouth Pier would never be able to handle cars. A new ferry terminal was therefore built and the harbour was dredged to make it suitably deep. In May 1939 the first car ferry began operating and was able to bring 400 passengers and 16 cars at a time from Lymington. It was also one of the first roll-on-roll-off ferries, but took an awful lot of traffic away from the pier, even though passenger steamers continued to use it as a disembarking point.

Since World War II shipping invariably used the new and improved Yarmouth Harbour, and despite being granted Grade II listed status in 1975 as the last totally wooden pier in Britain (with lattice handrails), it was running at a loss. In 1980 repairs were desperately needed and the owners requested demolition consent, but this was refused. Between 1983 and 1986 the Harbour Commissioners began an intensive programme of restoration which included renewing to the walkway (costing £250,000) and a further £100,000 was spent on other essential works.

By 1991 it was found that the pier head was in a dangerous condition and in 1993 a huge fundraising appeal was launched to raise £600,000 to put right all the problems. Balau (a tough hardwood) decking planks were sold at a minimum cost of £25, and engraved (there is one bought by His Royal Highness the Duke of Edinburgh, and from the National Piers Society, as well as planks bought by the local Women's Institute, yacht owners and individuals). Some 553 planks were sold on the walkway and another 70 on the pier head, while other work carried out on the pier included the building of a new pier-head pavilion, replacing the original Pier Masters' office (and now used as a fisherman's shelter). The handrails were also replaced using £200,000 that was spent the first winter. The pier reopened in 1994 but by July 2007 our old friend, the gribble, was making its presence known and the piles were found to have that worryingly cheesy texture associated with the gribble's tunnels.

Cue the best newspaper headline ever created (and I can't credit it to the genius creator, because all the archive online says is 'a reporter' – come forward and make yourself known!). *Gribble Versus Gribble – Let Worm Battle Commence* graced the *Isle of Wight County Press* pages and reported how the appointed project manager for fighting the gribble and making Yarmouth Pier fit for purpose for another 40 or 50 years was called... Richard Gribble! I can, after extensive research say that Richard doesn't look anything like his namesake (thankfully), he being more upright and definitely less woodlouse-looking than the marine isopod in question!

National Lottery funding provided a grant of £350,500 towards replacing 54 of the original wooden piles with new greenheart ones, much tougher and more resistant to gribble the marine woodlouse, and a 'Not the End of the Pier' campaign helped to raise the rest, which saw the renovated pier and education displays re-opened to the public by Alan Titchmarsh, the new High Sheriff to the island, on 26th April 2008.

Coming into Yarmouth we found our way into a car park at River Road, bordering the marsh lands on the edge of the River Yar. We leapt enthusiastically out and off to find Pier Square, although I know if we'd been having a leisurely holiday we would have gone to have a look around Henry's castle and perused a few of the interesting shops, but this was not going to be our sightseeing spot, this was kissing business!

At the end of Pier Square we were forced to walk past tempting smells of coffee from the little café next to the pier entrance, although if it hadn't been for the little arch supported by two grand lamp posts overseeing all who pass, like two stern policemen, we wouldn't have known where the way to Yarmouth Pier was!

We followed the footpath to the right of the sign and paused at the entrance to take in everything in front of us. There's a blue and white 'welcome' notice, with a brief history of the pier, a blue bell (and a request to make sure you have a fishing permit before you cast!) and a very interesting little section that contains lots of educational and interactive displays about the pier. Sadly the touch screen wasn't working, but you could look at old postcards, delve into the video vaults, look at how you can save the pier and rebuild it in jigsaw style (or that's what it looks like!). There is also a very interesting little wooden L-shaped bench on what looks suspiciously like pier piles, and on closer inspection it even has little wooden limpets and barnacles all over it! There's also a weighing machine here – I got the hint about eating anything else so soon after breakfast, thank you!

After all these distractions we made to step on to the pier, which stretched away smart and gorgeous and inviting into the sea, but first parted with a pocketful of change into the voluntary toll box. Would it really hurt every visitor to part with a £1? Of course not, we all spend more than that on things we don't really need when we go to the shop, and I can't understand why people are so reticent to put just the requested 30p in – and we saw you people. You still walked down the pier and appreciated all that hard work!

I'll calm down now. It's something that makes both of us cross, but I don't suppose it will change the 'oh it doesn't apply to me' brigade, however many times we moan!

Wow! The pier is just stunning. Everything looks very neat and tidy, and the wooden railings and lattice are exquisite. There are crabber and fishers, walkers and visitors and locals, all using the pier for their own enjoyment, which is great. The sponsored planks are clear and easy to read and we spent an age making sure we read them all! Being a bit thick (I'm sure I've got blonde roots) I looked at the pier in front of me and then back at the limpet bench. The penny dropped with a clang! It's a bench in the shape of the pier! Jay shook his head and walked on, smiling, and I suspect he'd seen the L-shaped connection much sooner!

We paused a short distance along and watched one of the huge Lymington ferries come in. They look as though they are going to run aground just behind the walls of Henry VIII's castle, such was the skill of constructing this deep water ro-ro ferry port. I do wonder what Old 'Enery would have thought, having these great behemoths docking so close to his fortress, but I suspect he'd have been quite happy at the thought that his castle had been turned into a semi with the pub next door (although he'd definitely have had the name changed. The *George*? That's treason!). The water, despite the recent churning by the ferry, was remarkably calm, apart from a patch that looked like constant Jacuzzi bubbles were going off in it. As we watched, they moved – what was it? A helpful passer-by put my mind at rest, explaining that the boiling water phenomenon was caused by a shoal of mackerel, and I wished I'd packed a net, deprived of fresh fish twice now!

Yarmouth Pier is in such a stunning setting, and walking along at our snail-like pace gave us loads of time to watch the very varied sea-traffic, watching the ferries cross mid-stream and the little yachts playing chicken in front of them. We trod on the Duke of Edinburgh's plank (sorry your Highness) and marvelled at the simple, but effective straight, clean lines of the lamp posts. At the end of the pier, the wooden lattice railings give way to metal gates and rails, where the *Waverley* and *Balmoral* tie up on their occasional visits, but it's not for a very large area and I'm sure it's more for good old 'elf and safety' reasons than anything else. I would have queried this with Jay, but he will admit that he could have been a fantastically stringent H&S inspector and has been known, on more than one occasion to go around pointing out where laws are being broken and safety compromised!

I prevented a spouting of why seaweed should be cleared from the decking, pressed him against the rails (ah, that's why they're reinforced then!) and engaged him in a bracing end-of-pier kiss. Unable to breathe, and therefore talk for a while, we carried on across the pier head, still reading planks and then back to read the plaques on the delightful hexagonal shelter, painted in sea-and-sky blue and white and topped with a weather vane in the shape of a dolphin. Robin the photographer appeared round the other side of the building and positioned us for a picture, thankfully standing up, not doing gymnastics and a bit further back along the neck of the pier. The final picture (looking a little more like a desperate grapple than romantic snog) was rather good and if I may say so, showed my Moomins off to great effect! We had a chat and had a few landmarks pointed out to us, Fort Victoria to the west, peeking out from the trees and now home to a planetarium and underwater archaeology centre. Having been to Hurst Castle on the opposite side of the water I was amazed at how close it looked (and when I checked, it's only three-quarters of a mile across the Solent here which is why it was so heavily fortified).

We were sorry to say goodbye to Yarmouth and its pier, a very welcoming and interesting spot on the island. We did pause at the pier café for a much needed latte, before hitting the road for the arduous journey to our next pier. Just four minutes later we pulled up on the promenade outside Totland Bay Pier, situated in the very quiet Totland village and in the warm and sheltered Totland Bay. Initially it seems an unlikely spot for a pier, with little to draw visitors here other than the sand and shingle beach and the secluded nature of the bay.

There's been a pier here since 1879, precipitated by steamer services bringing more visitors from Lymington to the surrounding area from 1870. A road from Totland Bay to Yarmouth was built in 1873 and this opened up visitors to this delightful area. S. H and S.W Yockney designed a wooden decked pier with light girder framework and cast-iron piles that was built in 1879, completed in 1880 and stretched 137m (450') out into the deeper water, thus allowing instant steamer access to the area. The pier had a small wooden shelter at the seaward end and a small amusement pavilion at the shore end. This ease of visiting pleased the Victorian visitors immensely, and the area soon became well-known for having smooth sands that were particularly suitable for bathing machines. The seabed was flat and sandy and the air had a 'restorative, bracing atmosphere', and a comment in 1883 said that the pier provided a 'pleasant promenade'. This same year also saw the opening of the Totland Bay Hotel, constructed at the top of the hill overlooking the bay in Victorian Gothic style to provide much-needed accommodation for all the new visitors.

Initially steamers visited from Lymington and Yarmouth, but popularity meant services were soon extended to include boats from Bournemouth, Southampton and Portsmouth and was also incorporated into the 'round-island' tours. Once the railway opened from Newport to Freshwater in 1890, tourism really boomed and regattas were regularly held and well attended, and the hotel had to be enlarged to cope with the extra trade.

By the 1900s increasing coastal erosion meant the pier had to be extended, and this was carried out in 1916 to keep the pier in line with the deep water which ranged from 6-8m at this point. Despite the First World War meaning pleasure cruises stopped, there was still a daily service to Lymington until May 1918, but demand was not like it had been and by 1927 this too stopped. Occasional round-the-island cruises visited, but by 1931 the condition of the pier was so dodgy, that these too ceased.

During World War II the pier was sectioned, a wartime postcard shows three landward spans missing and the little simple pier looking very subdued and desolate. Post-war repairs were carried out by Mr Humby and the Wall brothers (who sound like they should have been a 40's dance hall swing-band combo!) who replaced the corroded piles with wooden ones and sorted out the pier head. These repairs are evident today, the first two spans in chunky wood, with thicker cross-bracing and legs. The pier re-opened on 17th June 1951 with the arrival of the *Lorna Doone II*, which berthed at the pier and this saw the return of other steamers up until 1969.

In 1971 the pier was sold to Trinity House for £10,000 and was used as a base for pilot boats, but this lasted for only four years when the National Physical Laboratory used the pier as a base for their wave and weather monitoring equipment, information from which went into designing oil rigs, but the pier was again sold several times, by people who did not invest anything in maintaining the pier. A fire in 1978 destroyed the shore-end arcade, and because access to the pier had been through this building, the pier was closed. The arcade was then further damaged in the same hurricane that destroyed Shanklin Pier in 1987. (Shanklin Pier, between Sandown and Ventnor had also been a popular steamer and tourist venue since Victorian times, and I'd been lucky enough to visit back in August 1987, just months before it was destroyed.)

The pier was sold again and repairs carried out to the shoreward pavilion and pier, which meant that the MV *Balmoral* was able to visit in 1993, bringing much needed income to the pier funds, but vandalism to the arcade and no money forthcoming from any quarter (despite nearly £1 million being spent by the council on sea defences, groynes and new sea wall). The pier changed hands in 1997 again, this time for £19,500, but sold once more to local artist Derek Brannan in 1999, who used the pier-head building as an art studio. In December 2008 the pier was advertised for sale by auction, with a guide price of £100,000 which, on the face of it seemed a very reasonable amount for a piece of seaside history, although ten years previously, repairs were estimated at £150,000 to complete... Needless to say, the pier didn't sell, and sits waiting for someone to give it some TLC, which is how we found it today.

Today there is no grand hotel overlooking the bay, nor rowing boats for hire or people swimming in the sparkling waves, but there is a steady stream of visitors to the café fronting the pier, either driving down the little access road or coming along the little promenade from further along the coast. The welcome here is as warm as the weather, and you can either grab a snack to take away, or enter the long blue and white building to browse local books and artwork while drinking a hot beverage or eating cake or chips. The bonus here is that although the main body of the pier is closed, there is a short section that remains open just behind the café, and it was here that we sat with coffee and flapjack and I fell in love all over again.

Poor old Totland Bay Pier is in a bit of a state. If I had the income, lottery win or rich benefactor I would have bought it there and then, but it would have to be a labour of love as there is so much work that needs to be done. I'd have done it...

Galvanised rails at the café end have simple central decoration, and chairs and tables crammed in to make a few square metres of decking viable – then there is the wooden fence and a little gate with a polite 'private' sign, and the rest of the pier stretches out into the Solent rusting away. The original seat-back railings have no seats and are heavily corroded. On the westward side this is much worse, and in places the rails and lattice have thinned so much that parts of the metalwork have disappeared completely. The decking appears fairly solid, although covered with an attractive layer of the orange lichen *Xanthoria* showing there has been very little footfall here (but lots of gull poo!) for a long time.

A high security fence topped with barbed wire seals the end of the pier off from any unwanted landward attention, but would also stop any pirates making it to land too. The little art studio can be reached from its own landing stage at the pier head or along the neck and seems quite solid too, and we peered over the little star-topped wooden fence, contemplating how long it would take us to save up enough to buy the pier, and what we would do with it if we could. Sadly this is likely to be just a pipe-dream, but we'll keep buying our lottery tickets and keeping our fingers crossed, and just hope that someone else has the readies and the foresight to buy Totland quickly and save it from falling into the sea. It was a wistful kiss here (flavoured with chocolate-topped flapjack which for once I *can* recommend), and you may be wondering from the above description why the pier needs saving quite so quickly, when it doesn't seem in too bad a state.

Like icebergs, the important part of piers are under the water and it's only from looking at the underside and at the piles does the real problem with Totland Bay Pier become really (and shockingly) evident. Once you've 'got your eye in' with the levels of the pier against the skyline, you'll spot some alarming dips in the pier-head woodwork where piles under the water have subsided or collapsed, despite looking initially so solid. The wooden replacement piles that fixed the wartime breaching look as though they've been gnawed by beavers, the effects of the sea and marine creatures having consumed much of the timber, and even the sturdy reinforced concrete legs on the shingle have been substantially corroded, narrowing the cylinders in many places and exposing the metal inside.

It is such a lovely pier, simple but still evocative of days gone by and in what must be one of the most beautiful locations for seaside promenading, this is somewhere that wouldn't cost millions to repair and restore, unlike some of the grander, longer and more elaborate piers that we'd visited. We left Totland Bay really hoping the right person would come along soon to save the pier, and fervently dreaming it could be us... Look! Flying pigs over the bay – but no harm in wishing, right?

The rest of the day on the Isle of Wight was spent in glorious sunshine at Alum Bay and the Needles, exploring geology (amazing!), history (awesome!) and some pretty special views from above the Needles themselves and the chairlift down to Alum Bay (not recommended for the faint-hearted and I still don't know how Jay managed to persuade me on there). Even when sightseeing we couldn't get away from piers. Alum Bay, famed for its multicoloured sands was home to a pier, although no longer. The original had a pier head twice as wide as the length which opened in 1887 and remained extremely busy until after World War I. Declared unsafe in 1925, the pier was closed and in 1927 suffered severe storm damage and broke in half. There are no traces at all of the pier today, although there is a small landing stage for modern pleasure craft – but just not the same thing at all!

We reluctantly left the western end of the Island to catch our ferry back to mainland England, but it was a hard decision to take. Could we get away with throwing the keys in the sea? We could change our identity and camp in a wigwam on the beach, live off the land and... Back to earth with a bump we were being waved forward onto the Red Funnel vessel back to Southampton and reality. Bother! Missed my chance again! Consoled by the fact that we still had some piers left to go (is it so wrong to be easily bribed by kisses?), we watched the Isle of Wight slip away, but vowed we'd be back!

CHAPTER 19

A Bridge Too Far!
(Weston's Birnbeck Beauty)

Passing all three of Weston-super-Mare's piers twice a day I get to see them in all sorts of different weathers, tides, and lights. If I was being totally honest, the most beautiful of these has to be Birnbeck Pier, seen first through the trees along the Toll Road and then viewed from the higher ground at the 'old' end of Weston, sticking out at an angle into the sea and ending on an island. The tenth longest pier in the country at 317m (1,040'), it's one of Eugenius Birch's designs and its unique feature is the fact that it could, possibly, be described as just a bridge, going from land to island – and it's the only pier in the country that does. I think it's a combination of this setting and sadly, current dereliction and marine light quality that makes Birnbeck so appealing. I've seen it swathed in snow, backed by tempestuous storm clouds, lit up by the ruddy light of dawn, swathed spookily in thick sea fog and sparkling with some remaining glory from the 'good old days' in the summer sunshine.

Sadly, Birnbeck has been closed to the public since 1994 and, like Totland Bay has been passed from one well-meaning owner to another quite often, each unable to fulfil their vision for this structure before selling it on again. Because of this, all the buildings on the island are in a pretty shocking state of disrepair and the main neck of the pier has been saved from total collapse because it's still used as an access point by the R.N.L.I., who have lifeboats stationed here.

The three piers of Weston are a brilliant example of how fashions and requirements of tourists have changed over the centuries, and how our seaside towns have kept pace with these. Weston-super-Mare is the proud possessor of a wide, curving bay, protected by the promontories of Brean Down on one side and Sand Point on the other. There is plenty of sand (and acres of sticky treacherous mud at low tide too!), and the second highest tidal range in the world, which takes the estuarine waters of the River Severn startlingly high at certain times of the year. This and the savage currents that accompany the shifting tides obviously gave pier builders a bit of a headache as far as designing a robust structure far enough above the waves was concerned, but Weston has one end of its shoreline carved from black rocks and this proved the ideal place to build said pier.

Conveniently there was also a large flat island nearby too (approximately 1.2 hectares or 2.97 acres), and in 1864 Eugenius Birch came up with the design for this elegant structure that was originally intended just to be a bridge to the island, but metamorphosed into a pier. For a town that had been a popular seaside resort since the 1820s, 1864 seems very late to be thinking about building a pier, but there had been ideas afoot since 1845, although this started as a plan for a jetty first and then a suspension bridge right across to Birnbeck Island. James Dredge (who had unsuccessfully offered plans for building the Clifton Suspension Bridge) came up with a suitable design and work started in 1846 on the first of the supporting towers.

However, anyone who has watched the tide roar in or out at the point on the Severn Estuary will now be able to hazard a guess that any construction job here would not run smoothly. Treacherous currents coupled with a stonemasons' strike and then a severe storm washed away most of the work, then halted until the following spring. Dredge tried to get the work finished later that year, but by 1848 found himself on the receiving end of legal action and with an incomplete bridge and Weston without a tourist attraction.

It was not until the 1860s when the tourist trade was really booming here and promenade piers had become 'the' thing to have in your town (there were more than a dozen built during this decade) that a new proposal was put forward, abandoning the idea of solid embankments and stone pillars. Birch, who had become best known for designing promenade piers with decking above and architecturally pleasing (rather than just plain or functional) piles underneath, usually in groups, was commissioned for the Birnbeck 'bridge' and £20,000 was raised for the construction after a public campaign. At the time of Birnbeck Pier's construction, Birch was also supervising that of Brighton's Palace Pier, and there were many similarities between the finished structures.

Birnbeck was built by engineers R. and J. Laybourne, and the parts were prefabricated at the Isca Foundry in Newport before being assembled like a giant kit over the water in Weston. In total there were fifteen groups of four cast-iron piles installed, each pile driven just over a metre into the rock below. Support was given by way of cross-bracing and ties and a wooden decking with seven bays going out wider than the main walkway was constructed on top. The island had to be terraced to allow for development, and because the secondary reason for building a pier here was to provide a safe landing spot for steamers, a northern boating pier was added, stretching 76m (250') clear of the island and furnished with solid timbers and piles to help absorb the 'crunch' of docking boats as they battled with the tricky tide (I've experienced this effect on board the MV *Balmoral* as it tried to berth at Weston's Knightstone Island, and it's quite alarming, but better to lose a chunk of timber than hole your boat or take out a pier pile!). At the landward end there were two Gothic toll houses and gates, designed by local architect Hans Price (we've seen his work at Clevedon already) which completed the site – the pier was all set to go!

The bays and pier neck incorporated that now-familiar continuing seat and balustrade rail effect that we'd seen on so many piers already, but these were in fact a very new conception and one that marked out the deliberate construction of a pleasure pier as opposed to those that later evolved, and it was something that Eugenius Birch had helped to pioneer. Finding that little nugget out fairly late in our pier escapades made us think. Was this another way of defining what was a pier from a jetty? In reality I don't think there would be many piers at all if we just used that, and I still think the appearance of some kind of leisure and pleasure facility is more useful!

With the addition of gas pipes and lighting the length of the 'bridge', and reinforcing buttresses around the island, people were beginning to see the whole development as one 'pier' instead of separate identities, and since its opening on 15th June 1867, that is how it has been known ever since. The opening of the pier was carried out by the four-year-old son of the local Squire – brought in because of squabbling over who had the 'right' to do it, and on the day, he did a great job. Everyone in the town was granted a public holiday and the opening was done to the sounds of fireworks, cannons and ringing church bells! It would appear the rest of the day went well, although there did appear to be one slight problem with the completed construction, discovered only when a band marched along the pier, which set up resonance in the structure and caused it to start swaying. With a further incidence in 1886, extra cross braces were added and a Pier Bye-law was created, banning any further marches!

Despite looking like a sure-fire winning proposition, business wasn't great although the initial toll of 1d was increased to 2d after 120,000 people had visited in the first three months alone. Maintaining the structure proved costly, and a hoped-for railway branch line bringing people to the door was not going to materialise. Lack of interest was also in part down to the fact that the island hadn't really got anything on it to attract visitors – what an oversight! A plunge bath was built in 1872 (but there had been much better baths on neighbouring Knightstone Island since the 1820s) and the pavilion and reading rooms were only completed in 1884, along with a luggage tramway. Three years later saw one of the more dramatic installations opened to the public on the pier, the switchback, although further (and to my mind, more exciting, developments were to come!). By now Weston had grown from a tiny fishing village of just 150 people in 1811 to a thriving town with more than forty shops on the High Street and 161 lodging houses on or near the seafront to cater for all the tourists! The prospects of the pier were beginning to look up and were helped considerably by the arrival of Campbell's White Funnel steamers, also known as 'the swans', who were now plying their trade up and down the Bristol Channel and were happy to use Birnbeck Pier as a convenient port of call.

On Boxing Day 1897 a fire destroyed the main pavilion which contained the concert hall and refreshment rooms. Although the fire brigade were called and the tide was in, their hoses couldn't reach the water and they were unable to put out the blaze. The very next day though, local renowned architect Hans Price was called upon to draw up replacement buildings, and these were opened in July the following year, incorporating beautiful decorative iron columns and tops, not dissimilar to those found in a Victorian railway station and a good example of Price's beautiful work, much of which is evident around Weston. A new low-water jetty was also opened in 1898 to the south-west of the island, 38m (125') long and able to cope with bigger steamers wishing to ply their trade when the waters were falling, as there could be as many as six steamers waiting to land at any one time! A postcard from 1920 shows a steamer at the jetty at low tide, just out of the reach of the rocky ledge, but it must have been a daunting climb (especially for ladies) up several flights of stairs to get to the deck level of the pier towering far above them!

By the turn of the century Birnbeck had two well-established lifeboat houses, both still visible today. The first was built on the northward side of the pier neck and launched via a stone slipway, the second on the south side in 1902 with railed slipway for easier (and quicker!) launching. This was once the longest slipway of any lifeboat station in the country, but is sadly now also too dangerous to be used and the lifeboat has reverted to its original slipway on the northern side.

Town enlargement showed the increase in visitors was financially beneficial – there were 265 lodging houses and twenty hotels all over Weston by 1903, although it was also said that many people visiting by steamer never left the pier, such were the (obviously much improved) facilities there! (The truth may actually have been linked more with the fact that many of the steamers came from Wales and on a Sunday, there was no drink at home. However, the ships often had bars and the pier had plenty of alcohol available!) These now included tea-rooms, a band, coffee rooms, photo studios, an amusement park, shooting gallery and (unusually) a telephone, although this was intended for business use only, and a Pier Bye-law stated that visitors were forbidden to 'hallooo, shout or call out, or blow, strike or sound any gong, horn or other instrument, or make any other noise beyond that of ordinary speaking'. What spoilsports!

It was in 1903 that a second calamity was to occur. The 10th September saw the arrival of 'The Great Gale', which wreaked havoc across the town and severely damaged both steamer jetties on the pier. The pier was closed until June 1904, with the north jetty not opening until the following year (rebuilt using steel girders and extended to 91m or 300' long) and the south-west jetty left useless until 1910. This did not do trade at Birnbeck Pier any good at all, and developments elsewhere in the town were to strike a real blow and affect the future of this pier.

1902 saw a tramway taking visitors straight from the railway station in the centre of the town a short distance to the seafront and in 1904 the newly opened Grand Pier meant less people wanted to make the journey to Birnbeck. Large and fancy, with a huge pavilion that promised all the biggest and best stars, it was almost inconceivable that Birnbeck Pier would ever be able to compete. However, due to dangerous currents steamers refused to dock at the Grand Pier and boat trade was still popular to Birnbeck. This pier was not going to give up easily though and some amazing new amusements were built. There was your standard helter-skelter and the switchback, but also 'flying machines', a swing-boat roundabout that took you out over the sea, a maze, a bioscope (a kind of early cinema with dancing girls between films), a hurry skurry (a very high bendy slide with huge queues showing its popularity) and, the *pièce de résistance,* a water chute – the Edwardian equivalent of a log flume! This fantastic piece of engineering (that would've scared the pants off me) faced the island parallel to the pier and hauled boats up by chain to the top of the ride and let them go into a large purpose-built pool that filled with seawater when the tide came in.

In 1909 an extension on iron supports was built sticking out over the sea on the southern side of the island to make more room for amusements, but had to be demolished in 1912 as it hadn't been put up safely. Investigation of old postcards illustrates how thriving the pier was during the Edwardian era, and it's not surprising they wanted a bit more room! One from 1913 shows the road outside packed with horse-drawn vehicles, two electric trams and a steamer leaving the pier. The switchback is visible on the south side of the pier, the back of the water chute dominates the north side, and in between can be seen a roller-skating rink, refreshments room, prominent clock tower (essential for any pier with a busy steamer service) and so busy with people there was hardly any space to breathe!

The tramway finally brought visitors from town to the pier in 1908 and terminated at what is now the Friends of the Old Pier's Society Shop, but was then the tram signalling station. A huge fire at the Grand Pier in 1930 saw a new, amusement filled pavilion re-opened in 1933. The tramway to Birnbeck shut in 1937 and although the pier's earlier extension was reinstated (this time made from concrete on concrete 'stilts') on the south side for shops, visitor numbers weren't what they had been. World War II unusually saw Birnbeck spared from sectioning. Instead it was taken over by the Admiralty and in 1941 was re-named HMS *Birnbeck* and used by the Department of Miscellaneous Weapons Department. Surrounded by barbed wire on the land, and its own personal mine-field at sea, the island was now home to these 'Wheezers and Dodgers', scientists who devised and trialled new underwater weapons, and more famously, Barnes-Wallis' 'bouncing bomb'. The Pier Company received the princely sum of around £375 a year for the use of the island and pier, and there are many funny and interesting stories surrounding this period in the pier's history (including how a block of concrete was dropped on the pier by a Lancaster bomber, and the arrival of an 'enigma' machine), which lasted until 1946. Many of the exploits and those of the DMWD can be found in *The Wheezers and Dodgers: The Inside Story of Clandestine Weapon Development in World War II* by Derek Pawle (Seaforth Publishing, 2009) and *The Secret War* by Gerald Pawle, with a forward by Neville Shute who worked for the DMWD (now out of print).

Following the War, a real decline saw the end of the pier often in sight, although it invariably clung on tenaciously to life. 1971 saw the last of the regular boat traffic, which at its peak had seen around a thousand steamers a year visit the island. The pier changed hands in 1972 and Victorian themed amusements proved a popular attraction (and many people I have worked with that grew up in Weston can tell some great stories of going to the pier and using old pennies on the slot machines!), and the main pier, jetty and toll houses were granted listed status in 1974.

In 1978 planning permission was granted to build a 120-bed hotel with boat and car parking and a local outcry erupted – however, the work did not materialise. The pier changed hands again and another set of plans were passed in 1979 for a hotel, marina and causeway to link the island to the land. Maintenance work had to be carried out to the pier, but no other work materialised and the pier stayed the same. Also this year, the MV *Balmoral* visited for the very last time, which, looking back signalled the end of tourism on Birnbeck Pier.

Still open to the public, but used mainly by fishermen now (and the R.N.L.I.) the pier was hit by a loose pontoon in February 1984 that had escaped from engineering work in nearby Sand Bay. The damage (nearly £1 million) was swiftly rectified, but the pier was battered by a huge storm in 1990. It wreaked havoc with many parts of the seafront but damaged the lifeboat house slipway so badly it proved impossible to launch using it, and the windows, although made of toughened glass, were smashed. By 1994 a further stormy period meant the structure was deemed so unsafe that the pier was closed to everyone except lifeboat crew, who take their life in their hands every time they receive a call-out and have to make their way across the decking to the island using a walkway they had installed at a cost of £20,000 in 1999.

Birnbeck Pier is now on the English Heritage Buildings at Risk register and the future is still desperately uncertain for it. Bought again in 2006 by Urban Splash, there was a glimmer of hope for a while. £4 million of repairs were carried out and the following year they launched a competition for redevelopment plans and ideas from the public. In March 2008 the winning plan was announced which included, not surprisingly a hotel and apartments, but by the time of our visit (October 2009) nothing had changed. The pier was still clinging onto life by a thread, investment in redevelopment is not forthcoming (with Urban Splash citing the recession as its main reason for not carrying out any work), and it looks like the pier will probably be put back on the market in the near future.

Despite this deeply depressing scenario, there are still lots of people that care about Birnbeck Pier. It has a thriving Friends society (with a great website), who are determined to work with any new owners to get the pier rebuilt and reopened, and there are always members of the general public who want to know what the latest news is whenever the Friends' shop, Pier View, is open. It was thanks to the Friends that we found ourselves waiting outside the main security fence one sunny October morning to be allowed a kiss on the end of the pier. Sadly, like Queen's Pier, Ramsey, this was going to be a kiss on the landward end only. The Friends had tried to get permission for us to travel to the island, over the pier but it was felt that we wouldn't be covered by Urban Splash's insurance, and so we'd had to settle on a compromise, for which we were extremely grateful.

Pier View, the old two-storey tram signal box is in fairly good repair – it's battled vandals who repeatedly strip lead from the roof (plans are afoot to replace it with a lookalike material) and is in regular use as a shop. However, things on the other side of the fence are definitely *not* greener. The gates onto the pier are now modern security gates, wreathed with scribbles of razor and barbed wire, and not very welcoming... Neglected and overlooked in front of them are remnants of days gone by. A rubber-tyred luggage trolley lies abandoned next to a rusted turnstile, paint flaking and flanked by weeds.

There's the 'trunk' of a cast-iron lamp post, headless but still carrying some of its black and white paint, albeit spotted with rust and guarding a small piece of fleur-de-lys topped wrought-iron fence. This was so badly corroded that it looked as thin and fragile as a cobweb, ready for a sea breeze to snap it and sweep it away. The toll house still stands strong and sturdy, stone built and boarded up securely – it would make a wonderful house though, with a sloping (and now very overgrown) path down to the coast behind it.

The gates were now open and we were allowed to step onto the metal grid that links the land with the pier, where the lifeboat men can, with some element of daring, make their way over to the island where their boats are stationed. It felt incredibly sad to be allowed this far and no further onto the pier (we were out over the seabed though), but given the state of the structure, which we could now clearly see, it was wise to go no further.

From the vantage point next to Pier View, and especially when the tide is out, it can be seen how many bits of bracing on the pier legs are missing or corroded to a point where they are broken or dangling down – definitely no more marching across the pier now! Broken and missing planking and rotten balustrade railing are also obvious, and looking across to the island you can see the derelict buildings, some of which still remain (others have been knocked down to prevent them collapsing) but they are in a terribly precarious state with floors missing and slates that can fall from the roof without warning or even a puff of wind to help them.

It felt strange to be stood on the pier and see so many pieces of the original structure. There were Eugenius Birch's pier-edge bench supports, curling up like little metal dolphins and a lamp post stalk in the bay that would have been lit by gas over one hundred and forty years ago. The northern landing stage is still standing; sway backed and as wavy as the sea underneath. I am amazed it's still there, such are some of the dodgy angles, and after every bit of bad weather I drive past expecting to see a part of it missing, collapsed into the sea. So far the old girl is hanging on in there, but you really get the feeling that it won't be long before something has to give, and as we stood there we really, really hoped that salvation would be just around the corner.

We had our kiss, supervised by Lesley and Charles McCann of the Friends of the Old Pier Society and stepped away from the pier, so that it could be locked up securely again. We walked back to Pier View and stood at the sea wall to look objectively over the pier and its island before we left. On the rocks below us, two men worked their shrimping nets suspended on tall poles stuck in the mud, something that has been happening here since long before the pier was even thought about. Hopefully the pier will not end up collapsing and disappearing into the sea, and the shrimping men will still scoop up their catch in the shadow of the pier for many years to come – time will tell!

CHAPTER 20

Work in Progress!

After a bit of frantic counting on my fingers I realised it had been seven months since our last visit to a pier. Seven months? Well, we hadn't been sat back doing nothing you know! Another random set of thoughts on New Year's Day meant we now had... a wedding date! Noticing the date 01.01.10 I wondered what it meant in binary (22 in case you're itching to know). It didn't take much of a jump to think that there would be 10.10.10 this year, and so I punched this into the internet (you didn't seriously think I'd worked it out myself did you?) and the answer was 42. I'm a huge fan of Douglas Adam's work, so 42 had huge significance because it is the answer to the greatest question of all – what is the meaning of life, the universe and everything? I talked to Jay about this... could we? Was it possible to? Let's... get married on 10.10.10, and celebrate the meaning of life for each other. It sounded like a perfect idea! Now, the next great question was where?

Weston's Grand Pier was coming along steadily. From a deck devoid of anything it had now been re-timbered, and in November 2009 floating cranes were lifting the huge steels that were then rapidly fixed together to give the pavilion infrastructure, which looked a little like a giant aircraft hangar with its curved roof. Amazingly, by Christmas, the roof was on, the building now had a round turret at each corner and the sides were starting to be fixed in place. Sudden snow and freezing temperatures halted work unexpectedly at the start of the New Year, but the owners found ways round this, and it wasn't long before construction was underway again.

By February the floor was in and sides nearly on, although wreathed in scaffolding it looked like a fantastic giant Meccano kit!

The 12th April saw a huge spring high tide, and I went to work early in order to take some pictures. If I'm being truthful, I was hoping for a spring storm too to drive the tide in higher for a spot of flooding and some dramatic waves crashing over the sea front, but the day had dawned beautifully still and warm with blinding sunshine and sparkling blue sea, the total opposite! Really it was just as well, I'm not sure Birnbeck Pier would have stood up to a battering from such high water. As it was, the water reached to the very top of the lifeboat slipway and almost to the edge of the walkway of the northern landing jetty! As I stood by the railings to take a photograph, I was struck by the stillness of the morning. There wasn't a sound except for the gentle lapping sound of the water, eerily much louder than normal and almost insistently sucking at the pier structure.

At the Grand Pier, scaffolding supporting the neck of the pier was under water and the silver cladding going onto the sides and towers of the pier, although still wreathed in scaffolding, gleamed and reflected beautifully on the calm waters. There was only one word to describe the scene – wow!

At this point we were not sure if the pier would be finished and ready to conduct weddings by 10.10.10, so we had a ponder and decided that with only six months to go it might be an idea to come up with a contingency plan. We also realised that we still had five piers left to visit... better get a move on!

CHAPTER 21

The Battle for Hastings, the Number 52 and a Floating Beauty! (Hastings and Eastbourne)

Hastings, 1066 and all that and Harold with an arrow in his eye... and a very fierce modern day battle going on in the world of piers to illustrate how well loved they are and what lengths people will go to in order to save them! We had been conversing back and forth with the lovely people of the Hastings Pier and White Rock Trust and on 15th May set off to visit the pier they were valiantly trying to save, have a kiss on the bit we were allowed to access, and then later that evening attend the 'Mend of the Pier' fundraiser, which promised to be an evening of entertainment and cabaret.

And what a delight Hastings turned out to be! Nowadays much overlooked in favour of Brighton (unless you happen to live here and it's the centre of your universe), Hastings has a wonderful seafront, straight out of an Agatha Christie novel – we almost expected to see Miss Marple busybodying along the prom or Hercule Poirot hailing a taxi, but sadly, that was not to be! The sea was luminous shades of green, grey and blue and although there was a stiff chilly breeze coming off the sea, the sun was shining brightly as we arrived.

Hastings has a broad shingle beach with substantial sea defences and groynes, topped with a wide promenade. There is some stunning architecture across the road including what was once the Palace Hotel. Go and have a look through the big black doors and you'll see the wonderful hallway and elevator – although the hotel was built in the 1880s, this is straight out of the 1930s, a real time warp and I'd just LOVE to go inside and smell the history!

It is a really interesting promenade and we were intrigued by the odd little blue and white building opposite the old hotel. What was it? A subway? A convoluted entrance to a toilet block? Only by crossing the road are its origins revealed – this was where the White Rock Baths used to be, a Victorian spa complex that provided two pools, Turkish bath and health hydro facilities for people desperate to improve their health! Mostly subterranean it's been used as a swimming pool, skating rink and a skate park in recent years, but sadly it's now closed, oft vandalised and awaiting a decision as to its future. There are many parallels between Hastings and Weston, we have our Tropicana, they have their Baths! The town also grew at a similar rate to Weston, with a population of just 3,175 in 1801 and rising to 10,000 in just thirty years. By 1891 Hastings had grown to nearly 60,000, a huge increase.

We passed an interesting water feature, a large raised pond with benches incorporated along the geometric sides – obviously Art Deco and very likely the work of Sidney Little, also known as the 'Concrete King'. He was responsible for the double-decker promenade down by the seafront which was commissioned when quite substantial seafront renovations and upgrades were carried out in the 30s – more about Mr Little later! It was here that I warned a pigeon not to think about going in as it couldn't swim. The pigeon chose to ignore me and plopped in, disappearing up to its armpits. Jay said he was pretty sure it wasn't swimming and that we'd just walked past Hastings' unique pigeon bidet. I think Hastings may have something to say on that matter, dear...

We could see the distinctive squat little cream and silver towers of the pier entrance coming up, and walked past to see both sides of the pier. Hastings Pier has the most enormous gates and frontage that we'd ever seen! Walking west we found ourselves at the start of Sidney Little's promenade, the lower deck of which is known as 'Bottle Alley' thanks to thousands of pieces of coloured glass that were used to make a glass mosaic along the wall. Curved bays were frequented by deck chair enthusiasts, although now it's more likely that you'll bump into a resident alcoholic clutching a can while you dodge some suspicious yellow puddles...

Back on the top side of the promenade you can play human draughts on the red and white chequer board paving or admire the stupendous floral displays of different coloured tulips (it must have cost thousands, there were so many bulbs in different colours and species) and the ship that appeared to have been washed up a short distance away, dwarfing the other buildings along the seafront. This, amidst the Art Deco bus shelters and other delights is surely the jewel in the crown of the area. Marine Court (originally known as 'The Ship') is a 1930's block of flats that was styled on the RMS *Queen Mary*, and from many angles (even above) looks like an ocean liner! Apparently this building is so striking it can be seen up to twenty miles away (thirty two kilometres) on a clear day!

We turned back towards the pier, only to see that a small crowd had gathered, waving little flags. Oh dear! Big breaths... we'd not had this before! Even worse, they cheered when we arrived, having recognised us from photos. We were then told they'd also tried to get hold of a brass band – and boy, were we glad they hadn't! Eventually the gates were opened (the local council had not been all that keen to let us in) after a sticky moment when the key wouldn't turn – but we were in! As you may have worked out, there's some issue here over access, although it's more about ownership and responsibility, something the Hastings Pier and White Rock Trust want to put right, and are within a hair's breadth of doing so.

So how did Hastings come to have a pier? Now one of the most at risk piers in the country, it has been here since 1869, although it took nine years of wrangling before a site was approved and tenders invited. Eugenius Birch submitted a design and work started at 3 am on 18th December 1869, carried out by Richard Laidlaw and Sons of Glasgow. A grid of cast-iron screw piles were inserted by ten to twelve men stood on a wooden platform a metre or so off the seabed. Each pile was hand-screwed into the seabed using a wooden capstan which fitted over the top of the screw-tipped pile and, like donkeys, the men walked round and round until the 30cm (12") diameter pile was soundly in the seabed. At the landward end, this was into rock, but further out the seabed became clay, which, just like Ryde on the Isle of Wight, concealed an ancient forest of tree trunks. One pile broke as it collided with a submerged oak tree in 1872. The offending trunk was removed and found to weigh 1.81 tonnes (2 tons) and measured 7.3m (24') long and 1m (3') wide, and was put on display in the local park for many years.

There had been plans for a second pier, also designed by Birch, to be built a little further west at Warrior Square, but given the amount of arguing that had taken place over this one, plans were dropped. Hastings Pier finally opened on 5th August 1872, one of the first ever August Bank Holidays (and it should be noted, traditionally wet and windy). It had cost £23,250 to build and was modelled on Birch's pier in Brighton; although this one went a step further by having a stunning onion-domed 2,000 seat pavilion at the seaward end, the first pier to include an amusements pavilion specifically in its original design. The pier was 277m (910') long, with steps down to landing stages, each 61m (200') long, with another landing stage added in 1885. It featured all Birch's stipulations for a pier (lighting along the length, benches incorporated with the railings and thin decorative bracing) along with Turkish-looking toll booths, one of which was damaged by a storm on New Years' Day 1877 (but was repaired within six months at a cost of £1,650). The pier was an overnight success – in its first year of opening 482,000 visitors paid their 1d toll to enter, and this had risen to 584,000 by the end of the next.

A bowling alley was built half-way along the neck in 1910 and a 'joywheel' roundabout (no, I've no idea what it was either!) was built next to the seafront promenade at around the same time. The entrance to the pier was originally a wishbone shape, a narrow 'pierlet' coming in from both left and right, each arriving at a toll-booth. In 1913 the council proposed improvement plans for the whole seafront to boost the flagging tourist industry, and as part of its plans bought 67m (220') of the landward end of the pier from its owners, at a cost of £7,100. The council then spent £12,300 expanding the parade and merging it with the pier, to create an 'apron' four times the size it had been, designed to be a public amusement spot before the entrance to the pier was even reached. On this they had built a huge circular bandstand, with crescent-shaped shelters on either side. If you look at the old picture postcards from around this time the place was packed – the shelters held 650 people on proper seats, while the area around the bandstand was designed to take 2000 deckchairs. Two thousand! The old toll-booths and joywheel had been removed in 1914, and the new extension and bandstand were opened on the August Bank Holiday of 1916 (again, delightfully wet and windy – no change there then!).

The pier remained open and busy throughout the Great War, but a huge fire (thought to have been caused by a serviceman's discarded cigarette butt) in 1917 destroyed the seaward pavilion, with pictures reminiscent of Weston's Grand Pier fire so recently. A replacement, although somewhat less elaborate, re-opened in 1922 and the whole pier received a facelift and re-modelling in the 1930s, along with much of Hastings' seafront, something we'd already spotted. A shoreward pavilion was built in 1926 and given an Art Deco front in the facelift (even the clock got a fashionable hexagonal surround) and the theatre was also rebuilt, heralding one of the busiest and most profitable periods for the pier. The shoreward end now looked more Egyptian than Turkish, with squared shapes and repeated linear designs as was befitting of the day. The pier was so busy and so popular there was even a searchlight installed so that visitors could continue swimming at night! Once through the toll-gate there was a 645 seat 'Shore Pavilion' theatre, amusements centre, tea room, bar, refreshments room and the 1910 bowling alley. Oh, and steamers, ships, fishing and all marine entertainments at the seaward end! The first week of August 1931 saw 56,000 people going onto the pier, and I would imagine the local council were feeling very pleased with themselves!

In 1938 a huge storm shifted part of the seabed under the seaward end of the pier, necessitating £22,000 worth of repairs, and despite the outbreak of war, the pier stayed open until 1943. The pier was sectioned then by 23m (75') stopping just short of the rifle range. The pier suffered some minor bomb damage but was re-opened in 1946. Solariums (or more correctly, *solaria*) were built in 1951 and 1956, and in 1960 the Townsend hovercraft operated from the pier head, but the large bandstand on the apron was demolished in April 1961.

Extra concrete legs were added underneath the ex-bandstand apron for the installation of the aluminium Triodome, a 1950's fluted flying saucer, designed originally to display the Hastings Embroidery in 1966. It was later used as an amusement arcade and the bandstand shelters were converted to arcades and shops. The pier saw many big names play at the ballroom during the 60s and 70s (including the Rolling Stones, Pink Floyd and The Who), and the pier kept all its other amusements right up until the decline of the early 1980s (with the exception of a small zoo, which closed in 1974 and the animals, including ten hens and twenty rats, being sold off!).

In 1976 the pier received Grade II listed status but had begun to run at a loss, and in 1983 it was sold for £196,000 to Hamberglow Ltd. Despite a well-meaning approach, the continual maintenance programme underneath the pier wasn't carried out and it was also in the 1980s that the PS *Waverly* stopped visiting because of the state of the landing stage. There then followed a quick succession of changes in ownership, in 1996, 2000, 2002 and to an offshore enterprise in 2004. It's at this point in the pier's history that you need to sit down with a clear mind (and probably a strong coffee) in a quiet room and concentrate.

In July 2006 the pier was inspected by Hastings Borough Council and promptly closed to the public, owing to the structure being unsafe. Legal argy-bargy ensued between the two parties and it was only resolved when the council and one of the pier tenants paid for the £300,000 repairs and the closure was reversed. A storm in 2008 saw damage done to the seaward end and collapse imminent – barriers restricted public access and a bit of patching was done but when the tenant hung up their pier-owners boots, access was restricted and they have resisted contact from the council requesting a proper repair. We've seen from the other piers how important regular maintenance and repair is and that's without factoring in the effects of the sea.

And that brings us to our visit. The Hastings Pier and White Rock Trust (HPWRT) are a group of fervent (and slightly bonkers but very lovely) local people who are determined to acquire the pier (through compulsory purchase with the help of the council) and renovate, re-open and run it as a not-for-profit organisation. They oppose the option of demolishing the pier (which would cost over £4 million of local tax payers' money) and have worked out a plan to achieve re-opening for exactly the same cost as demolishing it! Starting from the apron the development plan would see the structure gradually renovated and opened in stages, ensuring that money would be coming in to fund further work – and also to keep the pier in the public focus, which helps to keep the money coming in too! It can be done, and with drive and enthusiasm like this Hastings Pier stands a very good chance of being a pier with a positive outcome!

Finding out about the history of a pier often makes clear what it is that we are looking at when we visit, especially in the case of closed piers where objects may not be in their original places or damage means certain bits are missing.

We now stepped through the open gates, escorted by HPWRT members (sounds now like we've done something really wrong) and stopped in awe at the sheer size of this part of the pier – it's big. Really, really big!

I dare say it helps that the space is not occupied by bandstand or flying saucer. It's decked (solidly here) and the buildings at each side of us are the remnants of the 1913 bandstand-on-the-apron improvement and there aren't many clues as to what the small colonnaded shops were last used for. We did have a good look round, and found one had been a pub and another an ice-cream concession, but apart from the broken glass and splintered wood caused by vandalism over the last eighteen months, little is left. We had our photo taken here (once the large dead gull had been unceremoniously chucked over the side), with the HPWRT members looking-on in suitably eccentric fashion while we kissed, for publication in the *Hastings Online Times*. For once it makes someone else look as mad as a box of frogs and not us!

Because of the dodgy nature of the rest of the pier (when last checked a piece fell off in the inspector's hand) we were only allowed to go this far, but it gave us the chance to look down the sides of the pier over the diamond lattice railings (made by Braithwaite and Kirk, West Bromwich). We spotted little metal Art Deco style pendants hanging down characteristically in pairs, and tiled columns on the sides of the building in clear green and blue, again perfect for the period. It's here the pigeons sit – perhaps because it complements their feathers, or maybe they appreciate the shape of the windows, we couldn't tell.

The main pavilion building with its hexagonal turrets is slightly at odds with the little round towers, but is still fairly pleasing on the eye, especially the round stained-glass window in the central one. As we stood there, as if by magic, a man with a key turned up and proceeded to open a door in this building. We edged across and craned our necks in the vain hope we'd be able to look inside (we're just too polite for our own good), and it was one of the other Trust members who had a word with him and said that we could have a quick look inside as long as we didn't move far from the door (in case something fell on us or we fell through the floor – lovely thought!).

Inside it's remarkably bright, mostly down to the roof being glass and the space was dedicated to little market-stall type amusements under green girders which was all we could really see behind the plywood and the pigeon poo. As we turned to leave, we read two notices on the wall – one telling us to leave the premises quietly (have we *ever* been rowdy on departure?) and the other giving a short potted history of the pier, left behind from its days under the Hastings Pier Company. We had a last look around on the pier before we were ushered out, and the gates were locked once more behind us (after a brief struggle with key and mutterings about getting some proprietary squirty lubricant next time). We said our farewells, but would be back later to attend the Mend of the Pier Fundraiser, an event which, we were told, would be unlike anything else we'd ever experienced. Gulp!

We went back to our temporary abode and decided to have an early meal – there was a football match on (sorry, I neglected to make a note of who was playing, but if you ask him, I'm sure Jay will remember!) and we sat at a conveniently positioned table in the totally empty eatery and ordered dinner. Jay noticed that the table had a number – 52, the same as his age, and we laughed at the strange coincidence. Later as we got ready to go out, I checked our paperwork... Hastings was our 52nd pier! How uncanny!

A breakneck taxi drive later (and we vowed not to use *him* again) saw us at the Crown House for the promised fun and frolics. It was well attended, funny, mad and delightfully eccentric with a half-time raffle, which we fancied supporting. Jay has the magic fingers when it comes to winning things (I can guarantee if I touch a ticket or even look at it we will not win!) and sat down with the tickets. The first number drawn... was ours! Jay went up to pick his prize and be introduced to the crowd. A couple of tickets later, we had another winner, and I was sent up for my prize and round of applause. The next ticket out of the hat was... ours again, and this time it was that number again, 52. What were the chances of that?!

We sat down, wildly excited with our success and heaped the goodies on the table (a DVD, bar of soap and a very pretty little incense burner) and watched the end of the show. We had a fantastic time and it was a shame (although very funny) that events were brought to a sudden and premature end when an exploding apple set off the smoke alarms and the building had to be evacuated until the fire brigade (two vehicles) came and re-set the alarms and wagged a cautionary finger at the performer (whose name will remain unpublished!). Our taxi (different driver) arrived at that point and we slipped away, but we had experienced a wonderful, if slightly surreal evening, and a wonderful, if slightly madcap, visit to Hastings Pier!

Tomorrow we would be visiting Eastbourne Pier but we knew we'd be keeping a close eye on the efforts of the HPWRT and looked forward to reading their success story in a paper soon.

Another sunny morning saw us leisurely heading the seventeen miles to Eastbourne along the East Sussex coast (although it was west we were travelling, not east, just to be confusing!). Now we'd seen most of Eugenius Birch's piers and learnt what to look for, we were quite looking forward to seeing another. Eastbourne Pier hadn't popped up on the radar since we'd been aware of piers around the country, again overshadowed perhaps by the two at Brighton, but the newspapers and media are missing a trick, and should head a bit further along the coast every time the sun comes out!

First proposed in 1863, the town's major landowner, William Cavendish, the 7th Duke of Devonshire was really keen to have a pier in Eastbourne and backed the idea. The Eastbourne Pier Company was registered in April 1865 and on 18th April 1866 the first pile was driven in by J.E. Dowson's engineering company. Officially opened on 13th July 1870 by Lord Edward Cavendish the pier wasn't actually finished, owing to Dowson's death, but was completed in 1872 having been taken over by Head Wrightson and Co.

The pier consisted of a landing stage, windbreak and six kiosks along the length with two larger, almost octagonal Gothic-style toll-booths flanking a smaller one between them at the entrance. Typically Birch (and we now feel qualified to say so), there were little lamps, integrated seating and wrought-iron railings along the 305m (1,000') length, and elegant, slightly raked piles with cross-bracing below. However, these legs disguise a unique feature of this pier, for the piles supporting the superstructure are sat in cups on the seabed. This means that in stormy weather the legs (and therefore the whole pier) can move slightly, absorbing the force of the waves and wind rather than being battered and suffering damage. This theory was tested using two six-pound cannons on the deck to illustrate that the pier was able to withstand huge forces, although this does appear to be a bit insignificant considering how forceful the sea can be on this part of the coast, but I'm sure the idea was well-meaning!

A violent storm on New Year's Day 1877 washed away the shoreward end, which was rebuilt at a higher level so that the pier sloped slightly as it made landfall. Eleven years later a 400-seater pavilion was built for the cost of £250 at the seaward end and a new arrow-shaped landing stage added in 1893, constructed just away from the edge of the pier to protect it from wayward steamers! Between 1899 and 1901 the original pavilion was replaced by a 1000-seater theatre (the first pavilion went off to become a cow shed in Lewes!), bar and two saloons midway along the deck. A camera obscura was also added, a novel invention whereby an image of the surroundings is projected by way of a pinhole camera into a darkened room below.

From 1906 P & A Campbell steamers regularly visited the pier, providing pleasure trips to France and south coast resorts, and in 1912 some new entrance buildings were erected and in 1922 a 900-seat music pavilion, also known as the 'blue room' at the shoreward end which was also used as a ballroom before being converted to its current incarnation of an amusement arcade. The 1920s saw an increase in visitors arriving by charabanc. An old postcard from 1925 shows two packed vehicles disembarking at the entrance to the pier, and interestingly there seems to be a vehicle park for some outlandish bath chairs just next to the formal gardens (also visible in an earlier picture too!).

In 1940 part of the decking was removed instead of radical sectioning, and machine guns were put into the theatre to repel potential enemy boarders, along with a Bofors anti-aircraft gun halfway along the pier. Local police were nearly responsible for the destruction of the pier in 1942 when they tied a mine to the pier legs in the mistaken belief that it was safe. The mine promptly exploded and damaged not only the pier but also local hotels – it's not recorded what happened to the policemen, but the betting is they were pretty red-faced, to say the least. In 1943 netting was added to the sides of the pier to provide camouflage for small landing craft hidden underneath, and a successful rescue that year by two engineers resulted in them being awarded the George Medal and British Empire Medal when they pulled a colleague who had fallen from the sectioned pier out of the sea.

Once peacetime had resumed, the decking was put back and a new kidney-shaped entrance with new buildings installed and the pier was back in action. Steamers continued to visit up until 1957, when they were gradually replaced by more conventional motorised vessels. The camera obscura had fallen into disrepair and disuse by 1960, and in 1970 the theatre was destroyed by a fire, but replaced by a 'Dixieland' show bar that was also used for discos and cabarets but remains today – in fact it's a rare thing among piers that so many of the early buildings and fittings can still be seen now.

Eastbourne Pier is also a fantastic example of how successful a pier can be if it's continually looked after and maintained, with £250,000 spent in 1985 on a facelift which included a big new arcade. The devastating 'not-really-a-hurricane' of October 1987 tried its best to have a go at the rocking pier, but the worst it could do was destroy the landing stage. On 15th June 1991 a new £500,000 entrance was opened by the Duke of Devonshire (obviously not the one from the 1860s, he'd be well crinkly by then) and all the hard work was rewarded when the pier was awarded 'Pier of the Year' by the National Piers Society in 1997.

More recent years have seen this wonderful pier go from strength to strength. The camera obscura was refurbished in 2003 and English Heritage upgraded the piers listed building status from Grade II to Grade II* in May 2009. Put on the market by owners Six Piers Ltd. in the same year it was removed from the market in October following a really successful summer season – you cynics! The following May the pier was treated to £250,000 worth of refurbishment leaving it sparkling and gorgeous for our visit!

The walk along the promenade was breezy but pleasant, the brick-paved walkway next to the wide expanse of shingle seemed to soak up the sunshine, and even though it was still relatively early on a Sunday morning, there were plenty of people strolling along, sitting on benches reading the Sunday papers or power walking in funny lycra outfits (watch out, the fashion police know where you live!).

Despite the relative newness of the entrance, it in no way looks out of place with the rest of the structure, the corner booths with linking canopy topped by a square clock-tower in Edwardian style are welcoming and shiny (and I am notoriously a sucker for shiny things!). It must be said it's also a very grand setting for the pier, opposite some very large and impressive Victorian buildings – many of these are still hotels and have Grade II listings, and in between these and the seafront are the equally impressive and attractive carpet gardens (formal-shaped beds amongst velvet lawns, and when we visited, planted with deliciously scented wallflowers). This, next to the blue and white Victorian lamp-standard is where we would have parked our bath-chairs all those years ago!

Inside the airy and deceptively large entrance there is an easy-to-read map of the pier, listing all the things we could expect to see. Would we feel the pier rocking? What was the state of the sea today? Stop panicking woman and go and explore! Ever susceptible to the powers of persuasion I know I convinced myself that the pier was gently rocking the entire time I was on it – for the faint-hearted visitor, I can assure you it doesn't move at all and it would take a considerably stormier sea than we had today before it did! Beyond the entrance is Funtasia, once the 'blue room' music pavilion, today an amusements arcade.

We decided to walk around the pier first, and revelled in the blue and white paintwork, continued all along Eastbourne seafront, a decidedly cheerful and seaside-y combination. The more modern lamp posts along the pier are rather unusual, featuring a very wide-mouthed fierce lion, which almost looks like he should be holding something in his mouth it's that agape! The original, more diminutive lamp posts are still there too although without tops, and they seem to be part of the railings. These are also painted blue and the start of the pier sees simple rails with a stylised flower panel at the bottom. Despite all that recent money spent, there is a lot of shabby paintwork and in places some rotten woodwork, but I've resolved to be a lot less scathing of cosmetic works because it takes a constant effort to maintain these piers and the underside is much more important!

The early panelled windbreak along the centre of the pier is absolutely beautiful. The original one ran the length of the pier and was a sheer confection of scrolled wrought ironwork painted white. Now there is a roof, decorated panelling at the bottom in blue and white and blue scrollwork not only holding the roof up but also running along the top. There are no benches at the foot of the windbreak any more, there's now more call for tables and chairs and places to eat the vast array of fast food that can be bought on the pier! We'd passed 'Sugar Rush' and the Waterfront café and bar before sidling round the back of the seaward pavilion to the end of the pier.

Now used mainly by anglers again, the end of the pier has a metal decked, lower and simpler staging today, rather than the huge substantial landing stage required before. Through gaps in the decking I could see the sparkly water below and noted that a couple of the cross bracing pieces were very corroded and could do with replacing! The end of Eastbourne pier is a relaxing, quiet and rather lovely place to while away some time, smoothly decked and with a simple white bench and blue handrail combo at the edge. The Pier Angling Club have a little hut at the end, where they also rent out fishing rods, but if angling isn't your thing, you could perhaps just sit and watch the little yachts go past, or the sparkles on the sea. Or have a kiss with someone lovely by the railings! We opted for all three options before carrying on our exploration of the pier's delights. This large pavilion at the end also has the camera obscura at the top of its pinnacle, reached by gleaming white steps, but sadly we were too early to be able to go up and have a look at the views of Eastbourne.

There is a rather alarming notice here, stating that it's advisable to hold the handrail when windy. Isn't this being a little bit *too* safety conscious? I can't ever recall having had wind that bad... Perhaps this is what comes of working with small children (the sense of humour, not the wind!), but it wasn't just me, and we both walked along chortling loudly. Sorry! You may have suspected what we were like, now you know you were right!

Back to some sort of sensibility (wiping our eyes dry), we marvelled at the older seats on the midsection of the pier, here with fewer wooden slats and more wrought-iron backing, and then we stopped and eyed-up the kiosk that houses the Glass Studio. It did nothing to quell my seasickness but compounded the wobbly feeling because the building has some pretty strange angles and looks like it might fall off the edge of the pier! Mr Sensible assured me there was no way that it would, and so we went inside to have a look at the some of the lovely glasswork. From the other side the little building in its bay looks totally straight and secure. I don't know what all the fuss is about!

We hadn't forgotten about the amusements pavilion, and on our way back slipped inside for a go on a few machines. However, rather than reaching for our pennies we were stopped in our tracks, because inside there are many of the original features of this 1920's building behind all the modern flashing lights and gaudy machinery. The main room is painted blue and has plasterwork swags, scrolls and urns around the walls and ceiling and these are painted tastefully in green, cream and terracotta. The ceiling has raised skylights, and at one end there is still a small stage, framed by Romanesque columns, some more swags and topped off in the centre with a large ornamental plasterwork roundel. On a mezzanine behind the stage front is a pool hall and this is reached by a delicate white spiral staircase. The view back from the top is impressive, especially if you pretend the modern machines aren't there, but it's a really sympathetic preservation of a building that's nearly a hundred years old but still needs to have a modern appeal.

We did succumb to some penny falls machines again before leaving the pier, past the charms of the fish stall but avoided purchasing tubs of anchovies, jellied eels and whelks, not a wise idea in a hot car for a long journey home! With Brighton's West Pier now sadly past all hope of restoration, Eastbourne Pier is well worth a visit, with the beautiful wrought ironwork along its length and it is regarded by many (including us!) as the best example of Eugenius Birch's outstanding engineering and design.

CHAPTER 22

The End's In Sight – But Up Pop Some Surprises!

We now had just three piers left to tick off on our list and a wedding to organise for October. We had a dress (although we were still fighting over who would wear it), bridesmaids (also dressed) – and now we also had a venue! With increasing worries that Weston's Grand Pier wouldn't be ready in time, we had a flash of inspiration. Our last pier to visit was Brighton Palace Pier, oft photographed (especially when the papers needed a picture of something 'English' or to illustrate a packed beach during a heatwave!) and usefully it was also in possession of a wedding licence. Emails whisked back and forth, phone calls were made... and the place was booked! Now the panic really set in – we needed to send out the invites, find someone to do flowers and a cake, book accommodation for us and the guests... and I needed a hairdresser, all in an area where we knew no one! Whose silly idea was this?

To top it all, some idle surfing of the web had thrown up another pier. Then Jay declared that he had somewhere special he wanted to take me, having organised access to a pier that I hadn't got on my list. Neither of us wanted to spoil the surprise, but we managed to discover that they were in roughly the same direction and somehow found a spare day to go visiting not one but two unexpected piers! Mine was first on the agenda and would take four hours to get to (including a much needed coffee break along the way!). Jay was mystified but deduced that we were heading towards London and the contentious issue of piers on rivers again.

Bother that man, he's just too clever for his own good, but he couldn't work out the exact location of Mystery Pier #1, which was in the London Borough of Bexley, and the delightful town of Erith. We swung into the car park of Morrison's supermarket, a vital component of this pier's story because they own it! Back when Erith was a quiet backwater of London, in the days before it was swallowed by the serpent of industrialisation, there had been a cunning plan. The idea was to cash in on the current fashion of tourists visiting resorts, by building a pier, thereby encouraging boats to visit and boost income in the area.

Money was stumped up by the Guardians of the local Wheatley Estate and a 135m (444') wooden pier (although technically a jetty, I suppose) was built. It opened amid great celebration on 22nd August 1842, the entertainment included duck hunting, jingling (not the hunting of Morris Men but men hitting each other with ash sticks until the last man was left standing!) and boat races. A grand public dinner was held in a marquee afterwards and the pier was up and running!

Although there are few records of the next couple of years, business must have done quite well because in 1844 the Pier Hotel was built, and in July of the following year some grand gardens opened for visitors that featured a fountain, maze, archery field and bowling green. Two ships, *The Diamond* and *The Star* brought passengers from Gravesend and London every day and on the face of it the pier at Erith should have continued to be a roaring success.

There were, however, several glaringly huge wasps in the jam jar. One was the river, which was tidal. When it went out there was an enormous amount of mud which offended Victorian sensibilities. This was compounded by a twice-daily release of raw sewage from the Southern Outfall Works at Crossness just as the high tide was turning. The idea was that the ebbing waters would swish the poo out to sea. It didn't, and instead from 1865 when the plant opened, it came swirling down the Thames and lingered at Erith. The second problem was the arrival of the railway in July 1849 meaning tourists coming to the Wheatley estate could arrive not only in style but without the smells (even without the effluent aroma from 1865 the Thames would have been in a pretty disgusting state with lots of gross things churning around in its sludge. The Pumping Station was just the icing on the cake and I don't recommend eating it!). It would have been preferable to travel faster and arrive fragrantly than risk the boat journey, and numbers landing there dwindled quickly.

The last thorny problem was the arrival of heavy industry in the area as a result of larger shipping and that bothersome railway. In 1864 the Erith Iron Works were opened, from 1881 William Callander's cable works was up and running and when looking at an 1897 map of the area, the waterfront had been swallowed up by huge depots, railway sidings and wharves for unloading coal. Not really the sort of place you'd fancy travelling to with your beau for a walk and cup of tea without a pomander the size of Wembley stadium!

The town swamped the old estate grounds and the pier site was taken over by a coal merchant. The pier survived both World Wars, despite being on the edge of London, in the neighbourhood of munitions factories and right underneath the German bombing routes! By 1957 the old wooden pier was well out of date and probably fairly unstable. Now that shipping was larger it needed deep-water berthing facilities, so a new concrete pier was built outside the line of the original wooden one with a railway running the entire length. The hotel was demolished to make room for warehouses and the days of tourism were now nothing more than a memory.

However, since the 1990s Erith has been subject to a huge rejuvenation and regeneration project and it's now a much changed area. Gone is the heavy industry and desolate drab scenery. The Thames has undergone a much needed clean-up operation, rendering the air with a much more pleasing aroma! Now there are new flats and smart riverside apartments, a big supermarket and new retail and commercial sites. The waterside has also been opened up as a Thameside path, suitable for walkers and cyclists. During the regeneration the land near the pier was sold to a supermarket for development but came with the caveat that the former pier was restored as a public amenity.

We walked across from our parking space towards the river which was marked by a large masthead flagpole with signalling flags whipping around in the breeze. I haven't decoded them for fear that the message was rude, but they did look suitably maritime, so we were impressed. To the right is an old building, now painted dark blue and sporting the title 'Erith Deep

Wharf'. There are also flood defences here in the shape of strong gates that would be pulled across if the tide threatened to breach the banks – and there is the start of the pier!

It is an L-shape, and we walked along the short leg of the L first. It is a wide pier and has been nicely done, with blue metal benches along its length and matching blue angle-poise lamps on each side to light the way. Once out over the water it is remarkably quiet and peaceful. The air has that lovely damp rivery smell (and thankfully no longer chemical pollution or thick sewage!) and we spotted several ducks in the river and a cormorant sunning itself on the other side of the water.

Although underfoot is brick paving it's been laid in patterns using three colours – red, cream and black. Once around the elbow we started out along the long bit of the L which runs parallel to the river bank, past other walkers, a couple of people sat on the benches watching the Thames slip silkily by and a gaggle of disaffected youths. Don't get me wrong, we're not sticking a label on them just because they were teenagers, and we're sure they were bored, but we suspect it was only the presence of us arriving at the end of the pier that made them stop disembowelling the workings of a lamp post (from the top) and smoking something that didn't smell like normal tobacco... They took off on their BMX bikes using colourful language, leaving two lads with their fishing rods behind. Fishing is really popular here, and now the river's been cleaned up there are a wide number of species available to catch including flounder, bass and the ubiquitous eel – we found graffiti on the little signal box at the end of the pier which read *13 Jly 2010 – Flounder 2lb* complete with a little picture of it on the line. Eleven day old graffiti! That makes a change; it's usually old and irrelevant!

We didn't pause for very long to have our end-of-pier kiss as it was a bit difficult to concentrate with lurking youth around the corner, but Erith Pier had been a lovely surprise addition to our journey and we had enjoyed the walk along it. The little white box at the end of the pier has two sets of buffers in front of it, memorials to the little loading railway that once ran along here, and in front of them is a circle of chequer plate metal where the turntable used to be for spinning the locomotives round ready for the return journey, a nice reminder of the pier's heritage.

As we walked back we watched some of the varied Thames shipping that increasingly work the river, and admired the new flats and apartments that have been built on the waterside. We had lunch in the supermarket café and then sat in the car while the co-pilot plotted a route to our next destination. I still had no idea where we were headed, and still didn't (despite driving) as we left Erith past the three mosaic fish on the roundabout and off in a north-west direction (by way of the M25!).

I was baffled. We weren't heading towards a coast.

"Is it on a river?" I asked.

"Nope!"

"And it's not the sea? So it must be a pier on a lake then!" I ventured.

"Up to a point..." replied Mr Enigma, "Keep driving and you'll find out!"

I hate a mystery, especially when it's at my expense! I was none the wiser as we drove into the leafy Buckinghamshire town of Beaconsfield.

"There's a model village here isn't there?" I asked.

I swear you could have heard the penny drop as far away as Australia it fell with such a clang. Again. Mystery Pier #2 was not going to be a full-size affair – it was a scale model at Bekonscot! We leapt out of the car leaving my adult self in the seat, and we made our way round to the entrance, situated in a real chocolate and cream railway carriage (it also contains a shop and a cash machine!). Jay explained who we were, the nice lady checked her book, and because the devious man had already arranged our visit, we were waved in *gratis*!

Bekonscot is an absolute delight and is generally considered to be the granddaddy of model villages everywhere. Its creator Roland Callingham was a London accountant who had a passion for model railways which he indulged in his spare time. In 1927 he had his gardeners dig a swimming pool in the garden to add to the tennis courts as entertainment for dinner guests. However, being a deliciously English eccentric chap, the pool soon acquired two islands and a pier. Mrs Callingham had, however, decided that enough was enough. She insisted that either the model railway went or she did.

The Callingham's garden soon had a large model railway running around the pool, soon added to following suggestions of buildings from the staff, who were often pinched from their duties to help construct new houses or scenes in the garden! Mr Callingham named his village 'Bekonscot' after Beaconsfield and Ascot where he had lived, and by 1929 it was open to the public. Eighty years on and Bekonscot has grown to a 1.5 acre site of six villages (all named), two lakes, a canal and a waterfall, a white horse, hunting horse and shire horse and ten (scale) miles of railway track and seven stations!

We entered the model village (following a discreet one-way system) and marvelled at the zoo, where we spotted an elephant ride, a little boy buying an ice cream and a chimp's tea party. There are superb details everywhere and a brilliant sense of humour – this isn't a serious place at all! We walked around Bekonscot castle and village (there are gardening nuns!) and some superb topiary. I think the garden element of the model village is what really makes it – all the plants have been chosen and then pruned and trimmed to be perfectly within scale of their setting with even the leaves the right size!

After leaving the model of Bekonscot Village we strolled around Southpool Village and there at the back of the lake was the pier! Actually you can hear it before you see it, because like all good Victorian piers, it has a bandstand and the smartly clad band here are playing loudly!

We closed in on the pier which is situated behind the Bekonscot Yacht Haven and sticking out into the cream and pink lilies of the Lake (that was meant to be a swimming pool!). There's a shoreward pavilion theatre that looks remarkably like Wellington Pier at Great Yarmouth, perhaps with a hint of Penarth. There are four square, terracotta and cream-coloured towers, each topped with a bell-shaped cap of green and revealing its Art Deco origins though the shapes and colours. There's a poster at the front of the pier advertising the bill – Max Miller, Arthur Askey, George Formby, Gracie Fields and Flanagan and Allen – that's an impressive concert!

The pier neck goes to a T-shaped pier head, with planking running along the length. The rails are white and not terribly decorative, and there aren't any integrated benches – so it's not one of Eugenius Birch's lost designs! With just a couple of rectangular shelters on the neck, the main focus is the large circular bandstand. It has a domed silver roof and blue ironwork, a colour scheme mirrored by the little shelters. The whole effect is topped off by strings of multi-coloured bunting along all the sides of the pier, and the scarlet-coated bandsmen, playing their lungs out to the two rather apprehensive onlookers!

We had a kiss at the end of the pier, although it wasn't the wet end! We kissed on the path and I have to admit it was a brilliantly witty joke to play and a very clever day out! The rest of the model villages were just as detailed and funny. The fishmonger's van leaving the harbour has 'Bert Zye' on the side, the soldiers in Wychwood Castle have a floral window box, and there are even men legging their barge through Hanton tunnel. It'd be easy to write a book about what you can see at Bekonscot – the high diver and wall of death at the fairground, lighthouses and gypsy camp. My favourites are (apart from the pier) the archaeological dig and white horse carved on the hill, but there is bound to be a lot I hadn't spotted, even though we eventually spent several hours there!

It makes a lovely change not to have to think of a different way to describe walking back along a pier – if it gets a bit predictable and tedious for you to read it, just think how hard it is for me to write it! Here at Bekonscot we didn't just walk back to the car; instead we saw the rest of the models and had an ice cream in the wasp-infested picnic area. We decided it was less likely that we'd ingest an insect with a grudge against humanity if we walked around a bit, and the shelters here have some interesting old posters advertising things such as Barnum and Bailey's balloon horse Jupiter. A 'sensational ascension act with a gorgeous pyrotechnic display' really caught my attention and I wanted to know more, but sadly I've not been able to find much out about this act at all, which is a shame because I'd love to know how they managed to get Jupiter used to a balloon and fireworks!

At last we'd finished our mystery pier tour, a day with many differences and delights and unexpected experiences but totally brilliant! And NOW we had only three more piers to visit. And a wedding to organise... AAARGH!

CHAPTER 23

The Birdmen Cometh...Along With Another Surprise (Worthing, Bognor and Mystery Pier #3!)

It was now the middle of August, eight weeks to go until the Big Day and we had some South Coast piers to finish – and also a trip to Brighton to see the venue! We realise that it was probably a bit close to the wedding to change our mind if we hadn't liked it, but how can you NOT like a pier! We'd also seen plenty of photos, so were more than happy with the venue. I also had an appointment with Lynnette the florist in Hove, the cake was under construction, the dresses fitted and ready to go – but still no hairdresser! We both felt a bit strange going to see a pier but not really looking at it – we felt it wouldn't have been right, so we took a chaperone with us to make sure we didn't see too much and ensure we behaved ourselves and didn't sneak a kiss in! (There's nothing scarier than a disapproving teenage daughter to make sure you behave yourself!)

We were blown away with the City and the pier – we knew we'd made the right choice! And I shan't say any more about it, as it needs saving for its own chapter! All the meetings went smoothly (flowers now discussed and sorted) and the following day we left our rather lovely hotel to visit Worthing Pier. Once a mackerel fishing hamlet, Worthing became an elegant Georgian seaside resort and much of the architecture remains today, with tall, grand buildings sweeping along the seafront. The first pile for the new pier was put in on 4th July 1861 under which was placed a simple time capsule consisting of a bottle that contained an inscribed parchment and some coins. The design of Sir Robert Rawlinson opened on 12th April 1862. Considered as the thirteenth pier to be built in England it was a simple promenade space 293m (960') long and 5m (15') wide with decking and flag poles and a single central toll gate. The pier remained an entertainment-free zone until 1874 when a local orchestra was hired to play for three hours a day as long as the weather was nice – it took another seven years for shelters to be built though!

In 1884 this single gate was replaced by two kiosks, one for collecting tolls and the other to sell souvenirs. The pier remained fairly building-free until 1888 when the neck was widened to 9m (30') and the pier head extended to 32m (105') so that a 650-seat pavilion could be built. The work cost £12,000 and the pavilion opened the following year. The very first moving picture show in Worthing was screened here in 1896 – a thrilling experience, no doubt!

Steamer traffic was regular, going all along the south coast, even to Brighton's Chain Pier (built in 1823 and demolished in 1896). Because the steamers often queued to berth at Worthing Pier when the tide was low, it was proposed to extend the pier into deeper water. However, it was discovered that even if the pier was doubled in length (and that would have meant a structure of 585m or 1,920'), it would only increase the depth of the water by 1.8m (6')! Not *really* worth all the trouble or expense!

Tourism in Worthing and on the pier was booming at the start of the twentieth century. In 1913 work started on enlarging the shoreward end of the pier, but a devastating event on 22nd March put paid to any plans for development. Easter Monday had seen unsettled weather all day, but in the evening during a concert the wind speed had picked up to an alarming extent, and it was decided that discretion was the better part of valour and everyone legged it to the shore. Here the crane being used for the heavy lifting was swaying alarmingly, and the concert goers joined a small group of onlookers who were by now very concerned about the wind speed. By 9 pm the wind was reaching 80 mph and just after midnight witnesses saw the arc lighting on the pier go out, accompanied by several loud bangs, and the neck and landward section of Worthing Pier was swept away.

Photographs taken the following day show hundreds of people on the beach, surveying the wreckage disbelievingly. All that was left was the pier-head pavilion out at sea (which locals affectionately dubbed Easter Island), the rest reduced to stumps of ironwork, twisted girders and shattered planking. The beach for nearly a mile was littered with debris that included iron seats, piles and woodwork.

However, the pier was reopened the following year on 29th May with neat planking and little 'button hook' lamp posts along the length. The pier head, now reunited with the land went back to being a popular entertainment spot, visited by steamers again. Worthing Borough Council bought the pier on 23rd March 1921 for the princely sum of £18,978 (and 15 shillings!). They charged 2d as a toll, and by 1926 decided to replace the kiosks at the promenade end with a grand new pavilion, designed by Adshead and Ramsey.

Still there today, the pavilion is a huge building for the £1,000 it cost back then – you couldn't get a comparable return for your money today – and inside was elaborately decorated. Outside, the huge dome sat low to the ground but dominated the promenade and proved an extremely popular venue. The new pavilion also incorporated a new souvenir shop to one side, to keep the visitors happy!

For nearly twenty years the pier operated successfully and without incident, and the 10th September 1933 dawned like any other with visitors enjoying the delights of the pier in the autumn sunshine. It may have been a cigarette butt thoughtlessly discarded, but wisps of smoke at the end of the pier soon became a huge conflagration. Staggeringly it wasn't until flames were licking at the pavilion walls at 3.40 p.m. that the alarm was raised, by which time sheets of fire, whipped up by a strong easterly wind were leaping some 20m (60') into the air.

Fishermen on the end of the pier had a narrow escape, as did a party of fifty enjoying a fine-dining experience in the pavilion – diners and waitresses fleeing for their lives. The fire brigade were called and joined forces with the public, trying to create a fire-break by ripping up decking and removing anything combustible to stop the fire from destroying the whole pier. The PS *Waverley*, passing by on its way to Littlehampton sailed close to give passengers a closer view – so involved were they that people were seen hanging over the railings, and the boat began to heel over dangerously in the water!

On the pier more than 300 holidaymakers, some still attired in their bathing costumes, carried off seats and became part of a bucket chain, or helped the firemen with crowbars and axes to remove planks. One man drove his car onto the pier with extra tools on board, and came back with a load of salvaged furniture from the pavilion. Even the womenfolk became involved in the rescue, forming a chain to remove deckchairs. Although everyone battled valiantly (and perhaps saved the entirety of the pier with their exertions), the thick smoke could be seen over 30 miles away and in less than an hour there was nothing left of the seaward end of Worthing Pier except charred and smoking timber and blackened ironwork hanging above the sea, all surrounded by the wall of sturdy timbers meant to stop damage by steamers.

A huge determination to reinstate the length of pier and rebuild a worthy pavilion saw the pier re-open in July 1935, 293m (960') long and topped with a 'Streamline Moderne' pavilion, the repairs costing around £18,000. This later type of Art Deco styling building was extremely elegant with sundecks giving the illusion to visitors that they were on the deck of a grand ocean liner. Inside attractions included a solarium with ultra-violet lights and 'vita glass' windows (a special glass containing quartz to allow even more ultra-violet rays in). This new building was soon being used with gusto and hosted dancing and provided refreshments for all, with steamer traffic resuming bringing visitors by sea once again.

Two years later an amusement pavilion and a windshield that ran the length of the pier were added, and an orchestra provided four performances a week up to the outbreak of World War II. Following the evacuation of Dunkirk, when the threat of German invasion was felt to be severe, a 37m (120') hole was blown in the pier to prevent it being used, but two years later when this threat was less, the landward end of the structure was used as a canteen for troops and as an amusement centre with billiard tables and a library.

Following the war, the Government stumped up the cost of repairs and renovations, and the landward pavilion re-opened to the public in June 1946, with the rest of the pier up and running by April 1949. With metal and other materials being in short supply following the war effort, old cast-iron water mains pipes were used to replace some of the missing piles! To put this lack of materials into context, greenheart timber, so necessary for solid marine piling and needed especially to repair bomb-damaged docks, was also scarce. Just one shipload arrived in Britain in 1947, and amazingly, despite the demand for the worm-resistant timber, half of this load was used to repair the piles of Worthing Pier.

Since then, the life of Worthing Pier has been considerably less dramatic. In March 1958 some shoreward refurbishment was carried out and an extra lounge added the following year. These buildings were closed between 1979 and 1982 to carry out important work on the pier's structure. In 2006 the pier was awarded the coveted 'Pier of the Year' award and had a somewhat notorious nightclub operating in the Southern pavilion for three years between 2007 and 2010, although after the war it had also been used as a café, dancehall and a model railway layout!

We hadn't really done any research about our visit that day, and as we walked along the lovely wide promenade, saw large banners advertising the Birdman competition. The date looked familiar... oh! It was this weekend! Originally held at Bognor Pier this rather eccentric and deliciously English annual competition involves inventors building flying machines and throwing themselves off a platform on the top of the pier into the sea. Whoever travels the furthest distance is the winner – obviously done when the tide is IN, or I would imagine the appeal (and the number of competitors) would be significantly less!

There are some lovely features of this broad seafront – mackerel adorned rubbish bins, pretty Art Deco style up-sweeping lamp posts and strings of white fairy lights (and other globe-topped lamps too), seaward facing benches and stacks of deckchairs placed along the prom ready for hordes of onlookers to watch the Birdmen in comfort. We could see the pier but had been sidetracked by the rather gorgeous Lido building adorning the beachside. Originally a birdcage bandstand that was built in 1897 but demolished in 1925, the current Grade II listed, horseshoe-shaped enclosure was designed by Adshead and Ramsey, the same designers of the pier's landward pavilion. It cost a whopping £25,000 (huge when you think that the whole end of the pier was rebuilt in the 1930s for £18,000), but could seat over 2000 people for its original use as a concert space. From 1957 this area was converted to a swimming pool and before its closure in the late 1980s was home (albeit temporarily) to some dolphins, who were having a home constructed elsewhere! It now looked like an amusement space, with a stage area under the central roof, slide and trampolines, pirate water blaster, deckchairs and remote-control cars available for your delight!

We had arranged to meet the local paper's photographer at the front of the pier, and it was a truly impressive entrance to a pier! The landward pavilion is huge, its large grey curved roofs and Corinthian columns adding to the grandness. Closer, there are decorated friezes between the columns, and a sweep of white steps up to the many glass-panelled doors. Across the road, opposite the pretty floral roundabout, the hugeness of this building becomes really apparent and if my resultant photo had not been at such a crazy drunken angle I could have shown you, but you'll have to take my word or go and have a look!

We introduced ourselves to the lonely loitering chap at the entrance and were escorted through tough security (because of the Birdman contest) onto the pier neck and were whisked to the end. The platform for the avian leapers rises an impressive 11m (35′) above the deck of the pier, and in order for people to take their flying machines to the top, has a long ramp extending to the back of the pier. The photographer stopped to talk to a burly security guard... what was he doing?

Suddenly we were beckoned towards the bottom of the ramp – we were going up! John Rodway, boss of the safety company overseeing the launch pad (and a thoroughly lovely man who manned our camera for us while we were up there) had allowed us permission up onto the platform so that we could have a very novel kiss and photograph! It was definitely the highest pier kiss we'd had... the tide was out and the ramp moved slightly in the wind. That looked an awfully long way down!

We headed back down the ramp with wobbly knees to have a look at the rest of wonderful Worthing Pier.

"So, where are you off to now?" asked the photographer. We told him it was Bognor (to meet another photographer) and then home.

"Um... so you're not going to Littlehampton then?" he enquired.

"Littlehampton? It has a pier?" We looked at each other in an alarmed way. He told us that indeed, it did, gave us directions and said he was quite happy to meet us there and take another picture. Right. So that's another one then! Our starting journey of fifty or so piers had now extended to sixty in total – that's a lot of piers and a lot of kisses (and as I can testify in the days afterwards, an awful lot of writing and research too!).

We rejoined our bemused chaperone, who had waited on the first-floor decking of the pavilion ("That man took a picture of me! What was all that about?!") and had a look at the rest of the pier, and our fifty-seventh kiss at the proper end of the pier. Worthing Pier really is delightfully English, and all that you could expect from a gentle seaside walk over the waves. It's not brash or flash, noisy or in-your-face but harks back to its 1930's heyday having retained so much of the furniture and style of its rebuilding. Down the centre of the planked deck is the long windshield, now painted brown and cream and keeping the stiff sea breeze off the stripy deckchairs. Sat on one of these you could look out over the sea (we spotted a lone egret stalking worms on the beach) through the simple but elegant railings studded with simple lamp standards and flagpoles.

We walked to the end of the delightful pavilion, also painted in cream and as it approached the end of the pier, curved sympathetically and mirrored the end of the pier, giving a nautical sweeping feel as you look out over the sea. With curved glass windows and a first-floor window with railed balcony that resembled the bridge of an old-fashioned liner, all it was lacking was a bit of Ragtime jazz and suitably attired holidaymakers! We kissed between sturdy lamp posts (avoiding disapproving tuts from You Know Who) and looked at the barnacled upright timbers of the boating jetty, still in its original position set away from the pier and sitting lower, looking incredibly solid and indestructible.

Along the sides there are occasional port-hole windows in the cream lapped woodwork and at the entrance to the building sweeping stairways on either side lead up to the balcony. Gosh it's beautiful!

We headed back admiring the little tops of the columns between each section of the windshield, marked with geometric patterns and then 'oohing' over the delightful clock set at the front of the 1937 amusements arcade part way along the pier neck. Also featuring curves instead of corners it is cream, with lots of tiny light bulbs set just under the roof line. At the front of the building is a clock tower, two large period rectangular clock-faces showing the time in stern monochrome Roman numerals above glazed panels of rectangular patterns.

After more windshield and so-gorgeous-I-could-eat-you paintwork we stumbled upon a curious sign – considering there would be several hundreds of competitors leaping from the pier that weekend, apparently diving or jumping from the pier is prohibited and carries a £50 penalty. Well, I suppose it's one way of making some money! We left down a slight incline back through the gateway and looked back at the pier and all its glory – appreciating the fact that although Worthing Pier has very little left of its original construction (perhaps the time capsule bottle is still there under the first pile!) it really is the most beautiful example of 30's design. It wouldn't have looked out of place on Hastings seafront – maybe they'll redesign any new buildings to blend in using this as a template, it would look stunning.

As we glanced towards the seafront and Lido, I stopped.

"Look! That Lido's on legs... it's been built out over the beach. D'you think it could be classed as a pier?" I asked excitedly.

"Don't. Be. Silly," dismissed husband-to-be curtly, knowing full well what was coming. "It's far too short. That's not a proper pier. Come on!"

Or is it...?

Back at the car we whizzed off to the next assignation, Littlehampton Pier, which I have since discovered is somewhere else that is regarded by many as 'not a proper pier'. It's a lovely little town, lots of low buildings set well-back from the seafront and acres of wide sandy beach studded with little flinty pebbles and divided into neat sections with wooden groynes. There's been a harbour here since Roman days, and the River Arun wends its way out into the Channel past the modern port. Today it has a Hanseatic feel, with tall wooden buildings overlooking the water, and there are still fifty to sixty commercial ships that dock here every year.

Littlehampton is famous for having the first ever *Blue Peter* sponsored lifeboat stationed here, for having the headquarters of a well-known ethically produced beauty products company here and also for having a number of famous people stay here (such as Shelley and Constable). But it's not famous for a pier, and we were intrigued as to what we would find. Littlehampton really became a well-known holiday spot when one certain Mr Billy Butlin opened a resort and pleasure park here in the 1930s, the castles of which tower in the background to the beach today (although it's no longer a Butlin's).

We could see a long wooden breakwater stretching into the sea as we approached a little white lighthouse and hoped *that* wasn't the pier, but we were pleasantly surprised. On the eastern side of the River Arun, stretching approximately 100m (328') out from the shore was something that did look remarkably like a pier. The tide was out, so we jumped down onto the soft sand and went in for a closer inspection. The pier is built on substantial wooden piles, protected from the tidal currents at the seaward end by corrugated metal barriers. There's a lot of marine rockery going on around the piles too, but again, I suspect this is to help provide some shelter from the power of the sea, BUT you can see underneath it – it's not like some of the 'piers' we've looked at which have been infilled by rocks or are sat on top of sea walls.

We made our way back up top and walked to the little white lighthouse. Looking along the pier, we couldn't even begin to doubt that we were about to walk along a pier – it's decked, it has railings and loads of benches (not sure what a collective noun for these might be. Perhaps it's a settle of benches?) and there were an awful lot of people walking along the pier or resting on the seats, even at 11 am on a Saturday morning!

"So, what do you think?" asked the photographer, who, like the shopkeeper in *Mr Benn* had appeared from nowhere.

We stood and considered our answer for a second.

"Well, it seems to be a pier," answered Jay "We're so glad you told us it was here!" I'll get a photographer to suggest that Worthing Lido's a pier next time we're there, Jay might agree with *them*!

We walked to the end and had our kiss, were duly photographed, and, as mysteriously as he'd arrived, the photographer had gone again.

Unlike some piers, it's easy to see why this one was built. Historically, and I feel a bit controversially, the first pier here was built in the 1700s. The River Arun has always been prone to silting up, and in 1730 the main shipping channel was a mere 1.5m (5') deep, so in 1735 a new channel was created and two piers built to help keep the harbour mouth clear. The West Pier was longer and caught the sand and silt that was swept along the coast, while the East Pier was shorter but kept the channel clear and deep. An oil painting from 1811-12 by Sir Augustus Wall Callcott shows a rough wooden pier looking more like a row of rough wooden fencing poles, which is probably more likely what it was similar to than our interpretation of a pier.

However, by the turn of the century this breakwater had become a more familiar sight. By now it had lengthwise decking, fencing, lights and a couple of lighthouses, the landward one larger and the smaller one on the seaward end smaller and clinging onto the side of the pier. More importantly, old postcards and photographs show hundreds of people taking the air and walking along the pier. There are men fishing, people watching the boats going up the river and people walking up to the end and sitting on benches. Littlehampton East breakwater had become a pier!

This success continued through the 30's, with the rather cute 'salt and pepper pot' lighthouses being demolished at the start of the Second World War because they were clear landmarks to the enemy that a harbour was nearby. In 1948 a lighthouse at the landward end was reinstated, and this is the one we see today, the seaward light being replaced by a coloured marine navigation light instead. There is little other information on the history of the pier here readily available – I'm sure people have some stories to compliment its past – but we were really glad we'd got there at all.

Littlehampton really is a pleasant little pier, the wooden 'walls' topped with metal railings. We watched a swan and some boats in the river from the boat-shaped wooden end of the pier and watched people fishing in the deep-water river channel from the edge of the beach where it had been created years ago (although now reinforced with concrete rather than wooden poles, so that at low tide the sand doesn't collapse into the river). There is also a very tranquil air here, rare in this crazy modern world of hustle-bustle where everyone tries to get things done yesterday. Here you really could watch life go by and appreciate the simple things in life for a few hours, before returning to the 'real' world much refreshed. We too walked from the pier feeling relaxed and refreshed, ready to travel to Bognor for our 59th, and penultimate pier... scary!

We arrived at Bognor – Bognor Regis, to give it its correct title, ready to investigate another seaside structure. Originally called 'Bucgan ora' (Saxon for Bucge's landing place), this coastal village became Bognor and was converted to a coastal resort in the 1700s by Sir Richard Hotham, an influential property developer and MP. It acquired its Royal suffix fairly recently in its history, following King George V's convalescence from an illness (although he is reported as having been rather rude about the town) in 1929.

We parked a little distance from the pier (mainly because someone needed a coffee) and enjoyed a pleasant walk along the seafront, taking in the sights of another seaside. Even though we'd done so many, they are all different, despite the obvious similarities such as sea, path, road and houses! Here, we admired the double-headed lamp posts, each with a fairy-light shape on the post, and a nice wide smooth promenade, studded with flag poles and little concessions (thankfully one of which sold coffee, Jay was getting desperate!). We chanced upon a sweet little birdcage bandstand, coyly resplendent in blue paint, then the more modern amusement of a bungee trampoline, watched over by bemused old folk on the many benches.

On the seaward side there is a shingly beach, sandy where the receding tide has uncovered something nicer to walk on, although a rather large pipe (hopefully just rainwater run-off and not sewage) has been cunningly hidden amongst the groynes and appears to empty straight onto the beach. There are other distractions though. Fancy a go on the multicoloured bouncy castle? Or how about some traditional little wooden swing boats? You could hire a deckchair, pop over the road for a pizza or indulge in a little carton of seafood. There are still some little fishing boats pulled up on the beach that still look like they may be in use. Have a cockle!

Behind the beacon on the seafront we got a good first view of the sadly now much truncated Bognor Pier, little cream coloured buildings adorned with a feathery fascinator of pigeons.

The entrance to the pier is opposite a little crazy golf-course and public toilets, and as we walked up, also home to a small tarot card and palm reader at a little stand. We declined all the attractions of the opposite side of the road and turned to look at the front of the pier, a large and not unattractive post-Victorian (but not quite First World War) building that now houses an amusement arcade (although some of the concessions here were shut).

Our photographer dashed up (not out of thin air this time, it was a vibrant lady) and introduced herself, pouring enthusiasms on our romantic story. We still had problems with the fact that other people might be interested in what we were doing, even more that they might find it romantic, so we blushed and asked where she'd like us for the pictures! As we walked around the side of the pier, it became apparent that we'd come to a pier that was a bit of a Cleethorpes – looks OK from a distance but is a bit of a state close up. A concrete wall with some expletives and names on it, a spiked security gate and broken glass strewn around the entrance shelter to a nightclub took us onto the planking on the pier proper.

The planks are a bit old and threadbare, like a well-loved teddy bear that no one wants any more, with gaps and little holes and the ends sticking out over the sides in an uneven, unfinished years old look to it. A sign warned us that jumpers or divers would be prosecuted – lucky then that I was wearing a long-sleeved tee shirt – I should be able to argue my way out of a fine on a technicality! The photographer took a look around the corner onto the wider body of the pier, disturbing two gentlemen speaking in foreign tones and mulling over last night whilst clutching cans of cheap cider.

"Erm, I think I'll take your picture here if you don't mind," she said "It's probably the most picturesque part of the pier. Could you sit down?"

We completed a complicated manoeuvre, and then had to lean forward into a kiss, looking something like a cross between a lotus position in the mirror and a nasty swing boat accident. She was quite happy with the shots, however, and even used to my camera to take a few more (I have to compliment everyone here that happily took pictures of us or we'd never have had any of our own pictures on a pier at all!). She bade us a cheery goodbye and left, leaving us trying to untangle limbs and then attempt to stand up, watched by the two serious drinkers who were looking at us with sheer bafflement across their faces!

Around the corner (which turned out to be the back of the nightclub) it was a bit of a sad sight. Decking at the edges was replaced by concrete in the centre, with a small out-building and some derelict pieces of patio furniture piled up in the corner were the only things to grace the view. The cider men shuffled off in disgust at having been disturbed by two mad people, and the wide body of the pier narrowed to a plank-covered thinner neck before stopping abruptly. Although underneath this decking there are some solid and newish looking girders, but the decking isn't great and the rails are pretty ropy, once silver paint but now more rust than silver.

Half a dozen fishermen's rods were propped up at the end (although only one fisherman – had the others jumped off the end in despair?), and a lone navigation light told us it was where we needed to have a kiss. We did, and turned back to survey the poor leftovers of the pier. We looked gingerly over the edge at the narrow piles and fragile cross-bracing, draped with seaweed and peppered with barnacles – they looked sturdy enough (the legs not the barnacles!), which was heartening to see.

The outbuilding seen from the back was also dire. Garlanded in barbed wire and looking like a run-down shack it was home to some startled pigeons and a large amount of rot, and the few little sections of slightly decorative railing were adorned with polystyrene cups and crushed cans. There was nothing else to see or say. The main pavilion seemed solid enough and in fairly decent repair from the outside, but back on the land I think we enthused more about the designs moulded into the sea wall and the nice bit of brickwork than we had about anything on the pier.

It's really sad to see a pier ignored and unloved like this. Even while we were there several people walked onto the decking and up to the end and back, it seems to be just the structure itself that's enough of a draw, but some simple attractions would be a good distraction from the decay. It wasn't always like this for Bognor's pier, although it does seem to have had a fairly unexciting life.

There'd been plans for a pier here since 1835, but it wasn't until 1864 that the first pile was driven into the seabed to a design by Sir Charles Fox and J.W. Wilson and paid for by the Bognor Promenade Company. The pier opened the following year on 4th May and had cost the bargain bucket price of £5000 to build, partly because it was built using a local workforce and not outside contractors. It was essentially a basic jetty that extended 305m (1,000') over the gently sloping seabed, entered after paying 1d at the entrance kiosk. The pier stayed exactly the same, a rather low-key affair, until 1876 when it changed hands to the local council for £1,200, who installed a small bandstand.

A small pavilion opened for business at the seaward end in 1900 and a little landing stage was added the next year so that steamer trade could visit. This only lasted for six years, by which time the size of steamers had increased to the point where they were unable to pull up or disembark passengers easily and eventually stopped coming at all. The seaward end of the pier was neglected and unloved and was so dangerous by 1908 that it was sold for the paltry sum of 10 shillings and sixpence (about 50p in today's money) to Shanley and Carter, with the proviso that repairs must be carried out.

The new owners lavished all sorts of expenses on their pier (I think I would have done the same!), and spent £30,000 on major restoration works, ensuring the pier could open for the 1909 holiday season. Between 1911 and 1912 they widened the shoreward end of the pier to 24m (80') across to accommodate a 1400-seat theatre, the first cinema in Bognor, twelve shops and a restaurant with a roof garden. The outbreak of World War I saw 200 men billeted here (what a place to be based!), and the pier remained a tad more successful than it had been in the hands of the previous owners.

In 1936 it was decided to encourage steamer traffic back to the town and pier, now there was more on offer. A 33m (109') three-tier landing stage was built, designed, like so many of them were for the higher level to accommodate steamers and the lower decks for smaller boats. It was reached from the main body of the pier by a little walkway, and unusually had not been built parallel to the end of the pier or off to one side, but across the eastward corner of the pier head – not terribly aesthetically pleasing, but it worked. I can't find any record of the octagonal pavilion at the end of the pier having been enlarged, but it certainly looks bigger in the old photos and postcards, and this would make sense to cope with the increased number of visitors via boat. Further amusement was provided for people by way of diving displays. These had been really popular since the inception of piers, providing a handy deep-water pool to go into, and Bognor Pier was no exception. Popularity for these shows peaked in the 1930s and here (weather permitting) you could watch two shows a day.

In World War II the pier was taken over on 10th September 1943 and renamed HMS St. Barbara. It was used by the Royal Navy as an observation post and gunnery range and was attached to HMS Dinosaur (love the names of some of these bases. There was also HMS Armadillo, Squid, Newt, Rodent and Monster!). The Navy departed from the pier on 14th June 1945, and although I can't find out if the pier was sectioned or not, there is one black and white postcard showing an aerial shot of the pier, and it does look like there is a gap in the pier neck just after the landward buildings, possibly linked by a narrow bridge. It certainly doesn't look like the normal pier neck, and many piers that were sectioned and used by the military maintained contact with the land by means of a temporary bridge. On 27th June 2010 the RAFA marked the use of the pier as a naval station by unveiling a plaque to commemorate its part in the war.

Following the war, it would seem that the pier returned to normal everyday use without event, until 1964 when the first of two winter storms caused the seaward end of the pier to collapse, taking the octagonal pavilion with it. The pier was sold in 1966 to The American Novelty Company, but closed again in December 1974 following two fires in the previous three months. This looked like the end of Bognor Pier, with little care being given to the future of the place, but someone had come up with a bright idea. Remember those crazy people at Worthing who throw themselves off the pier in an attempt to fly? The International Birdman Competition had started in Selsey in 1971, but within seven years needed a bigger arena and better facilities. Bognor Pier was deemed to be a wholly suitable spot, and thus became the venue for this annual competition. In doing so it brought a guaranteed annual income to the pier, and also created a need to keep up some sort of maintenance programme to enable the competition to return again the following year.

On 27th April 1989 the pier was awarded Grade II listed status by English Heritage, but the state of the structure continued to decline and by 1992 the cost of carrying out all the necessary repairs was estimated to be in the region of half a million pounds. Two years later an application was made for a grant from the Heritage Lottery fund, but this was rejected, resulting in an application to demolish the seaward end of the pier being put forward in 1994. Another bid for £2 million was put forward to the Lottery Fund and the pier was sold to Bognor Pier Leisure Company in 1996. The bid for much needed funding was rejected again in 1998 and now the derelict seaward end was increasingly fragile and looked like being swept away in the first storm of the winter.

Storms in 1999 saw some of the decaying pier swept away, and further storms over each subsequent winter caused more devastation. Despite £50,000 of remedial work being carried out on it in 2003, the 24m (80') end section of the pier was finally removed in 2008, and saw the Birdman competition move to Worthing over fears that the sea wasn't deep enough at this distance from the shore to be safe. The pier still has the backing of the local residents who want to preserve the tenth oldest pier in the country and have it back in full working order as a respectable tourist attraction, and quite rightly so. All that remains of the once grand theatre are a few marks on the concrete decking and part of the other buildings, now much reduced in height, are used as 'Visions' nightclub. How about visions for the pier? The good news is that the Birdmen are back, and this year is the first time that there will be two competitions. I'd love to know how they tested the depth of the water. Did they throw a birdman and his craft off the end of Bognor Pier to see if he was in deep enough water? And how many did it take?

And so we left Bognor Pier, with one last (very important) visit to make on 10th October. There seemed to be a lot still to organise, and hopefully nobody would discover an extra pier to go to... fingers crossed!

CHAPTER 24

It Was Brighton - The Big Day!

Despite being one of the world's biggest worriers, wedding plans seemed to be proceeding ok. Contingency plans for disasters on the big day had been planned with military precision, a hairdresser had been found and everything was now in the lap of the gods, including the weather, which was alarmingly forecast as stormy! The week was marred however, with news that there had been a devastating fire on the 5th October at Hastings Pier. Spotted in the early hours of the morning, and despite the valiant attempts of ten fire crews who arrived within five minutes, by daylight it was clear that 95% of the pier had been destroyed. What awful news, especially when we knew that the Hastings White Rock and Pier Trust had been so close to ensuring the future of the pier. Closer to home, Weston's Grand Pier was nearing completion but was still not open to the public, and we felt we'd made the right decision to plan elsewhere for our wedding.

Saturday 9th October dawned cloudy and cool and we set off with a packed car for Brighton. Curling tongs, heels, sewing kit and sparkly make-up were all packed, and I had my things too in a separate bag... Brighton had once been the venue for three famous piers, but now there's sadly only one to visit, being the Palace Pier as the darkened bones of the West Pier still manage to look elegant marooned out in the water to the west but are no longer accessible. The first pier here had been the Royal Suspension Pier, first proposed as early as 1806 to make offloading coal and goods brought in by ship less backbreaking. Brighton was also the shortest sea route between Britain and France, and a pier would mean a safe and more decorous landing for tourists.

The Brighthelmston Suspension Pier Company was formed in 1821 and the building of a suspended deck pier to the designs of Captain Samuel Brown were begun on 18th September 1822. This meant working throughout the winter storms and conditions were awful for the workers, one of whom died, several others were seriously injured. This new construction created a popular tourist sensation, so much so that viewers were charged 6d to watch the workers, as long as they didn't distract them!

The finished pier was 352m (1,154') long and just 4m (13') wide, and had cost £30,000 to build. The one-ended suspension bridge had four towers, made from large slabs of cast iron and shaped like Egyptian prisms or pylons, (topped with a yoke-shaped arch) spaced 79m (260') feet apart and sitting on 20 oak piles that had been sunk 3m (10') onto the bedrock. Staggeringly, each tower measured over 7m (25') tall and weighed 14 tonnes (15 tons). The bar chains (patented by Captain Brown for use on suspension bridges) consisted of wrought-iron bars around 3m (10') long coupled with bolts and hung on 362 suspension rods, supporting the weight of the deck and towers, and anchored at the landward end some 16m (54') into the cliffs at East Cliff.

The pier opened on 25th November 1823 amid typical Victorian pomp, and the T-shaped pier-head landing stage decked in 30cm (1') thick Purbeck stone blocks provided a classy departure point for seagoing journeys. The landing stage was 24m (80') by 12m (40') and supported by 150 oak piles – these needed to be strong, as the finished structure weighed in excess of 181 tonnes (200 tons)!

Despite providing sail-driven ferry trips to France, the pier also had many entertainments for the inquisitive Victorian visitors, who paid 2d at little toll kiosks to enter the wonders of this elegant bridge out to sea. This sum gave the visitor access to kiosks at the bottom of every tower where they could buy sweets and souvenirs, have their fortune told or silhouette drawn. There was a brass band to entertain, and for the hardy souls, seawater baths suspended under the pier head. We tend to think of the Victorians as being terribly modest people, but here was the only place in the city where men or women could swim without using a bathing machine or (shock, horror!) even without a bathing costume! On the pier head there was also a sundial, lounge, reading room and little roofed wooden seats across the landing stage area. A bell suspended under the arch of the last tower rang to announce imminent boat departures and when a boat set sail, a 6lb cannon was fired accompanied by the raising of blue and white flags. With its elegant shape, green and black chains between stone-coloured towers and all the novelties provided by walking out over the sea, the Chain Pier proved extremely popular.

Steam boats superseded the power of sail by the mid 1820s, the railway arrived in 1841 and new deep-water facilities in Newhaven meant that ferry services from the pier were threatened, but this didn't faze the owners, they simply transferred their energies to providing popular steamer-driven day trips up and down the coast, and as more piers opened along the south coast, business boomed with up to 4,000 people a day using the pier. The dawn of the pleasure pier had truly arrived, and Brighton's Chain Pier had inspired painters like Turner and Constable to immortalise it on canvas, songs to be written about it and visitors no less than King William IV, who landed there.

Brighton's second pier, West Pier opened further to the erm... west in 1866 but didn't really impact on the popularity of the Chain Pier because it had been built primarily as a pleasure pier, not as a pleasure steamer point. Sadly, and I'm no engineer, but I think the narrowness of the Chain Pier and its enormous weight must have contributed to its demise, as did the exposed nature of Brighton's coastline, often battered by wild storms and waves. November 1824 saw the pier battle a huge storm, giant waves causing some damage and washing away bits of decorative ironwork. In 1833 a tempest brought waves that smashed over the pier and broke the chains supporting the third tower. Funds were raised and the tower eventually repaired, with the same incident occurring again in 1836. These storms showed how delicate this seemingly solid pier was, and proved how important regular maintenance was to ensure its integrity.

In 1889 the condition of the pier was looking a bit ropy, and was bought out by the Marine Palace and Pier Company. It stayed open until October 1896 when it was inspected by the Borough Engineer. He discovered that the pier head was an alarming 2m (6'9") out of perpendicular and ordered that the pier be immediately closed. Work had begun on the nearby Palace Pier (also to the west of the Chain Pier), and part of the contractual obligations to build it had been that the Chain Pier would be demolished, such was the state of disrepair, back when the company had purchased it. However, they were to be saved a job, as Mother Nature stepped in and did the work for them.

A real monster of a storm on the evening and night of 4th December 1896 saw watchman of forty years Edward Fogden struggle to complete his last job of the day, lighting the lamps at the end of the pier. He managed to get off the pier, which, as a structure that is built to move in times of bad weather to absorb some of the forces of the wind, must have been heaving up and down appallingly. At around ten thirty that night, a sightseer saw the pier 'shiver convulsively from end to end' then collapse completely. Edward Fogden's carefully lit lamps were the last thing to go, disappearing into the sucking, greedy waves. The next day, all that was left of the once elegant Chain Pier was a smashed first tower and some broken piles. Edward Fogden was pictured, standing alone and bereft, looking out where his beloved pier had once been, described by a newspaper as cutting a 'sturdy but forlorn figure'.

Wreckage from the Chain Pier wreaked havoc for a while, smashing into the construction work going on for the new Palace Pier and causing the destruction of Volks' Daddy Long Legs. I have *really* got to digress at this point and go off at a tangent to explain what this bizarre contraption was (yes, I know you want to find out about the wedding, but you'll have to wait!). If you thought the Birdmen of Worthing and Bognor were eccentric, you ain't seen nothing yet, trust me! Imagine, if you will, a section of a Eugenius Birch pier. Then meld it with a tram and a paddle boat, with sumptuous leather seating for 160 and a trained sea captain to drive it. On railway bogies. On rails. In the sea. Oh, and it was powered by an overhead electrical wire. Now you have a (disturbing) image of Volks' Daddy Long Legs, something that sounds oh, so wrong, but was surprisingly popular and provided rides for 6d to a staggering 44,000 passengers. That's PER year, not in total!

The sea-going tram began service on 2nd September 1894 going from Banjo Groyne to Rottingdean, more than two miles away (this just gets more and more unbelievable!). The brainchild of eccentric inventor Magnus Volk, it was reached by way of a lightweight metal pier and travelled some 55m (180') out from the shore on two sets of railway tracks set 5m (18') apart. Each bogey had little scrapers (looking rather like upturned tin bath tubs) to remove shingle, seaweed and marine life from the rails. By all accounts it travelled quite briskly at low tides and calm water, but was invariably reduced to a crawl at high tide as the motors were just not powerful enough. It was into this bizarre apparition that pieces of the Chain Pier collided, just one week after the service had started.

Amazingly it was rebuilt and re-opened by the following July and would probably have continued for a lot longer than 1901, when seafront groynes needed to be installed along the beach. Preliminary work scoured away the seabed around the tram rails and the only remedy would be moving the lines to deeper water. Now facing total doom, the company went bust and the tram had rusted away by 1910. There are still remnants of the weird beast, who was called *Pioneer* visible at extreme low tides – concrete sleepers at Rottingdean and some iron platform pieces to the east side of Banjo Groyne. (Volks also created what is currently the world's oldest operating electric railway in the world. It still runs along Brighton seafront to this day, and you can look up more about the railway and Daddy Long Legs on the Volk's Electric Railway website. Which just proves I'm not the world's biggest fibber!) There are also remnants of the Chain Pier still visible to this day. If you walk along the Max Miller Walk, some 100m (304') east of the Palace Pier, you will come across a plaque that marks where the Chain Pier came ashore, and if you visit this spot at very low tides, tucked behind the groyne you will see stumps of the oak piles and some masonry blocks, which may be part of the Portland stone blocks of the pier-head landing stage.

Brighton's second pier is probably now one of the most iconic ruins in the country, instantly recognisable and with a special place in the hearts of a good many people. Along with Clevedon Pier, the West Pier, Brighton was the only other Grade I listed pier in existence. I'm not sure when the listing fails to be applicable, given the current state of the pier today, but this listing hints at what a fantastic creation this once was.

The West Pier was started in 1863 to one of Eugenius Birch's now classic designs, although the first cast-iron screw pile wasn't sunk until March 1864. Compared to the skinny Chain Pier, the screw piles meant that a wider deck could be used with the resultant width being around 17m (55'), rather than the Chain Pier's 4m (13'). West Pier was also considerably longer, at 340m (1,115') and when it opened (after a long delay) on 5th October 1866 it consisted of a long deck for promenading with glass screens at the pier head to protect the dignified gentry from an undignified blasting, a few little oriental-style kiosks (two of which provided retiring rooms for both gentlemen and ladies!) and a couple of ornately decorated toll houses where the inevitable 2d toll was collected.

Interestingly West Pier had the same design flaw as Weston's Birnbeck Pier. One August Bank Holiday in 1867 the pier deck began to move as thousands of people walked along the planking. When this developed into an alarming sway and oscillation, people forgot their propriety and ran for their lives. Remedial work was carried out swiftly with some more bracing, although it doesn't appear that Birnbeck's Bye-laws were copied! The basic promenading pier experience remained at the West Pier until 1875 when a widened platform halfway along the neck was built to accommodate a bandstand – shelter at last for some very windswept musicians! Further improvements were made in 1890 with a central windshield down the centre of the deck and them some impressive additions in 1893. The pier head was widened to make a landing stage for steamers and a pavilion that was capable of seating 1,400 people was built at the pier head. The engineering of the project was guided by R.W. Peregrine Birch, Eugenius Birch's nephew (much like the Brunel family, genius for design seems to run in families!). The steamer landing stages from above not only widened the pier on both sides but extended out from the pier head, creating an enclosed polygonal lagoon – was this where the famous divers plied their trade?

The pier then went through a few years of fine tweaking – in 1903 the pavilion was converted to a 1000-seat theatre and between 1914-16 the bandstand was demolished and an octagonal concert hall built around an underskirt of iron arches. All this redevelopment was carried out because so many people were using the pier (over 700,000 a year for the first twenty years of its existence). This huge and beautiful pavilion kept the pier a booming business prospect through the First World War and into the Roaring Twenties. Between 1918 and 1919 there were over two million visitors to the West Pier, and although this was down to 900,000 by the late 1930s, concerts and theatrical performances continued in the theatre and entertainments such as the West Pier Divers (both men and women) plunged amazingly right up until the 1960s (although hopefully with a break between shows).

The pier was sectioned in World War II, and afterwards became more of a funfair pier with dodgems and rides, cafés, restaurants and games, but this was the beginning of the end as less people came to the Great British seaside, now travelling abroad for reliable sunshine and exotic beaches. The owners couldn't even blame the nearby Palace Pier for stealing trade, as this pleasure pier was also struggling to survive in the post-war climate.

By the 1970s it was decided better to demolish bits of the pier than throw money at restoration and in 1975 it was closed after being declared unsafe. Conservationists signed a huge petition which resulted in the pier being declared a listed structure, something that ironically sealed its fate. Now presented with a huge repair and maintenance bill, the owners went bankrupt. The local council refused to buy the pier, not being able to find a way of making it a viable business proposition.

Lovers of West Pier refused to give up and in 1984 it became the property of the West Pier Trust, and offers of money came in from charitable and private donors. Despite the pier neck being severed, some repair work was carried out using the money, and private guided tours given to keep interest fresh in people's minds (I wish we'd known how the story would end and been conducting our tour of piers then...), although an aerial shot from 1991 shows the sturdy landing stages either missing or sliding into the sea. It was really from 2002 that the structural weaknesses visibly made themselves known and this beautiful, dignified pier that had been a graceful, unaltered example of post-Edwardian architecture descended swiftly into a broken-backed white elephant that no one could save.

A partial collapse of the pier happened on 29th December 2002 and the tours ceased because of worries about the structure. These were well-founded, when less than a month later the concert hall in the middle of the pier collapsed. At the end of March 2003 the huge pavilion caught fire, and although arson was the most likely cause, has never been proved. Because of the previous breaks, the fire brigade were unable to reach the inferno, but the fire went out. Another blaze on 11th May 2003 destroyed the rest of the concert hall. It was extinguished but reignited the next day, and again it was unlikely that the fire had been as a result of natural causes.

A year later, stormy summer winds were more than the collapsed and fire-ravaged middle section could take and it crashed unceremoniously into the sea. The West Pier Trust finally waved the white flag and admitted defeat when a final bid for Heritage Lottery Funding was rejected on the grounds that any money donated would have to be raised by the Trust. Time had run out for the West Pier. Despite brave regeneration plans put forward now and again it is highly unlikely that there will ever be a West Pier in Brighton that will host members of the public, eager to eat candyfloss over the waves ever again.

Much of the debris along the low water mark was removed at the beginning of 2010 due to safety concerns, and even the much-photographed murmurations of roosting starlings that once used the isolated pier as a safe night-time refuge have shifted allegiance to the Palace Pier (a survey in 2004 showing that only 3000 birds used the West Pier, compared with an estimated 20,000 under the Palace Pier. Just how do you count 20,000 high speed little birds intent on zooming in fancy patterns under the pier?). The only glimmer on the horizon occurred in 2006 when a proposed development on the seafront where the pier entrance had once been was put forward. The i360 observation tower looked like being a really great proposition, bringing tourists to this part of the seafront for a spectacular view 25 miles in all directions. At a cost of £15-20 million this would also have included a partial rebuild of the pier, but the sudden economic collapse in 2007 meant work didn't start, and when we got to Brighton on the Saturday before our wedding and walked along to look at the West Pier and read the promising hoarding, there was no sign of it ever starting either.

Now on the seafront, there is little left of the West Pier. Just some of Birch's screw piles firmly drilled into the beach (a handy place to string your makeshift tightrope over the shingle), and the curved skeletal remains of the pavilion trying to maintain its graceful shape over the waves even though there are no fine drapes and coverings.

Up on the promenade, where the pier would have made landfall, behind safety fencing and hoardings advertising the i360 but still sat on some wooden decking is a small building, a little many-sided hut in cream with the words 'West Pier' picked out forlornly in blue, next to it a larger rectangular building, the surviving one of a pair of original entrance kiosks, arches picked out along the wall in the red and white paintwork and a curved grey top, that in its heyday would have been a miniature counterpart to the grand pavilion roof, held aloft by elaborate wrought-iron brackets. This building found use as Lewington's Rock Shop – Graham Greene could have bought real Brighton Rock here – but when we went past it looked as though it hadn't sold any sticky pink and white sticks with Brighton through the middle for a while. It's not as elaborate as when seen in the old postcards and photos from the pre-war period, but at least they're still in existence. Underneath the shop, if you look closely is another little curio – a one-man pill box from the Second World War, designed to be a major threat to any unlucky invader coming up the beach, hopefully on his own!

So now Brighton has just the one pier, a testament to bit of English bloody-mindedness (as far as the owners are concerned) ensures its success, where you can have one of the best days out on the epitome of an English pier... or are we biased?!

You really have got to sit through a bit more history – promise I'll keep it as brief as possible, but it's a necessary thing to do, because Brighton's Palace Pier (now more commonly known as plain old Brighton Pier) has a lot to say – and some echoes of days gone by that you may recognise too!

Originally called The Brighton Marine Palace Pier but shortened to Palace Pier, the first piles were wormed into the seabed on 7th November 1891. Despite a promising start, Richard St. George More's design wasn't fully finished until nearly ten years later, beset with money problems, being beaten up in 1896 by its older sibling, the Chain Pier, and people not realising *quite* how much work would be entailed with this mammoth project! The first part of the pier was declared open on 20th May 1899 with a grand procession that included the Mayor of Brighton. The party walked to the end of the pier and back, and then the Mayor and Mayoress did it all again, but this time paid their 2d admission fee and did it properly!

Finally completed on 3rd April 1901, the pier was 537m (1,760') long, had cost an unprecedented £137,000 and covered two and a half acres. The neck was wider than usual, wrought-iron railings decorative and curling in design, a total of 85 miles of planking (!) and eight beautiful iron and steel arches that carried around 3,000 light bulbs to illuminate evening walkers. Apart from the toll booths at the entrance, there were two kiosks midway along and a 1,500-seat pavilion at the end of the pier that were used for dining rooms, smoking and reading rooms. 1905 saw some amusement machines installed, including the Lady Palmist (I've had a go on one of these machines, where little buttons 'read' your palm, and the one I've used has always been spookily accurate!) and punch-ball machines. Two years later the Concert Hall opened, which by 1911 had become the theatre, with beautiful Oriental domes and wedding-cake wrought-iron work.

Also open by then was the fabulous Winter Gardens building, a huge domed confection of ornate ironwork girders and platforms, where you could sit and partake of tea and stickies by the fountain under a huge glass roof. A proper pier-head landing stage now catered for steamer traffic. With such stunning architecture on not one but two piers, Brighton became *the* place to visit, and there was always something happening along the seafront and on the West Pier or Palace Pier. If you'd visited Palace Pier in 1917 you would have been assailed by the Professor of Laughter, one Charles Zeidler, who essentially made his money (for many years too) laughing at (and hopefully with) people as they entered and left the Hall of Mirrors!

There were continual changes made on the pier, with newer games added (something that has continued up to the present day) and attractions. The entrance was upgraded in 1930 to its current incarnation, a wide canopied gateway overlooked by the tall, proud, square-faced clock tower. The pier was also widened at the same time, and the Mayor of the day came and opened it again, although I suspect with a touch less exuberance than in 1899! In 1932, only four years after their first outing in Britain, Palace Pier had its own dodgems ride, to go alongside a Ferris wheel. The pier was extended again in 1938, and the overall effect was extraordinarily popular. In 1939 there were over 2 million visitors to the Palace Pier, a figure that many piers today would give their right-hand to have (or possibly right-pile!).

The pier was closed in May 1940 and then sectioned. Residents remember not even being able to walk on the beach because of 'walls' of barbed wire and even mines along the beach (a common occurrence all across the country, such was the worry of invasion by the Germans). The pier did suffer a little from bomb damage during the war, but was reopened to the public again in 1946. Steamers and boat traffic continued to ply their trade until the 1960s, and the pier remained a popular draw for holidaymakers, although numbers eventually began to dwindle as people chose to go to highly fashionable Spain instead.

A fantastic Pathé film clip from 1946 shows a huge post-war crowd enjoying the pier on a very breezy day. The delightfully plummy Mr Cholmondley-Warner voice talks us through all the delights that people could expect to experience. There were shooting galleries and darts, ball rolling and a shellfish shop, a portrait painter and a children's roundabout. Deckchairs cost 3d to hire for the day (and there would still have been an entrance charge) and if you were feeling daring you could pick a seashell and have it tell you your horoscope. Slightly more mind boggling, there was a packed demonstration of a potato peeler, but the narrator tells us there was *'so much to listen to, so much to see!'* and that you could go for a good blow on the pier (ahem!).

For once, regular maintenance has always been religiously carried out here, preventing any of those nasty surprises that had befallen The West Pier. The piermasters had, until the 1970s been responsible for looking after the day-to-day running of the pier. Captain Weeks worked from 1928-1955 and was often seen in his gold-braided uniform, parading his war ribbons as he oversaw the maintenance men doing their work. This diligence paid off when the pier was granted Grade II* listed status on 20th August 1971.

In October 1973 it was decided to get rid of the unused landing stage. A 70 tonne (77 tons) floating barge was brought in to help do the job, the unreliable weather blew up a storm, ripped the barge from its mooring and then repeatedly smashed it into the pier. Unsurprisingly, quite considerable damage was caused, most devastatingly to the Oriental theatre, which was left leaning over the edge of the pier like a limp sock. The landing stage was finally removed in 1975, but the theatre was to hang on a bit longer.

In March 1984 the pier was bought by the Noble Organisation, who wanted to keep the pier as a financially viable enterprise and promptly scrapped the entrance toll and charge on deckchairs. They introduced state-of-the-art amusement machines that included games, slot-machines and bigger, better, wilder rides too but still managing to retain those old traditional things that people expect, like a carousel and helter-skelter. They announced that they were going to restore the poor theatre, and it was painstakingly taken apart and put into storage in 1986, only to disappear into the ether, never to be seen again. The general public were not best pleased. In its place at the wider pier head came the replacement Pleasure Dome (aha, so this is where Frankie Goes to Hollywood got their inspiration from, not Kipling's poem!), wherein reside the great thrills of basketball, gaming machines and good old air hockey!

August 1995 saw a nasty accident take place whereby an electrical substation underneath the seaward end exploded. Fortunately the subsequent fire was quickly extinguished and there were no casualties. In 2000, Noble decided to rename the pier, something that has caused a bit of a stink ever since. No longer do illuminated signs display the words 'Palace Pier' proudly as you walk through the gates. Instead they have been replaced with the simpler 'Brighton Pier'. The grumbling and unhappiness still rumbles on to this day – we'd be foolish to intervene, but perhaps an alternative would be to combine the two and call it 'Brighton Palace Pier'...

The pier had so far had a relatively accident-free life, but didn't quite escape unscathed on the night of 4th February 2003. A fire was spotted at 7.20 pm, and although fifty firemen battled the blaze for four hours, the ghost train and a couple of other rides were destroyed and decking had burnt through, falling into the sea in a shower of sparks. Fortunately the entertainment was replaced and the gradual and continual upgrade and improvement have unequivocally meant that Brighton (Palace) Pier has stayed well-attended and well loved. There are now over 500 employees and maintenance people who look after the pier every day (the maintenance team are known as Deck Hands) and see to the visitors' every whim.

The maintenance is pretty thorough and impressive. Painting is carried out every year and takes three months to complete, divers regularly survey and maintain the marine substructure to keep it sound – several million pounds have been invested in keeping the pier shipshape over the past decade, and long may it continue! Even if you've never been to Brighton, you'll know Palace Pier – it's *always* in the papers and on the news when we have a heatwave, behind the million sizzling people on Brighton beach. It's in magazine, newspaper and TV advertising campaigns for many well-known products, and the pier has also been in films since 1896, most famously appearing in *Carry on at Your Convenience* in 1971 (when the staff of a toilet factory go on a day trip to the seaside). There is even a space for the Palace Pier on the front cover of countless books, and it would appear to be obligatory that any television series visiting the city films with the pier in the background at some point!

And now we were there... Family and friends that had travelled down the day before joined us for an evening do at a seafront tavern and then we stormed onto the pier to while away the rest of the evening (being a hedonistic bunch) on the amusements. The pier looks stunning at night, now lit by over 62,000 bulbs, and the main place to go is inside the building that used to be the Winter Gardens, now the Palace of Fun. We squealed wildly as we lost money on the horses, won two pences by the handful and then lost them again and had games of air hockey that resulted in tears (mostly from hysteria, not because we were bad losers!). Mindful of the big day tomorrow, we left at pier closing-time and made our way back to our lovely hotel just across the road (thoughtfully painted red to go with my wedding dress – next door was purple for the bridesmaids' dresses, very uncanny!).

Amazingly the 10th October dawned bright and sparkly with bright blue skies. We could see the pier from our room, which added to the excitement of the day. We managed to eat breakfast (washed down with a bucket of Bucks Fizz) then Jay dressed for the occasion and left in the safe hands of guests and the florist to go and sit somewhere while I got ready, attended by three giggly bridesmaids (it got worse, the champagne had been left in the room...). I'd found a local hairdresser who had saved the day, and she turned up to tweak my hair into some semblance of style (it doesn't like being told what to do). With the bottles empty and everyone suitably attired, looking gorgeous and clutching fantastic bunches of flowers we decided it was time to make our way over to the pier.

For a woman who has walked along Weston seafront dressed in spotty pyjamas and wellington boots, shopped in the local supermarket dressed as a rat and been known to dress up as a bright orange squirrel, I felt very conscientious as we made our way over the main road to the pier – lots of people were looking! We hadn't realised that today was also the day of Brighton's annual bike show and on the prom, so it wasn't just tourists we had to contend with as we tottered on heels down the hill, but lots of leather-clad bikers too! The day was now searingly hot, more what you'd have expected on the Continent than England in October and the pier was packed. We met our flower girl and page-boy at the entrance, along with Jay's son who was going to ring the school bell as we went to clear the crowds! At 2 p.m. the pier's radio station announced us to anyone that could hear, and Ian Brown's *Stellify* began to play. This was it! We were off!

The crowds parted curiously and it wasn't long before we were at Victoria's Bar, half-way along the pier, well above the fantastic blue sea and ready for the ceremony to start. Victoria's is a stunning room, totally quirky and English – the bar has a fantastic Art Nouveau feel with big mirrors and dark woodwork, but the rest of the room is adorned with bits and pieces. There's a hanging pram, a trombone and a railway sign. Over there an aeroplane and a set of old skis. And a whole crowd of people (although not hanging from the ceiling)! Sam Cooke singing *You Send Me* started the ceremony, and apart from a bit of undignified squealing when I thought I'd been given the wrong ring ('Where are the sparkly bits? Mine's got sparkly bits on it!'), it went well, and we had our Palace Pier kiss as man and wife while Elbow's *One Day Like This* played. Magic!

Outside we posed for pictures against the railings, mostly taken by a group of tourists from the Far East. We weren't sure why they were so enthusiastic but apparently the number 10 is considered to be very lucky, so to get married on this day with three of them was triple luck. And then the bride was wearing pillar-box red, also regarded as a lucky colour – I'll uncross my fingers then, things seem to be going OK! Tossers of the confetti found it is always best practice to check what direction the wind is coming from prior to hurling huge handfuls of it, as we remained un-sullied and they disappeared in a pastel rice-paper cloud! The deckchairs at the side of the pier provided an ideal photo opportunity too!

A national newspaper had sent a photographer along and we walked to the front of the pier for some pictures, before heading to the carousel. We'd been granted a free ride for everyone in the wedding party, and so innocent visitors to the pier were unceremoniously told to wait while we boarded (sorry!). We'd chosen not to have formal photos taken, instead requesting copies of any that other people took, and there are some brilliant snaps taken during the ride. I can't say the following experience yielded such good snaps as bride, groom and attendants then went on the helter-skelter (apparently from the top on a clear day you can see the Isle of Wight. I don't know about that, heights and slides terrify me so I had my eyes shut). I went after the groom but at a velocity of 1cm a minute as I clung for dear life to the rubber. It was only the imminent arrival of a high-speed daughter behind me that made me let go and do the last bit howling like a banshee… and I can honestly say I shan't be doing that again in a hurry!

We'd had to wait while Victoria's was turned from being a ceremony room to a reception venue, and we walked around the rest of the pier taking in the sights (and we even managed to sneak away for a proper end-of-the-piers kiss at the end-of-the-pier. It was a real bittersweet moment, surprisingly. Here we were on the most special day of our lives so far, celebrating our love for each other, but we were on our last pier. We'd kissed on sixty piers and there were no more to visit – it was the end of something that had become part of our lives and filled so many weekends. Whatever would we do now?

We made our way back to the room for our reception (appropriately seaside-themed too) and cut our spectacular cake. Despite being sorely tempted to have a pier, we realised that this would probably be way beyond our budget. We did manage to secure a pier-linked cake-maker however, and it was the fair (and very skilled) hands of Gemma McFarlane who crafted our stunning sandcastle cake. In 2004 she was responsible for making Lord Richard Attenborough's 80th birthday cake, a faithful replica of Brighton West pier made from white icing. We cut our cake with a plastic spade and enjoyed the rest of the afternoon with everyone who had made the journey to share our day with us.

As the sun made a firework display over the ruins of West Pier, we went out to look, but were rewarded with something much more spectacular. Remember how many starlings roost on the Palace Pier? We stood on the east side of the pier and watched thousands of birds whirl and wheel, turning at incredible speeds and angles and making stunning shapes in the sky. We couldn't have asked for a more stunning show, and watched looking up (mouths firmly closed) until they suddenly, to a bird, disappeared under the seaward end of the pier, and all was silent again. Most of the onlookers said they felt like cheering and clapping as they went, and if you've never witnessed such a display then go to your local starling roost and watch!

It was very late when we eventually made our way off the pier, thanking all the guests, staff and wedding organisers for making the day so special for us. Organising a grand day at a distance was always going to be a risk, but hair lady, florist and cake maker really pulled the stops out and we were extremely grateful. Back at Millard's Hotel we collapsed exhaustedly into our room and watched the lights on the pier twinkling in the darkness...

The next morning we were due to set off home, but decided we needed a closer pier-kisser investigation of the Palace Pier (sorry, Brighton Pier) – we'd been a bit busy the day before and probably hadn't looked at all the details properly! The approach to the pier took us past the Sealife Centre, and a plaque in the pavement linked it to the pier! Apparently it's the world's oldest operating aquarium, which opened in 1872 and was designed by Eugenius Birch! He kept that quiet! Brighton seafront has some iconic railings that run from horizon to horizon, pale sea-green and simple rectangles with a diagonal cross and central little doughnut. The street lamps, also adorned in pale green look as though they've been spirited from a novel by C.S. Lewis, glass lanterns with delicate metal icicles towering grandly over the promenade.

The entrance apron is neatly bricked and lined with a welcoming committee of little food stalls and Victorian kiosks at each end, each with a little bell-shaped roof. The gateway to the pier is huge, stretching across the entire substantial width of the neck and covered by a canopy, out of the middle of which rises the nephew of The Clock Tower in London (more commonly referred to as Big Ben!), painted a stern but shiny black with a bit of gold pinstriping to glam it up a bit for the job of pier timepiece.

Running over everything are little lines of bulbs catching the bright autumnal sunshine that after dark transform the pier into an even more magical twinkling wonderland, and at the bottom of the front canopy where it declares this to be 'Brighton Pier' (just in case you've lost your way) there are four very lovely little golden seahorses, probably overlooked by many that pass underneath!

Once back on the pier we embarked on our circular stroll down the right-hand side admiring the beautiful iron work of the railings and the globe lighting as we held hands and ambled in a loved-up fug of happiness. There's an awful lot going on here, not just as far as amusements and shops go but in the stunning buildings, architecture and pier furniture – I'll apologise now if we've missed anything, I don't think that even in several visits we'd have spotted it all!

We decided to go into the Palace of Fun on our return circuit and headed for the right wall, but paused to look at the little kiosk from the Chain Pier with its fish-scale domed roof and little Gothic windows on every side. At the other end of the Palace of Fun is Moo Moos, and if you're lucky you'll meet the resident Friesian cow and calf here – *not* I should stress, real, but some brilliant life-sized fibreglass models to advertise the milkshake bar! On our earlier pre-wedding visit, the chaperone was highly amused by these and the tables, which are supported on four elegantly bovine legs and hooves!

Once through this tempting delight and back in the sunshine, we admired the elegance of the central windbreak just in front of the Palm Court fish and chip restaurant and take-away. Here at the end of the windshield some of the original Victorian decorative iron arches have been retained and incorporated into the modern day experience. In general, although there has been a lot of modernisation on the pier, there have been many efforts to keep the original Victorian architectural style going, with the huge amount of scrolled and attractive wrought-ironwork helping immensely! Palm Court is also the site of the original pier bandstand, although the only reference to having a good time and partying on down to the band is the huge glitter-ball up on the roof, topped with a lovely sailing galleon weather vane.

Behind Palm Court is Victoria's Bar, a delightful room which I would recommend you visit, but you already know why, and once past this mid-section of the pier, it opens up again for the amusements and entertainments of the pier head. There really is something for everyone here, from the traditionalists to modernists, from the young to the young at heart – it's great, and doesn't give the impression of all being crammed in just to make a fast buck, but still feels spacious even when it's busy. Fantasia is a novel driving track where little vehicles that look like they've escaped from a children's roundabout can be whizzed up and down roadways – lots of flashing lights and bright colours here! Outside are the more traditional carousel and helter-skelter, the former in fabulous gold and fairground colours (and still sporting 'Brighton Marine and Palace Pier' on its boards), the latter in striking red, white and blue topped with a flag and managing to induce a nervous grin from me as we walked past!

Behind the helter-skelter is the Horror Hotel ghost train and some of the whiter knuckle rides (depending on your level of thrill seeking!) like the Turbo roller coaster and The Booster, a 40m (130') spinny thing that was daringly experienced by Jay's son and grandson on the wedding day. They came off the ride a funny colour and quaveringly said it had been fun! Much braver than both of us! There are dodgems, a Crazy Mouse roller coaster (have you ever seen a mouse on any of these?), a log flume and even the kiosk for Brighton Pier radio on this 58m (189') wide section of pier.

If you look carefully there are some older pieces of architecture and design, harking back to the grand old days of the Palace Pier. Some kiosks still sport the initials of the Brighton Marine Palace Pier company, and I'd love to find out the history of the lion (chained up to stop him attacking punters) at Horatio's bar and the two horse riders mounted on grand white steeds opposite the bouncy castles. The elegant lady rides side-saddle, while the gentleman raises an arm that maybe once held a lance or sword. Both are attired and styled in that classical turn of the twentieth century take on medieval fashion. Who are they? Where did they come from and who made them?

After declining to try and beat the rodeo bull machine and skirting the huge geodesic dome of The Dome, Jay stopped to pat a sheep and goat (no really!) and as we poked around found the tiny little signalling cannon from the Chain Pier! It's mounted on a block of wood and covered in shiny black paint, with a plaque that almost dwarfs it! Tucked in an overlooked corner, it's another thing that may well be missed, but we were glad to have spotted it. There are also lots of information boards around the railings of the pier that give you a brilliant history of the pier and some of the things you can still see today, which is a nice touch.

Back past Victoria's there is a little green and cream 'traditional' gypsy caravan where Ivor will divine your tarot cards, and it's another thing that used to be found on many a traditional pier that isn't that common these days and adds to the feel of the place. We giggled at memories of the day before as we passed the 'we married on Brighton Pier' head-in-the-hole photo opportunity and entered the delights of the Palace of Fun.

Even if you don't want to go inside and have your ears assaulted by the cacophony of all the machines, you can walk around the outside of the old Winter Gardens and appreciate the stunning stained glass in the port-hole windows, although they look better inside illuminated by the sun. I'm not sure when they date from or who they were made by, but they are undeniably beautiful. You can find coastal scenes and lighthouses, cliffs and sailboats, rowing boats and a galleon, Brighton Pavilion and even the pier at sunset! Much of the original decorated iron girders can still be seen inside, reaching up to a centre point in the dome like a huge pyrotechnic explosion. There's plasterwork decoration on the walls and green, cream and gold columns – it's not hard to imagine what it would have been like in the 30s (I'll have a scone with my Earl Grey thank you), and a little bit of me would love to see this stripped out and given over to a quieter, more original use. Perhaps classical music performances, tea dances and refreshments, full of pot plants and the clink of fine china tea sets!

However, we had to be off. Reluctantly we left after saying goodbye to Sarah-Jane and Anne (our wedding planners), walked back to the hotel and said farewell to Tony who had been our exemplary host there and got into the car to head home. To use an overused cliché, it had been an amazing journey. We'd taken two years to visit sixty piers and travelled just over 7,000 miles (11,200km) in order to do so. We'd met so many fantastic people who'd helped us achieve this (and it'd be impossible to thank them all, the list would be pages long!), and even more help via emails and phone calls. We'd given loads of radio and newspaper interviews, posed in some interesting positions for photos and even been on TV twice! We had never expected a simple jokey idea would have led to such an adventure, to have learnt so much and to have fallen in love so head-over-heels with piers while we did with each other!

CHAPTER 25
A Grand Reopening!

You may think that was the end of the story, and leafing back through the chapters, the eagle-eyed amongst you would have already realised that there has been no mention or description of Weston's Grand Pier. What about its history and its future? We'd seen the devastation at first hand, watching a piece of history disappear in such dramatic circumstances, and then tentatively seeing the rebuilding process and awaiting the re-opening date with baited breath. The pier where this love story began and blossomed – would it or wouldn't it be the same? We'd find out on 23rd October (2010), just thirteen days after our wedding because that was the Grand Pier's grand re-opening!

Casting back a bit, you'll remember that Weston-super-Mare already had a pier at the start of the twentieth century to Birnbeck Island. Plans had been bandied around since 1880 for a second pier in Weston, to cash in on the tourist boom that was happening in the town. Since the arrival of the railway, even more day-trippers and holidaymakers were coming to the town and it was thought that a pier positioned more centrally would mean they would essentially have a shorter distance to go before spending their money and having some fun! The board of directors included representatives from the Cardiff Docks and Light Railway Company, who were also major financial backers for the proposed promenade, pavilion and landing stage which were to be the shortest walking distance in a straight line from the railway station as possible.

Work began on 7th November 1903 when the first of 600 piles was driven in by engineering firm Mayoh and Haley (who had also built the pier at Mumbles and Britannia Pier at Great Yarmouth). With the pier being built relatively late on in terms of pier evolution, the building of the Grand Pier was documented really well by photographers, and these resultant pictures are really fascinating. They show steam cranes lifting the piles into place and then helping to drive them in. The man-powered capstan days of the Brighton Chain Pier had been replaced with a steam-driven version here putting the screw piles into the seabed much faster! The extreme distance the tide goes out here meant work could be carried out for longer periods than somewhere with water lapping around the legs, and also saved one workman who fell from the first floor level of the pavilion as it was being constructed at the pier head. He fortunately hit the mud and it cushioned his fall – although he needed some serious pulling out, he was unhurt!

The first part of the pier up to the pavilion was opened at half-past three on the afternoon of June 11th 1904. The pier was 329m (1,080') long with a broad, angled ramp up to the pier neck where a planked deck passed some rectangular buildings (containing stores and cloakrooms) and led to the pavilion at the seaward end. The completed pavilion had a tower at each corner, looking vaguely Oriental in design. It housed a 2,000 seat theatre which was to be used for everything from concerts to boxing and ballet! The pier had cost £120,000 to complete, but had been finished quickly, thanks to the diligence and hard work of the building crews who had sometimes worked throughout 24 hours to finish the pier on time. A section of pier decking was kept clear to the left-hand side of the neck for the intended installation of an electric tram to carry steamer passenger's luggage once boats started to call.

To cope with the disappearing sea and to enable the steamers to dock safely at the end of the pier, it had originally been intended to build the pier 1,828m (6,000') out from the shore, but financially this was a staggering feat so initially an extension was constructed a further 457m (1,500') from the seaward end. While the main pier had stunning wrought-iron railings, each panel featuring the initials of the Grand Pier Company cast in the centre, the extension had simple, plain rails and lacked the electric lighting that graced the main part of the pier as it was only intended to use the extension deck during the day. Visitors to the main pier were charged the standard 2d toll to walk up as far as the pavilion, however a further toll was payable if people wished to walk along the new bit!

This extension opened on 16th May 1907, with over 10,000 visiting this extra bit of pier and it was hoped that regular steamer traffic would visit from Wales. However, the vicious swirling currents in this part of the Severn Estuary, sometimes reaching in excess of six knots made docking a steamer extremely dangerous. Despite this long extension, at low tide the end of the pier was still some distance from the sea, so even when the mud was covered by water it took a skilled Captain to dock. In order to overcome the tide a ship had to approach the end of the pier at considerable speed, and after several hair-raising experiences, only three steamers ever tied up successfully, managing nearly twenty visits between them. However, it wasn't long before the Chairman of the steamer company decided it was just too risky and stopped the service to the pier.

For a short while in 1914 the pier was closed due to financial problems but was reopened and put up for sale. The author Laurie Lee mentioned the Grand Pier in his well-known book *Cider With Rosie*, likening it to a sleeping dragon on the rippled mud! The extension of the pier was removed during 1916-1918, relegating the pier from one of the longest in the country to the second division on the table of length, and it was sold in 1919 to the Weston-super-Mare grand Pier Company, dedicated to keeping this central tourist magnet open for the benefit of the town.

With the steamer extension gone, the site for the electric tram line was redundant and reinstated as a normal piece of decking. Postcards from this era show the pier teeming with visitors. There were around fourteen shops around the pavilion at this time, deckchairs by the bandstand where audiences often listened to Mogg's Band playing. Some light amusements were added in 1926 and glass sectional screening that ran the length of the pier neck the following year.

At half-past six on the evening of 13th January 1930, flames were spotted coming from the bottom of the front right-hand tower of the pavilion and the fire-brigade called. Despite their best efforts, the fire soon took a hold on the whole pavilion. Workmen's oxygen cylinders exploded, blowing the turret where the fire had started onto the sand below in a flurry of sparks and flames. Eventually the fire burnt itself out, but everything on the end of the pier had been lost. Amusement machines burned and the fire was so intense, money melted together into blobs and fell through the spaces where the decking had burned, falling onto the beach. Some of these were collected by locals and donated to the local museum, where they can still be seen today.

It has to be said at this point that if I hadn't mentioned that this fire was in 1930, it could have been taken in virtually every point as being the later fire in 2008. Even the cause of the fire from both was undetermined, started in the same turret and resulted in total destruction of the pavilion and pier head. Even the photographs of the morning after the night before are eerily similar, showing twisted girders like some kind of nightmarish roller coaster, everything blackened and twisted. The pier in the 1930 conflagration had been underinsured and a huge sum of money was needed to rebuild it and the pavilion. The fire was so intense that some of the superstructure needed replacing and the whole thing needed re-planking. The pier was sold to Leonard Guy who was able to invest £60,000 into the rebuilding effort. The pier was decked and temporary amusements installed to keep the money flowing while funds were raised for a pavilion, a very canny piece of marketing!

With 36 piles added below the enlarged pier head to support a new, bigger pavilion the Grand Pier re-opened in 1933. The pier now sported the largest pavilion in the country and unusually for the day it housed a huge undercover fun fair – more spooky parallels to the modern replacement after the recent fire! The pavilion construction was a classic example of 30's architecture, but still retained elements of the original. There were four taller, rounded towers and the huge low, long-line pavilion had a graduated roof, like a slice through a crème patisserie tart topped with strawberries!

This change of use effectively meant the end of Birnbeck Pier, far away from the hustle and bustle of the town centre and with old-fashioned amusements. Why would people go there when they could have such a new amusement centre within easy reach? The only thing Birnbeck now had going for it was the steamer landing stage... the Grand Pier had high diving, water dodgems (a potentially lethal version of dodgems in a pond, complete with overhead pickup – strictly no splashing please!) and a looping waltzer. There were all the traditional offerings too; candy floss and ice cream and hoardings that told the visitor to expect 'Happiness, Mirth, Enjoyment'. In 1935 a ballroom and front café were added, with other rides added as they came out, such as the Figure of Eight wooden roller coaster which regularly deafened people as it hurtled round the track inside the pavilion!

Unusually the pier wasn't sectioned during World War II (knockers of Weston would say this is because not even the Germans would want to invade here), but the pier was used by soldiers who practised climbing down it onto the mud below in readiness for D-Day. In 1946 the pier was sold again, to Mr Brenner who kept it in the family until 2008, lavishing much attention on the old girl to keep it popular. Shops, an amusement arcade and a rebuilt entrance were added in the early 1970s. Those old wrought-iron railings were removed in 1971 and replaced by some fairly boring plain (but corrosion-free) aluminium ones. Some of the originals are in the local museum, but apparently the rest ended up on a Texas ranch!

The Grand Pier received Grade II listed status in 1974, and more modern improvements included a £250,000 bowling alley in 1993, and redecking, a two-storey funhouse and an indoors Ferris wheel the following year. Other reliable delights on the pier included the tractor-driven trains up and down the pier neck (Golden Arrow and Silver Arrow) and annual displays by the Red Arrows and other aerial teams. The National Piers Society awarded it Pier of the Year in 2001 and it's fair to say, that although regularly closed over the winter for importance maintenance, the pier has played a huge part in thousands of people's happy holidays.

Having lived in Weston since 2004 my children and I also have many fond memories of the pier and everything inside it. At night it glowed green all along the length, visible even from Wales. There were bumper cars and the Castle of Doom ghost train (whose squealing siren you could hear a mile away if the weather was right!), the balloon Ferris wheel and the air hockey! We ate the compulsorily greasy fish and chips and tried scoops of ice cream in blackberry or honeycomb. We played the slot machines and won thousands of tickets that we saved and eventually redeemed in the Prize Shop for two pier mugs. No visit was complete without a visit to the end of the pier. On the old extension stump was a children's monorail driving ride that wend its way around a model village, and some air-driven bumper cars – but it was opposite this that our hearts lay with the firemen's water shoot. Many a twenty pence was spent here, amid much squealing and back spray, even in the howling bitter sea winds that often blew on this part of the pier!

And of course, it was where Jay and I first met and fell in love. We'd arranged to meet here (as just friends) for a coffee and a chat in 2007. As we walked along the pier there was an undeniable spark, and other meetings here led to a first kiss. Maybe it was the magic of the seaside pier that had a hand in it, but there at the end of the pier the first kiss was shared and something started that has carried on for many more years and many more pier kisses! It was therefore with some disbelief that I first heard about the fire on the Grand Pier in 2008 on the local news as I woke up on that fateful morning of 28th July, a day with a deceptively cheerful blue sky and bright sunshine.

In the early hours of the morning an automatic fire alarm had been triggered. Unable to raise the key holder, the alarm company took no further action, and it was not until a quarter to seven that a passer-by noticed smoke and flames coming from the front of the right-hand tower near the shore. Thirteen fire engines and over eighty-five fire-fighters tackled the blaze. By half-past seven it looked like the pier might be saved. This was when I had also looked out of my window and seen the tower of smoke, looking for all the world like a plume from an erupting volcano, thick billows of grey and dove white rolling thickly straight up in the sky. I drove like the wind. I can't even remember whether I locked the front door, but I know I grabbed my camera and took it with me.

Brave fire crews and staff faced the blaze as it then took hold on the rest of the pavilion, running down the side and removing oxy-acetylene cylinders before they exploded in the heat. As I arrived an hour after the blaze had been seen it was horribly clear that this was going to end in tears with the complete destruction of the pavilion and pier head in a repeat of the 1930 fire.

There were some people watching, hardly a word was said, all being struck silent and trying to process what they were seeing. The roar of the flames and the occasional explosions as combustibles could take no more and succumbed to the fire filled the air. There was much cracking and snapping, as pieces of the decking fell through to the damp sand like Bonfire Night rockets gone astray. I watched the cars at the side of the pavilion dissolve into flames and the other three towers disappear into the blaze.

Half a mile away from the Grand Pier where I'd parked my car, ash was falling like grey snow, along with larger pieces of plastic and wood. Seared by the flames, these large pieces of debris had been swirled into the sky by the amazing heat that had created powerful thermal currents. These currents had gone up into the air probably half a mile, then along the coast the same distance before the thermals had cooled so much they could no longer support the chunks of pier, and they were falling with little smacks and thumps onto the road and parked cars.

By 9.30 or thereabouts, it was all over. The pier was nothing now except a twisted pile of girders. It was just discernible where the towers had been – ironically the one where the fire had started was fairly upright, whilst the others had literally melted with the intensity of the blaze and had folded over like dying flowers onto the pier deck girders. The extension at the seaward end was surreally unscathed, the decking providing a natural firebreak and the flags and children's monorail sitting forlornly at the end of the pier. Weak smoke continued to drift skyward, but the blaze had burnt itself out, finding no more combustible objects in its path. Firemen continued to damp the fire down over the next couple of days, security fencing was erected around the pier on the beach and assessment began to find out if anything was salvageable of the Grand Pier. As messages of disbelief flooded in, we waited with baited breath to see what would become of it.

There will always be doubters who cry 'arson', but why would you set fire to your new investment – and worse, why would you do it when you'd just spent so much money on new rides? People are such sceptics! The pier neck was opened within just a few days, allowing people to view the wreckage. A superb aerial photograph in one of the big daily papers showed how the fire had obliterated everything in its path, but not strayed from the wall of the pavilion, leaving the planks a metre or so away totally unscathed. The globe-topped lamps were relatively unscathed too, except at the front of where the pavilion had been. Here, one side of the glass was grotesquely melted into candle-wax drips, the other side untouched.

True to their claims, the owners set about fixing their pier and bringing it not just back to the entertainment facility it had been but to make it the biggest and best pier in the world, fit for the twenty-first century and beyond. Work to remove all the twisted metalwork and charred timbers began on 12th September, and the following month the official cause of the fire was recorded as 'unknown' despite extensive forensic work, with an electrical fault thought to be the most likely reason. The naked deck looked strangely small and forlorn through the winter, while plans for a new pavilion were chosen and the superstructure integrity assessed. All was well in this department and it looked like it would just have to be re-decked before a new pavilion was built!

Angus Meek won the contract to design a new pavilion and by January 2009 the last of the wreckage had been cleared. Planning permission was granted that spring and people watched and waited... As you've heard, the rebuild was almost as fascinating to witness as building the original structure had been! Extra piles had to be put in to support the new increased weight of the pavilion and these thick black poles were lifted into place by floating cranes before being walloped into place! Once the new ironwork was in place, reinstating the decking began. It was pretty tricky to see any changes going on from the land during this period, and if it hadn't been for regular updates in the local paper it would have felt as though there was no progression at all!

It was with a little thrill of delight that in October 2009 the first steels of the pavilion superstructure were winched into place and it felt like things were definitely underway in the right direction! Sometimes it seemed to be deathly slow and that nothing was happening. Then suddenly, a side had been completed, the huge curved roof outlines were clear – and there were four huge corner towers once more! Hooray! Of course there were setbacks – the council got a bit stroppy at one point, the weather played havoc with plans, either raining too much or freezing so hard that concrete for flooring couldn't be poured, but by the start of 2010 the main framework had been completed, cladding was being slapped on the sides and unseen hordes of Oompaloompas toiled inside to create a modern fantastic wonderland away from prying eyes.

Outside the cladding was nearly finished, still obscured in places by scaffolding. A very pleasing glass-sided, wave-topped walkway along the neck of the pier promised protection from the elements, but there was one thing missing. It had been part of the original design to build an 85m (279') tall observation tower at the seaward end of the pier, a viewing platform reached by a lift from the deck below. The piles had been driven in at the end of the old pier extension but no further work was undertaken, as the credit crunch hit and the firm went bump. By summer 2010 it looked like the tower was going to have to be put on hold, another project for the future perhaps?

Eventually, after many 'perhaps' dates, the grand opening of the Grand Pier was announced for October 23rd 2010. I'd like to say it was a bright, sunny day, but it sadly wasn't, it was wet, windy and not very warm either, but this didn't dampen the spirits of the 52,000 people who had come to celebrate the unveiling of this huge pavilion and its box of delights. The pier, all 366m (1,200') of it now sported the biggest and best pavilion in the world and we were ready for a look! Armed with camera, we also had an assignation. Well, two really. One was to have a kiss at the end of the pier, bringing the whole story and road trip full circle; the other was an interview for BBC Radio 4 with Paddy O'Connell!

We were expecting huge queues after hearing that people had spent a very cold and wet night on the promenade in order to get in, but by the time we got there it were pretty much like any busy summer day, quite a few visitors but not crowded. A good many were making use of the new central covered walkway. Many piers have a glass windbreak on the pier neck, but the Grand Pier now has one like a long glass tunnel, with doors that can be opened in the summer. It still gives the experience of walking along a pier, but without the inconvenience of the weather!

The pavilion is stunning, all curved surfaces that give the illusion of light even on a day like this. The surfaces are white or grey or silver and the front of the pavilion has an uncharacteristically small red neon signs that say 'Grand Pier 2010'. This frontage is guarded on either side by grand towers, and unlike the old decorative turrets, these each house something interesting. The two front ones also sport discreet balconies (and I hope that front right-hand tower has a large fire extinguisher and a sprinkler system too!), and the rear right-hand one hiding something rather exciting!

We thought we'd walk round the left side first to 'kissing corner', impressed by the new look pavilion that still managed to retain the lines of the old one only in a more modern way. The railings appear to be the same as before, but maybe they're just a modern version of the old, and it was nice to squish into our old spot there at the end of the pier and have a kiss, reminiscing about where it all began and reliving some warm, fuzzy feelings as we did, despite the rain!

There's a new look to this part of the pier. Originally the pavilion ended and there was a wide decked space before the rides on the extension. Now we were faced with a large two-storey building that grows out continuously from the main body of the pavilion right to the end of the pier. It's also a light-reflecting white and silver, with loads of glass to make the most of the view and sun (when it's out!). The lower of the pier-end rooms is a classy tea room, the upper intended to be the way into the lift for going up the viewing tower. On the opening day, the maintenance walkways right around the edges of the decking were open, and so we walked right to the end of the pier, looked over at the twelve stumps of the tower piles and mused that perhaps this wasn't a modern engineering palimpsest but something archaeological. Pierhenge perhaps?!

The wind was blooming biting here at the end, and we scuttled like beetles round to the north side of the pier, which had always been more sheltered. We went in to the connecting corridor by way of an enormous door and joined rather a lot of people who were investigating the inside of the pavilion. If we said it was big, we'd be underestimating things a bit – this is one HUGE pavilion and the noise from the plethora of machines and amusements contained herein is pretty loud! We the great unwashed public had been promised rides and amusements from all four corners of the known universe, and here they were, and there really is something for everyone here.

If you're a Weston Pier traditionalist, there's a ghost train, a much taller freefall ride, dodgems, crazy house and kids' adventure play area. Games and amusement machines include the good old penny falls, racing horses and arcade machines – and there are lots of air hockey tables too – hooray!

If you are the pier modernist who wants all their amusements up to date and high tech, the Grand Pier can cater for you too! There's a go-karting track that comes down from the first floor, a crazy house and Psychedelia, where you'll need 3D glasses to negotiate your way round. There's the sidewinder ride, Crystal Maze full of mirrors and a Laser Maze full of... lasers! (Think *Mission Impossible* – you have to escape without breaking the beams as quickly as possible.) Oooh, and there's the Robocoaster, an evil robotic arm with a chair on the end that promises to twist and turn you 'til you're sick and a 4D cinema that will squirt water, bubbles and fog at you whilst giving you a moving, 3D film experience. If you don't fancy any of that, there in the corner tower is a two-lane helter-skelter, so you can race a friend to the bottom!

There are also loads of shooting arcade games, but you can also try your hand at racing various vehicles or playing umpteen sports! There are even F1 simulator rides upstairs too! Speaking of upstairs, it's the only pier we've been to with escalators on it, and if all this has left you whacked out and in need of refreshment, there's a plethora of cafés and restaurants and bars and food concessions to reinvigorate you before you go up to the Prize Shop to redeem your miles of tokens or buy a souvenir of the pier.

We did at this point get horribly lost and it took a while to find the down escalator and the way back to the tearoom where we met our Radio 4 presenter. Because the wind was so fierce, it was hard to get out of the gale, but we found a spot behind the back tower containing the helter-skelter (also the scene of a passionate pier kiss – ahem!), and had a pleasant chat with Paddy before he went off to interview the pier owners. So, what did we think of the new all-singing, all-dancing pavilion? It's hats off to the Michaels, because it's an incredibly difficult thing to do, rebuilding a pier as a going concern whilst also maintaining an essence of what was there before. Yes, the pavilion is much bigger and no, it's not the same as the old one!

What it does do is capture the airy, 'shed-like' feel inside the building – and it's been arranged so that machines and rides can be moved to host concerts in the huge space too. There is something for everyone in terms of amusements and refreshments too, but it just doesn't have that old, ingrained character – which of course it won't, because it's brand new! If I do get my time machine perfected in time we'll pop into the future and see what it feels like in seventy years' time and check on potential fire risks in that corner tower too while we're there!

These improvements also mean that the pier will become an all-year round facility, something that Weston as a town has desperately needed, because if you've come away on holiday and the weather turns (as it so often does in this country), the pier will give you somewhere to go. Yes, the rides and amusements aren't cheap, but teach the children of today a little prudence and give them a pot of two pence pieces – it's still fun! We left the pier (still raining) and walked down the new covered walkway, which was also very pleasant. The buildings at the shoreward end are still the same as they had been before the disaster, the clock above the exit showing you'd missed your train home! 'Come back again!' it says as you go – and I think we just might!

There's just one more little surprise that the new improved pier has to offer, and one best viewed from the beach. Here you can appreciate the beautiful curves of the pavilion and pier-neck walkway, but once the sun goes down, the pier is illuminated by thousands of multi-coloured led lights! Computer controlled, they can be all one colour, random multi-colours or flash and wash from one end to the other. I personally like that, having always been a sucker for things sparkly and bright (give me a string of fairy lights in a darkened room at Christmas and I'm happy for hours), but others we've asked feel it makes the pier look a bit tacky and cheap. Hmm, the jury's out, the journey's finished, the kissing's done – it's over to you now, what do YOU think?!

EPILOGUE

So, an enormous 'thank you' to you, dear reader, for travelling with us as we hurtled around those seven thousand miles of our glorious country, waffling on about the boring old history of seaside boardwalks on legs and snogging in stiff breezes. We also have to extend our grateful hugs to all those people that helped to make it possible, whether or not we met you in person (and if we did, you were delightful) – it would be impossible to name everyone, but you know who you are.

We'd also like to offer our sincerest apologies too. It's highly likely we've got things wrong somewhere, or offended someone by saying something they consider rather rude and unfeeling about their local pier or town. Generally we hurtled in to your town and looked at the pier in as much detail as we could, kissed and ran away again (unless we stopped for a coffee to reinvigorate the co-pilot). Something I have learned is that when researching and writing about piers, even the ones we were a bit dismissive of had positive things about them, unique features that made me feel very defensive of them as I wrote.

So what of the future, for piers and for us? If we had a magic wand we'd save them all NOW – heaven alone knows they need saving, there are so many wonderful stories and lives linked with each one. In reality, October 2010 showed us both sides and the edges of the pier coin. Hastings was destroyed, Weston was rebuilt and Brighton maintains a fantastic midline of how to keep a pier traditional but modern in the same breath. We hope to keep supporting piers now for as long as we can, and we hope this book has done a little bit to reignite enthusiasm for these pieces of living seaside history and make people realise they need saving. We'd also love to hear people's opinions on their pier, and anecdotes too, for I know that there will be worthy stories I've missed or overlooked!

Because piers aren't exclusively an English oddity we've cast our eye abroad where there are probably at least another sixty piers to visit, but can't think of a book title for that one (I did suggest *Around the World in Sixty Piers* but got a stern look, so we're still thinking!). We have decided to re-visit all of the piers in this book again, ten years from our original starting date and there is a working title for this subsequent tome – *Pier Head's Revisited*! There have already been many changes, for good and bad that have happened to some of the piers we'd visited and we both keep an eye out for piers in the news and in adverts. The latter sad hobby often involves cries of 'which one's that?' and 'I recognise that railing, it's... (insert pier name here)'! Piers have even inspired Jay to write a poem – would you like to read it? Here you are...

Victorian Splendour

"We are going to build a platform
To withstand the strongest storm
So people can walk over the sea"
What a crazy idea; could it ever be?
Design engineers worked hard day and night,
Determined to get the details just right.
The piles were driven, deep into the bed
And decking was laid for people to tread.
Cast iron railings, lamp posts and seats,
Pavilion and theatre, places to meet.
Gentlemen strolling, doffing their hats;
Ladies promenading, lacy parasols twirling;
Children excited – look at this! Look at that!
Far beneath them, the sea gently swirling.
Customers waiting for short pleasure trips,
Steamships tied up to the head of the pier;
Walking down gangways, be careful, don't slip!
Smoke billowing from stacks as the ship pulls clear.

What a sight to behold when finally complete,
A Victorian splendour; a Victorian feat!

If any good comes of this book it's that someone will go and visit their local pier, see it in a new light and want to keep it preserved for the future. The National Piers Society have now altered their website to include jetties and river piers, not just in England and Wales but Scotland and around the world too – that would have been *so* useful before our trip had started, maybe we'll use it next time! And, if you go to the pier and see a couple having a discreet kiss at the end it might just be us... Grab your partner and do it too!

Hazel Preller is a primary school teacher and lives in Weston-super-Mare, North Somerset. When not kissing her husband Jay at the end of a pier she is often found covered in glitter and paint, walking the dog or wearing fancy dress (but generally not all at once).

She is as passionate about British history, wildlife and the countryside as she is about piers (and kissing on them!), and this is her first book. However, she has enjoyed the experience so much she suspects it won't be her last.

Hazel and Jay have a website, pierkissers.co.uk where you can find out what they have been up to recently or drop them a line. You can also find Hazel on Twitter @pierkisser, and *From Piers to Eternity* also has its own Facebook page.